OLYMPIC HOUSING

Olympic Housing
A Critical Review of London 2012's Legacy

PENNY BERNSTOCK
University of East London, UK

LONDON AND NEW YORK

First published 2014 by Ashgate Publishing

2 Park Square, Milton Park, Abingdon, Oxon OX14 4RN
711 Third Avenue, New York, NY 10017, USA

Routledge is an imprint of the Taylor & Francis Group, an informa business

First issued in paperback 2016

Copyright © 2014 Penny Bernstock

Penny Bernstock has asserted her right under the Copyright, Designs and Patents Act, 1988, to be identified as the author of this work.

All rights reserved. No part of this book may be reprinted or reproduced or utilised in any form or by any electronic, mechanical, or other means, now known or hereafter invented, including photocopying and recording, or in any information storage or retrieval system, without permission in writing from the publishers.

Notice:
Product or corporate names may be trademarks or registered trademarks, and are used only for identification and explanation without intent to infringe.

British Library Cataloguing in Publication Data
A catalogue record for this book is available from the British Library

Library of Congress Cataloging-in-Publication Data
Bernstock, Penny.
  Olympic housing : a critical review of London 2012's legacy / by Penny Bernstock.
    pages cm
  Includes bibliographical references and index.
  ISBN 978-1-4094-2005-7 (hbk)
  1. Housing--England--London--History--21st century.
  2. Olympic Games (30th : 2012 : London, England) I. Title.

HD7334.L6B47 2013
363.5'987964809421--dc23

2013020853

ISBN 978-1-4094-2005-7 (hbk)
ISBN 978-1-138-24675-1 (pbk)

Contents

List of Tables		*vii*
List of Abbreviations		*ix*
Introduction		1
1	Housing Legacy in Context	5
2	Moving Out: Experiences of Those Decanted to Make Way for the Olympic Park	29
A Note on the Carpenters Estate		65
3	London Housing Legacy: An Overview	71
4	The Shifting Terrain of Housing Legacy Plans	93
5	From Athletes' Village to East Village	113
6	Accelerated Regeneration – A Case Study of Stratford High Street	139
7	New Migrants to Stratford City	169
Conclusion: Imagining the Housing Futures of London 2012		191
Index		*203*

List of Tables

3.1	Rough sleeping in the 'Legacy' boroughs	76
3.2	Housing tenure in 'Legacy' boroughs 2001 and 2011 census	78
3.3	Overcrowding in the 'Legacy' boroughs	79
3.4	Housing waiting lists in 'Legacy' boroughs 2009–2011 and proportion of population on housing waiting lists	80
3.5	New affordable homes and homes for social rent in 'Legacy' boroughs	81
6.1	Housing schemes completed or planned along Stratford High Street – numbers and proportions of affordable housing 2000–2012	156
6.2	Other dimensions of community gain on schemes along Stratford High Street	161

List of Abbreviations

COHRE	Centre on Human Rights and Eviction
CPO	Compulsory Purchase Order
EIP	Examination in Practice
GLA	Greater London Authority
LCS	Legacies Community Schemes
LDA	London Development Agency
LGTU	London Gypsy and Travellers Unit
LLDC	London Legacy Development Corporation
LOCOG	London Organising Committee of the Games
LTGDC	London Thames Gateway Development Corporation
ODA	Olympic Development Authority
OPLC	Olympic Park Legacy Company
OPLSG	Olympic Park Legacy Supplementary Guidance
PDZ	Planning Delivery Zone
QDD	Qatari Diar Delancey
SNU	Safer Neighbourhoods Unit
WFCBHA	Waltham Forest Community Based Housing Association

Introduction

Now that the London 2012 Olympic and Paralympic Games are over the issue of legacy, including housing legacy, has come the fore. In 2005 when London won its bid to host the Olympic and Paralympic Games I like many other Londoners welcomed the news. A compelling vision was set out that had at its heart the potential to transform this part of East London for 'the benefit of all who lived there'. East London had been at the centre of a number of high profile regeneration projects over the last thirty year such as the regeneration of London Docklands. I had previously worked for the Dockland Forum – an umbrella organisation that monitored the Docklands development from the perspective of local communities. The Forum demonstrated the limitations of an alleged 'market led' approach (huge public investment was invested in Docklands) that led to physical rather than social regeneration and overlooked local needs. London Docklands has come to symbolise the contradictions of this approach where growing levels of housing need were exacerbated by building mainly unaffordable dwellings for private sale – the 'Isle of Dogs' serving as the most potent symbol of these contradictions. London 2012 on the other hand appeared to take at its starting point inclusivity and local need and therefore it appeared that the regeneration of Stratford and surrounding areas would evolve in a very different way underpinned by a partnership between state and market.

I was working as housing consultant for the London East Research Institute (Research Centre at the University of East London) in 2005 when London won the bid and decided to monitor and log a number of different dimensions of the housing legacy by asking a range of questions:

1. What were the experiences of travellers and residents at Clays Lane decanted from the park? How much housing was lost? Were other residents displaced as an indirect effect of London hosting the games?
2. What were the housing legacies of other host cities? How does the experience of London to date compare?
3. Would London 2012 result in the accelerated regeneration of East London and what would be the nature of that accelerated regeneration?
4. How would the athletes' village be financed, developed and converted into housing after the games? Who would have access to this housing? To what extent were original commitments to addressing local need reflected in this housing?

5. How would commitments to inclusivity be reflected in plans at the athletes' village and on the park?
6. Would the area attract a more professional population and would this displace existing populations?
7. What kinds of plans and policy instruments would be developed to realise the housing 'legacy'? Would they be adequate? Would the initial focus on legacy be maintained?
8. How and in what ways would the massive investment in this area translate into benefits for deprived communities living in East London?
9. What would be the relationship between State and Market in terms of delivering London 2012 and its intended legacy?
10. How would this part of London change over the coming decades?

I set out to answer these questions by establishing a number of empirical investigations and undertaking an extensive literature review. The findings are discussed here. We begin in Chapter 1 with an overview of housing legacies in other host cities and we include London Docklands as an interesting case study arguing that the approach in Docklands has more in common with that adopted at London 2012 than was initially envisaged and serves as a salient reminder of the risks involved in achieving an inclusive housing legacy.

The story of the housing legacy in London begins in Chapter 2 with an exploration of housing loss and displacement associated with the displacement of Travellers from Newham and Hackney and residents and Clays Lane. These case studies demonstrate that far from this part of East London being a desolate wasteland the area was home to a relatively unique form of affordable housing and strong community and neighbourly networks. Moreover, the need to expedite construction meant that the residents and travellers were forced to move to a time scale that led to compromises in the choices they were able to make. The displacement issue has become more far reaching than originally anticipated and we explore plans for the Carpenters Estate. In Chapter 3 we focus specifically on key dimensions of housing legacy associated with hosting mega events such as rising house and rent prices and treatment of homeless groups. We argue that despite London experiencing a housing boom in the years after winning the bid, this has not been the case in Stratford with limited house price inflation. On the other hand rental prices have increased considerably in Stratford and there was evidence of an increase in evictions and rental prices as investors sought to capitalise on their locational advantage prior to the games, however, there is no evidence of the victimisation of the poor in London as has happened elsewhere. We also examine the mechanisms for governing legacy and the 'convergence' agenda.

In Chapter 4 we move on to explore initial legacy commitments and argue that over time there has been a dilution of these initial commitments. We look in detail at a range of plans including the Lower Lea Valley Plan; The London Plan; the Legacy Communities Scheme and the Stratford Metropolitan

Masterplan and suggest that there is a huge gap between planning documents and outcome, with plans essentially serving as 'policy desires' rather than realisable mechanisms for achieving policy objectives.

The athletes' village or East Village is a key dimension of housing legacy (including a substantial proportion of affordable housing) and this is explored in detail in Chapter 5. We consider its connection with the Stratford City Project; finance arrangements; design issues and analyse in detail housing allocation policies and access issues that reflect a return to the past in terms of allocating housing based on categories of desert rather than need. We also interrogate housing plans associated with Stratford City and identify ways in which the high proportion of affordable housing included at the village has been used to justify lower levels of affordable housing elsewhere.

In Chapters 6 and 7 we report on the findings of two empirical studies undertaken along Stratford High Street which runs parallel to the Olympic Park and serves as a good example of the anticipated accelerated development/ regeneration that was anticipated to follow if London hosted the games. We analyse planning gain (S106) agreements on all schemes of 50 units or more built since 2000. We identify a trend away from the 'mixed communities agenda'; a decline in the value of planning gain; a substantial decrease in levels of affordable housing provided on site and a shift towards more offsite affordable housing. More generally we highlight the significant weaknesses of current mechanisms for extracting and distributing 'public gain' from regeneration projects.

Finally, in Chapter 7 we ask whether Stratford will become 'gentrified'. This is based on primary research undertaken in Stratford with Estate Agents, Developers and people who were either purchasing or renting properties in the new developments along Stratford High Street. The intention was to understand more about the characteristics of people choosing to live in Stratford and their reasons for moving to the area. We conclude that there is evidence of class change with Stratford now attracting a young professional class drawn to the area by the extent of regeneration; affordability and the potential for capital gains. Assumptions that an increase in market housing will reduce population churn was not borne out in these interviews with most residents planning to move on relatively quickly with limited connections with place. Moreover, there was a sense that residents increasingly identify two distinctive Stratford's emerging resonating with previous projects such as the regeneration of London Docklands.

Acknowledgements

I would like to thank the following: Doreen Bernstock; Kate Bernstock; Fiona Fairweather; Liz Fekete; Gavin Poynter; Sydney Jeffers; Prossy Mubiru; Francesca Webernorth; and staff working within the Sociology and Social Policy subject area for their support whilst writing this book. I would also like to thank all of those people who gave up their time to be interviewed for this project.

Chapter 1
Housing Legacy in Context

This chapter provides an overview of housing legacy impacts in other host cities. There are both intended and unintended housing impacts associated with hosting Olympic and Paralympic events and both dimensions are explored here. The conversion of the athletes' village into housing after the games is presented as one of the key dimensions of London's housing legacy, however, there is nothing unique about this. The first permanent athletes' village was built at the Helsinki Games (1952) and converted into a residential district after the games. Melbourne (1956) used the village to house immigrants. In Munich (1972) the athletes' village was converted to housing for low- and middle-income families and in Moscow (1980) the village was converted into housing for around 14,500 residents (Baim 2009). The literature on housing legacy is relatively scant. However, it has been possible to explore displacement; the utilisation of the athletes' village; trends in property prices; and the treatment of homeless groups during the games which have emerged as key themes/issues in a number of cities. One issue that is not addressed is trends in evictions as landlords capitalise on renting properties, as data was limited. We also include London Docklands as an interesting case study arguing that the approach in Docklands has more in common with that adopted at London 2012 than was initially envisaged and serves as a salient reminder of the risks involved in achieving an inclusive housing legacy.

We begin by exploring the housing legacy in each city that hosted the summer games from 1992. It is argued that from this point onwards Olympic and Paralympic projects became much more associated with significant urban renewal/transformation. We also include Vancouver (host to Winter Games 2010) as there are a range of housing legacy issues that are pertinent to London's housing legacy.

Over the last three decades urban regeneration and transformation have been key but not exclusive drivers associated with hosting the games, evident to varying degrees from Barcelona onwards. The IOC has come under pressure to ensure that those hosting the games place a greater emphasis on issues both of sustainability and legacy. Agenda 21 originated at the Earth Summit in Rio in 1992 and was adopted by the Olympic movement in 1999. This committed the Olympic movement to a sustainable agenda that addressed environmental, socio-economic and health issues that were subsequently translated into criteria for assessing bids. The concept of 'legacy' was first prioritised by the IOC in 2002 where they introduced a new requirement for host cities to demonstrate that the games would leave a lasting legacy beyond the event.[1] Therefore it is unsurprising in many ways that London's bid prioritised the issue of legacy, given that this was a key requirement, or that it was successful given its emphasis on legacy.

Barcelona – 1992

Barcelona is generally perceived to be a major success with regard to urban transformation. There were a number of housing impacts arising from Barcelona including displacement; conversion of the athletes' village into private housing; rising house prices resulting in indirect displacement via the price mechanism along with a small proportion of affordable housing provision.

It is estimated that some 624 families (a significant proportion of whom were of Roma origin) were displaced and subsequently rehoused and/or compensated from different sites in Barcelona and it appears that this displacement was generally uncontroversial. There were three main reasons for displacement: the construction of the Olympic Park leading to the displacement of 147 families, the elimination of informal settlements or shanty towns leading to the displacement of 282 families and the construction of a new ring road leading to the displacement of 165 families (COHRE 2007).

Initially the authorities offered residents the option of being re-housed in the secondary market or on purpose-built sites. However, the policy of using purpose-built sites was abandoned following a campaign in one area against re-housing a group of mainly Roma families to this site and households were subsequently re-housed on an individual basis into the secondary market to avoid a concentration of residents in one particular area. Quite often, existing housing conditions were poor and therefore re-housing would have improved the housing conditions of these residents (COHRE 2007).

The athletes' village provided a major source of high quality housing and was converted into 2,048 apartments, housing around 5,783 residents after the games. The village was built on derelict land close to the waterfront and its design was intended to provide continuity with the urban pattern of nineteenth-century Barcelona. The village was developed by two private development companies and sold on the open market, with 60 per cent of units sold prior to the games. Sales were slightly slower after the games and the final apartment was sold in 1996 (Carbonnell 2005). The village has become a desirable place to live and house prices have risen. For example, when the village was first constructed units were sold for prices similar to the Barcelona average but after ten years prices had multiplied to 2.5–3 times the Barcelona average and were comparable with the most expensive districts in

---

1   Rule 2 of Article 14 stresses that an important role of the IOC is to ensure that the Host city and country promote a positive legacy from the Olympic Games to host cities and host countries with benefits beyond the games. Guidance is provided on how this might be incorporated in the bid. See IOC Factsheet – Legacies of the Games updated in July 2012.

Barcelona. This premium has been explained in terms of location next to the sea, architectural quality and urban design.[2] Research has demonstrated that the profile of residents living at the village were younger, more educated and more affluent than residents in Barcelona as a whole and a higher proportion of disabled people live at the village, attracted by its inclusive design (Carbonell 2005).

Initial plans were to have included a proportion of affordable housing at the village, however, it was argued that the cost was prohibitive. Affordable housing was provided on three sites originally built to house the media and Olympic and Paralympic officials. On one site 68 (one third) of 205 units were designated affordable and included a mix of housing for social rent, cooperative housing and discounted housing for sale. At another site, 150 of 488 houses were sold to families with limited resources and on a third site 842 multi-family houses and 56 single-family houses, built to house the media, were sold at moderate prices after the games. The Barcelona Games then did include an affordable housing legacy (COHRE 2007).

Barcelona's success in transforming itself has been associated with substantial house price inflation and growing inequality (Raco 2008). According to research undertaken by Halifax Bank (2004), house prices increased by 131 per cent in Barcelona as a whole compared to 83 per cent in Spain (the highest of any recent Olympic host). Rental prices also increased significantly rising by 145 per cent between 1986 and 1993. However, in the period following the Olympic Games 1992–1995, Barcelona entered recession and developers encountered difficulties selling properties. Nevertheless, prices increased significantly after 1999 (GLA 2007). There is also some evidence that homeless people were subject to increased controls in Barcelona during the Olympic Games (COHRE 2007).

Atlanta – 1996

The Atlanta games have been associated with high levels of displacement linked to the restructuring of public housing in the city under the auspices of an Olympic housing legacy programme, a lack of concern for low income (mainly Black) sections of the population and poor treatment/criminalisation of the homeless.

The games in Atlanta were underpinned by a private sector/business-led approach with a limited role for the public sector. The focus was on a commercial model of regeneration aimed at attracting inward investment into the city and raising the global profile of Atlanta and in this regard it was successful with 18 companies relocating to Atlanta after the games (Poynter, Roberts 2010).

The Atlanta Housing Authority (AHA) launched its own Olympic Legacy Housing Programme in 1999 which effectively resulted in the dismantling of

---

2   In 1993, apartments at the Olympic village were selling for 1,444 million Euros (compared to Barcelona average of 1,409 million Euros) and by 2003 they had risen to 3,375 million Euros (compared to Barcelona average of 2,367).

public-only housing schemes and their replacement with 'mixed tenure' schemes aimed at stemming/reversing the flow of the middle classes from the city. The programme committed itself more generally to abolishing mono tenure housing projects in the city.³

The programme was part of an approach to inner city revitalisation underpinned by private/public initiatives and a perception that public sector housing projects had been a failure. Atlanta had the largest number of residents living in public housing in the US and this housing had come to be associated with a range of problems such as high crime, high unemployment, high rates of poverty and poor academic achievement. From this perspective, concentrations of poverty reinforced cultures of poverty which were more to do with attitude than opportunity. According to the Director of the AHA:

> In the early 1990s after Atlanta had won bragging rights to be the host of the 1996 games, they had been handed a blessing and a liability. Atlanta would be showcased to the world..but not all of what it would see was showcase material... behind all these problems were more than forty public housing projects that distilled concentrated poverty into a toxicity from which there was no escape... Most daunting to civic leaders was the location of one of the most decrepit and foreboding projects – Techwood/Clarke Homes directly adjacent to the planned Olympic Village. (AHA 2005, p. 5)

The Techwood/Clark Howell Homes comprised 1,195 homes and were located north of the Olympic Park. Techwood was the first public housing scheme in the US, established in 1938 and would serve as a test case for this the new approach. There were debates as to whether this was the best way forward. For example, Keating (1992) noted that this was an established neighbourhood with long-standing residents and strong community ties. Moreover, residents had been working with planners on revitalisation schemes which would ensure it would continue to provide affordable housing for the poor, whereas Ambrose and Gribsby (1999, p. 7) suggest that the scheme was characterised by poor design, lack of resident screening, lack of maintenance and was a 'typical crime infested urban ghetto'.

Residents had the opportunity to vote on whether they wanted to be relocated, with 147 voting to sell the land and 42 voting against (Channel Five News 1992). The subsequent process of displacement was controversial in that the Atlanta Housing Authority had begun to run down the estates and increased evictions in the lead up to demolition. The Atlanta Housing Authority executive director confirmed to residents in a meeting that 16 families had been evicted in the first two days of

---

3   There had previously been a rule whereby any affordable housing demolished had to be replaced by another affordable unit, however, this rule was amended by congress enabling policy makers to move away from public provision.

that week (Jan. 1993) for rule violations and bad behaviour.[4] In 1993 around one third of the 1,195 apartments were vacant. Those that remained in housing received section eight vouchers entitling them to either move permanently using these vouchers or temporarily pending a return to Centennial Place although there were far fewer public housing units included in the new scheme and resident screening was high, limiting the actual number who were able to return to these developments.[5] In order to be eligible for the housing residents needed to be up-to-date with utility bills, not have committed certain crimes within five years, either have a job or be participating in self-sufficiency programmes or in study (Piper 2005). According to Ambrose and Grigsby the success of schemes such as Centennial Place was due to ensuring only residents with middle-class behaviour patterns were accepted (Ambrose and Grigsby, p. 10). The low proportion of residents returning has been explained in relation to residents' satisfaction with housing accessed through section eight vouchers, failure to meet criteria, not wanting to move twice and not wanting to participate in self-sufficiency schemes. Of those responding to the invitation to return to the redeveloped schemes, 24 per cent had their applications rejected.

Centennial Place replaced Techwood/Howell Homes. The replacement was a mixed tenure scheme comprising 756 units, 300 designated as public low-cost rental units, 300 units designated as private units for sale and 126 units designated as tax credit units aimed at those on incomes below 60 per cent median income. A magnet school was built to attract people to the area. There is evidence that there has been a significant change in the demographic profile of residents which has become more ethnically and socially mixed. For example, the Median Income of residents at Techwood was $3,129 per year and at Centennial Place this had increased to $34,000 for a two-person household in 2000 (Keating, 2000). Rental and property values increased and for some this signalled success, however, for others the process of area improvement has contributed to wider gentrification and secondary displacement (Brice 2003).

The Atlanta Housing Authority included three other schemes in its Olympic Legacy programme that were not directly related to the Olympic project but appear to have been included opportunistically. These schemes included East Lake Meadows where 470 households were displaced, Eagan Homes where 370 were displaced and Hope Homes where 64 families were displaced. Martin Hill Plaza (Summerhill) was more directly linked to the Olympics as it was adjacent to the stadium (Newman 1999). Residents at Martin Hill Plaza (Summerhill) were moved out and initial plans were to create a private scheme, however, after the Games the scheme was upgraded and remained public housing which residents were able to return to. According to Newman (1999) the community development corporation at Summerhill was able to capitalise on its locational advantage and attract private sector resources to bring neighbourhood benefits such as improved

---

4   Jan. 5 1993, Techwood Planning committee.
5   According to Bayor (2000), of the 1,128 residents at Techwood Howell only 78 moved into apartments at Centennial Place.

housing. Moreover, he suggests that this one area received 80 per cent of the funding invested in low income neighbourhoods between 1990 and 1996.

Atlanta was a polarised city and the regeneration projects accentuated a process of gentrification. The clean-up of poor neighbourhoods was reflected in the treatment of the homeless. Atlanta is identified as a city that treated the homeless population very badly in the run-up to the games and the Atlanta Homelessness Task Force documented a massive increase in arrests in the period preceding the games. The city also attempted to introduce a range of ordinances enabling it to remove the homeless from the streets and the potential to imprison them. One such ordinance enabled the police to arrest people 'acting in a manner not usual for law-abiding individuals' in parking lots and garages. Conviction under the measure would carry a sentence of two to six months in prison or assignment to a public works project and probation, however, this was successfully challenged (New York Times News Service 1996). Funds were made available to an organisation called 'Travellers Aid' to distribute one-way tickets out of Atlanta and according to COHRE (2007) police mass-produced arrest citations with 'African American Male Homeless' on them with space for the charge and date.

House price increases were not as high as other Olympic cities, rising by 19 per cent in Atlanta and 7 per cent in the US as a whole in the five years leading up to the games, however, closer analysis of the Olympic area suggests a much lower increase, with prices increasing just 0.5 per cent above the city average for the period (GLA 2007). The athletes' village at Georgia State was purchased by the Georgia Institute of Technology after the games and used for student housing.

The political context is particularly important for making sense of the impact of the Atlanta games on low income groups. The commitment to private enterprise central to the Atlanta bid was reflected more generally in housing with a withdrawal of state commitments to housing under the auspice of rebalancing populations, similar to arguments being made in East London about tenure mix. The games were used as a vehicle for withdrawing public support for state housing and as a means to reinvest in mixed-tenure schemes. More generally a disdain for the poor was evident, similar to the kind of rhetoric now emerging in London about 'strivers' and 'scroungers'. The poor lost a vital source of housing and the homeless were criminalised and whilst some lower income groups did benefit from new housing at Centennial Place, the net loss of public housing was much greater and income inequalities already marked in the city became more pronounced:

> The low income predominantly African American areas of Atlanta were most affected by the games...Residents were relocated from at least six public housing projects. For these individuals the games cost them the use value of their homes and neighbourhoods. (Newman 1999, p. 153)

Sydney – 2000

Sydney was unique with regard to Olympic projects in that the games were developed on surplus government land and therefore there was no direct displacement as a result of the games. The centrepiece of Sydney's housing legacy was the transformation of the athletes' village into housing after the games, creating a new neighbourhood 'Newington'. The games in Sydney were heralded as the green games and this was translated into a high eco specification for the athletes' village. Sydney is one of the most populated and expensive cities in Australia: in the 1970s the cost of purchasing a property was three to four times median income and this had increased to nine times median income by 2004 (COHRE 2007). The cutting-edge and progressive design of the scheme was not translated into the distribution of housing at the athletes' village which failed to include any affordable housing despite the need for it.

The Mirvac Village Industry Consortium (including Lend Lease) built the athletes' village and converted it to housing for sale after the Games. The village comprised 1,900 properties and was financed by a mix of private/public finance with a clause to ensure that if profits reached a certain level there would be a return to the public sector. There has been considerable price inflation at the village (rising at an annual rate of 4.1 per cent) since they were first sold in 2001. According to Mirvac's development director for Master Communities, the high quality of the build, town planning, parks and green space and mix of housing all contributed to a development that was more successful than anticipated, with green space and infrastructure ensuring ongoing demand (Walsh 2012). The profile of residents living at Newington (former site of the athletes' village) indicates a higher proportion of managers and professionals and a lower proportion of trades people than for Sydney as a whole (Auburn Council 2012).

Sydney experienced a considerable increase in house prices in the period leading up to the Games, however, this increase is not attributed solely to the Olympic Games. Bounds, Dwyer and Mali (2000) argue that this is actually more marked in areas outside of the Olympic Corridor in Sydney. They argue that the Olympics has had an impact on this, but that price increases are associated with an ongoing process of gentrification linked to the restoration of brownfield sites and construction of high/medium density apartments in South Sydney more generally. There is also evidence that Sydney's property prices peaked three years after the Games and began to fall. COHRE (2007) also concur with this analysis suggesting that there had been a rise in homes for rent and sale exacerbated but not explained exclusively by the Olympic Games and that this levelled out after the Olympics.

In the period prior to the Olympic games there was evidence also of an increase in evictions of residents in order to capitalise on rising house prices and this was discussed in parliament:

> To date the Sydney Organising Committee for the Olympic Games has refrained from the street-sweeping activities that marred the Atlanta Games and saw

thousands of homeless people forcibly moved out of that city. Although we have not gone down that path, the Sydney Olympics stand to be remembered as the homeless Games. According to the Tenants Union, currently 120 eviction-related cases go before the tribunal each day. (Lee 2000)

On the other hand, there were efforts to ensure that Sydney did not undertake the kind of sweep-cleaning operations that occurred in Atlanta, and Sydney produced a protocol setting out guidance for the treatment of homeless people in the lead up to the games. In 1998 the Premier of New South Wales, Bob Carr made a statement indicating that 'unfortunates would not be removed from the streets just to make an impression for the Olympic games'. Nevertheless, legislation was introduced in 1999 which provided the potential to move people on from specific areas in Sydney, including homeless people, though research indicated that this was rarely used. On the other hand, one news station reported that the homeless were being intimidated in the lead up to the games (COHRE 2007; ABC News 2000).

Athens – 2004

There were both positive and negative dimensions of Athens' housing legacy. Athens was relatively unique in that the whole of the athletes' village was converted to low-cost housing after the games. On the other hand, there were serious concerns about the treatment and displacement of Roma families and their subsequent rehousing, and victimisation of the homeless. There was little evidence of a significant increase in house prices after the games.

Athens came under a considerable degree of criticism in the lead up to the games with regard to the treatment of mainly Roma residents. According to COHRE (2007) a number of landowners were displaced and adequately compensated, in some instances at above the market value for their properties. Concern focussed on the displacement and poor treatment of Roma families. Both the Greek National Commission on Human Rights and UNCESCR in a report raised concerns about this:

> The Committee is gravely concerned about numerous reports on the extra judicial demolition of dwellings and forced evictions of Roma from Settlements by municipal authorities often under the pretext of construction projects for the 2004 Olympic games without payment of adequate compensation or provision of alternative housing. (United Nations Committee on Economic, Cultural and Social Rights 2004, p. 7, para. 121)

Amnesty International has raised concerns about the treatment of Roma in a number of European countries over several years, however, we focus here exclusively on displacement linked to the Olympics. COHRE (2007) identify three key concerns that have emerged with regard to Olympics and displacement. Firstly they highlight the way in which the construction of an Olympic site or potential construction of an Olympic site was used to justify evictions. For example, in 2001 the President of the Special Committee for the Roma, with the Council of Europe, raised concerns about the clearance of tents and tent dwellers in Aspyropygos under the auspice of Olympic projects.

Secondly, there was a failure to honour formal agreements with regard to displacement. For example, in the town of Masouri (a suburb outside Athens) land settled by Greek and Albanian Roma families was required to enable the construction of a car park for the Olympic Games. A formal agreement was reached with regard to displacement between the authority and 50 Greek Roma families. The agreement set out terms for the voluntary vacation of the plot in exchange for financial compensation to pay for housing on a temporary basis, and the provision of permanent, metal, prefabricated housing. The agreement excluded the Albanian Roma families, leaving them to find suitable alternative accommodation themselves. The agreement with the 50 Greek Roma Families was not adhered to and the families filed complaints with regard to the considerable delays in the payment of monies compounded with problems finding alternative accommodation because of both discrimination and lack of monies. The Greek Helsinki Monitor filed a criminal complaint with the Athens Misdemeanours prosecutors' office leading to an investigation. The Mayor of Masouri, in a letter dated February 2004, confirmed that only 14 families had been paid in full. However, it was subsequently reported that subsidies were eventually paid to all families (Amnesty International 2004). Amnesty International expressed concern that residents had been evicted without securing alternative accommodation and the authorities were therefore in violation of the International Covenant on Economic, Social and Cultural Rights to which Greece was a signatory. Amnesty International reported that by 2005 payments had still not been paid in full and residents were not clear where they were going to live (Amnesty International 2009).

Thirdly, Greece had an integration programme linked to improving the living standards of the Roma through the construction of new settlements in prefabricated housing, basic services and security of tenure. According to COHRE (2007) three schemes were not progressed because of the Olympics. For example in Crete, in the Municipality of Nea Alikarnoss, 200 families were to be resettled on a location adjacent to a basketball court that was to be used for the games. It is alleged that the mayor blocked this and in an interview commented:

> You cannot have a gypsy settlement next to a basketball court, part of the Olympic 2004 facilities, because gypsies blemish one's sense of good taste. (COHRE, p. 77)

He proposed the site be used as a car park. The housing project did not progress on this site. A trial ensued on the basis that the Mayor was in violation of its own anti-racism law, however, the Mayor was found not guilty.

Greece is relatively unique in that the athletes' village was converted into the largest social scheme designed and targeted at low-income workers. The Workers Housing Organisation developed the scheme through the establishment of a separate subsidiary Olympic Village 2004 S.A. who built the athletes' village and converted it into housing following the games. The Workers Housing Organisation had experience of developing large-scale projects, whereas the private sector had developed only small-scale projects and therefore this was one of the key rationales for the Workers Housing Organisation leading the project.

The athletes' village was converted into 2,292 units housing around 10,000 individuals after the Games. The housing was sold at half market value to members of the Workers Housing Organisation (EOK) and was allocated via a lottery in October 2004 to those who met the criteria. More than 17,000 families applied for the housing (Hellenic Republic 2004). The lottery was open to all workers despite calls for the housing to prioritise Greek Nationals. It was targeted at public sector workers or pensioners who did not have sufficient income to purchase a property and had worked for a predetermined number of days and a small proportion of units targeted at people living in a particular district.

The new district has encountered lots of problems. The strong environmental standards set out in the candidature file were not adhered to. Plans for the village included new infrastructure such as libraries, cinemas and schools which were identified as central to the establishment of a successful community, however, these were not developed, placing an additional burden on existing provision. The Local Authority was not given additional resources to cater for the substantial increase in population arising from this new housing (East Thames, 2007). There was a general lack of clarity about responsibilities for key services such as rubbish collection and this lack of clarity resulted in the local municipality refusing to collect rubbish from the village. The conversion into housing was also slow and by April 2006 only 400 families had moved in. This meant that, despite being allocated the housing in 2004, some two years later the houses were not ready for occupation. Currently the village has high vacancy rates and is strewn with litter and graffiti (Smith 2012).

Clearly Greece's problems have become much more significant since this time to the extent that the government has stripped the assets of the Workers Housing Organisation to pay debt and the Olympic Stadium is being used to house increasing numbers of homeless families (Nunns 2012; Ekathimeniri 2012).

Data on house price increases is complex. There is evidence of increases in house prices in the 4.25 years preceding the games. For example, in this period property prices in Greece increased by 53 per cent compared to 62 per cent in Athens. This additional premium was relatively low in comparison to other cities (Halifax 2004). Moreover, even this 9 per cent premium is problematic as detailed analysis of property trends in Athens revealed that above-average price increases did not correlate with proximity to Olympic infrastructure and reflected a more general trend across Athens at this time (COHRE 2007).

There was also evidence of a heavy policing operation targeted at the poor in the lead up to the games: A substantial force of 70,000 police and military officers was drafted in to police the city. There were reports of victimisation and relocation of the homeless, a significant increase in deportations of asylum seekers and increased use of the mental health legislation to section drug addicts and the mentally ill. According to the European observatory on the Homeless '…a lot of undesirables were thought to have been moved on to other districts' (quoted in Smith 2004).

Beijing – 2008

The Beijing Olympics housing legacy was marked by significant displacement and rising house prices. The transformation of Beijing was far-reaching with the construction of new roads and venues and is estimated to have cost in excess of £20 billion making it the most expensive Olympic and Paralympic Games to date (Bristow 2008). The rationale for hosting the Olympic Games was less about direct economic benefits and more about demonstrating China's strength as an economically successful global superpower.

There is some debate as to the extent of displacement linked directly with the Olympic and Paralympic Games. For example COHRE (2007) estimated that 1.5 million were displaced whereas Beijing's Olympic organising committee argue that the figure was around 6,037 households with each of them receiving a compensation package (Beck 2007). Amnesty International and COHRE highlighted the wider context of repression that had impacted on lawyers' ability/willingness to take on issues of tenants' rights, coupled with a lack of freedom of expression which makes it difficult to assess the actual number of residents displaced and the compensation given. Amnesty International took up the case of a housing rights campaigner imprisoned for trying to organise protests against the demolition of housing for the Olympic Games (Amnesty International 2008; COHRE 2007).

As is the case in many cities, it is difficult to identify and isolate displacement related to the Olympic Games as compared to other processes of development. In Beijing there has been a process of transformation going on for some time and this in itself has been leading to significant displacement of the poor from inner cities to outer suburbs. Nevertheless the delivery of the Games was dependent on a range of new infrastructure, such as 22 new stadia, two ring roads, 142 miles of new infrastructure and eight new subway lines and therefore, it is hard to imagine that widespread displacement could have been avoided.

Shin and Li (2012) argue that in 2004 the municipality committed to undertaking 'environmental' improvements that would involve demolishing 171 Villages in the City (VIC) housing more than 33,000 residents. According to Shin this meant that 'areas most likely to be visited by Olympic tourists in Beijing would be clear of urban eyesores' (Shin 2009, p. 134). In reality progress was much slower and a lower number of VICs were demolished – this was estimated at 63 VICs. Villages in the City are not unique to Beijing and are found in cities across China; housing provided is privately rented and mainly occupied by migrant workers who find it difficult accessing either public or private housing for sale. The housing tends to be poorly regulated and of poor quality. They conclude that the loss of this housing did not impact negatively on the residents as they were able to secure affordable housing elsewhere, however, they suggest that the process has contributed to a spatial restructuring of Beijing:

> It is possible that the slow death of VICs in relatively central districts of Beijing in its promotion as a world city would accompany the growth of VICs in Outer Suburban districts, thus producing a bifurcated city with spatial segregation.
> (Shin, Li, p. 20)

Both Beijing and China have experienced significant house price increases from 1990 onwards. Real estate investment made a significant contribution to GDP and expanded in Beijing at an annual rate of 22 per cent between 1999 and 2006, reflecting a growing demand for housing with the growth of people living in cities and also by investors/speculators. Real estate development is significant in Beijing with almost half of fixed-asset investment invested in real estate since 2000 (*Economist* 2007). There is evidence of significant price increases both in the years preceding and following the games. For example, between January 2006 and 2007 property prices in Beijing rose by 9.9 per cent which was the second highest rate of 70 cities surveyed in China. Moreover, the significant physical improvements associated with the Games clearly had the effect of uplifting land values further, however, it is difficult to locate the specific contribution that hosting the games has played as distinct from the ongoing transformation of cities across China and Beijing in particular. According to a report in the *Economist* there was a slowdown in new builds in the year directly preceding the games as the city wanted to avoid lots of cranes and building sites and it is argued that this slow-down in supply contributed to increased demand. Moreover the slow-down disproportionately affected the supply of low-cost housing schemes which was cut by 57 per cent in 2006 compared to 6 per cent for all housing projects (*Economist* 2007). What is clear is that the ongoing issue of access for low income groups in Beijing has been exacerbated as a result of Beijing hosting the Games.

The athletes' village was converted into luxury housing after the games and renamed Dream World. The scheme comprised 1,800 units and was developed by the Beijing Urban Construction Investment and Development Corporation and a subsidiary established to develop the village and subsequent housing – the Beijing Goa Investment Development Company Limited – the scheme did not include any 'affordable housing' units. The majority of the units (more than 1,000) were sold in 2006 helping to capitalise the projects and two years later prices had doubled. The scheme won an LEED Gold award for its environmentally friendly design. It is claimed that actual construction costs were not higher than any new build in Beijing and there was a limited need for marketing as the fact that it was built for the Olympics effectively acted as a guarantor of quality. The transport, green environment and access to sports facilities were perceived to be key attractions (China.org.cn 2008). We can conclude that this scheme was aimed at better-off sections of the population.

There is evidence of a 'social clean-up' of the city prior to the games and the relocation of the homeless. The head of the organising team for the Beijing Olympic and Paralympic Games ordered the relocation of what were seen as problematic businesses or people in the lead up to the games including prostitutes, hawkers and the homeless, though he argued that the police operated with restraint when undertaking their duties (Watts 2008).

Vancouver Winter Games – 2010

We will not be exploring the housing legacies of Winter Games in general. However, the Vancouver Games has some strong similarities with the London Games with regard to its commitment to an inclusive housing legacy and its bid was formulated when the issue of legacy had become more significant. Vancouver's bid included an ambitious affordable housing legacy accompanied by an Inner City Inclusivity Commitment statement that formed part of the bid, setting out a commitment to maximise the benefits and minimise the impact on inner city communities including pledges to ensure that people were not made homeless as a result of the winter games, residents were not involuntarily displaced, evicted or made to face unreasonable increases in rent during the Games and that an affordable housing legacy would be provided.

The decision to incorporate an inclusivity agenda into its original legacy bid was clearly in response both to the legacy criteria and the city's serious housing problems both in terms of lack of affordable housing and homelessness. Vancouver has the highest percentage of households with serious affordable issues of any city in Canada and is ranked the eleventh least affordable city in the world. This is explained by a huge demand for housing, in part fuelled by immigration to the region. The population increased by 19.5 per cent between 2000 and 2010 (Mohtes-Chan 2011). The 2003 bid document claimed that one of the lasting legacies of the games would be to end homelessness in the city, however, between 2002 and 2008 homelessness in the city increased by 134 per cent. Researchers undertaking an Olympic Games Impact Study indicated that it was not clear whether homelessness has been caused by homeless people moving there from elsewhere in Canada or because of the Olympics, and overall they identified a 'very slight positive impact' on homelessness (Hui 2010). This was explained in terms of the implementation of strategies to strengthen housing rights, for example, a voluntary organisation was funded to provide advice to residents unfairly evicted (though it is claimed that this applied to very few residents). A tenant registry was established for tenants concerned about eviction, a bye-law was introduced prohibiting the conversion of housing to tourist hotels and night shelters were provided. Nevertheless, the Chief of Police did advise the homeless that they would be moved to shelters if they were too close to official games venues and security zones (Mauboules 2010).

There were two key dimensions to the affordable housing legacy: temporary housing used to house athletes and officials at Whistler were re-used as 156 rental apartments for low-income households and distributed across six neighbourhoods after the Games.

The athletes' village was built on former industrial land owned by the government along the waterfront and comprises 1,108 units including 252 affordable units. The contract to build the village was awarded to a private consortium. The original plans included a strong commitment to affordable housing with the largest component of housing (66 per cent) designated as affordable, including 33 per cent of units targeted at low-income families i.e. those unable to afford median rent and 33 per cent targeted at houses in the middle third of income. The affordable housing was to be pepper-potted throughout the development. In 2006 affordable housing targets were revised downwards and by 2007 the affordable housing element was reduced to 252 (20 per cent) units located in distinct blocks (Markle 2010).

The athletes' village has encountered a number of problems. One key problem that has arisen has related to the financing of the scheme linked to an underestimation of costs. The Vancouver Organising Committee provided a $30 million subsidy towards the cost of affordable housing at the scheme which was initially estimated to cost $65 million. This increased to $95 million in 2006 and the final cost was $110 million. The increasing costs were explained in terms of initial under-estimation with regard to the clean-up costs at the site, an upgrading from LEED Silver to LEED Gold which required much more demanding adherence to green technologies and a slowness in commencing the project which resulted in the need to pay additional overtime to ensure completion (Enchin 2010).

In 2010 a debate ensued related to the high cost of affordable housing at the village. Questions were raised as to whether it was appropriate to invest this much money into affordable housing when a much larger supply of housing could be built elsewhere for the same cost. Eventually it was agreed to rent half of the 252 units to essential workers who earn no more than five times the monthly rent with the remainder targeted at low income households. There were concerns that any change in policy linked to selling the units would have impacted on the existing stock of housing for sale at the village. Initial commitments to substantial affordable housing then had been compromised.

There were also problems with regard to identifying a 'not-for-profit' provider who was willing to take on the affordable housing element. There were a number of requirements placed on potential providers which were perceived as prohibitive. For example a clause specified that any surplus from the units would be returned to the government whilst losses would be absorbed by the providers. There were no subsidies for operating the scheme and they would be required to purchase properties on 60-year leases. It was argued that this would translate into rents that would be unaffordable for many residents on low incomes. There was also caution with regard to new forms of green technologies used at the apartments

(*Globe and Mail* 2010). The units remained empty for months whilst issues of management were resolved. At the end of 2010 the first social housing units were let and a management agency COHO Property Management was established as a subsidiary of the Cooperative Housing Federation of British Columbia.

Private Developers were appointed to deliver the scheme, however, following the downturn in the property market the City of Vancouver had to provide an additional bail-out to ensure that the project was completed. A number of private sale units were sold off-plan in 2008 to assist with the capitalisation of the project and the long-term plan was for the government to cover its cost through the sale of the units. By December 2010 only 30 per cent had been sold and receivers were called in and the scheme rebranded 'The Village on False Creek' and prices reduced by an average of 30 per cent with many properties converted to luxury rentals pending recovery of the market (CBC News 2011). By 2012 there was evidence of increased demand and the perception of a 'ghost town' was beginning to fade with shops and services opening at the village. Moreover, by September 2012, 551 of the 737 units for sale had been sold (*Globe and Mail* 2012). In August 2013 it was reported that a Canadian Investment Group had purchased a number of units that would form part of a private rental investment product similar to that offered by QDD in London (Bula 2013).

The athletes' village in Vancouver initially set out ambitious targets for sustainability and affordability. Whilst it was successful in meeting sustainability objectives (which have contributed to the marketability of the apartments) it has been much less successful with regard to the provision of affordable housing. In part the waning commitment to affordable housing reflected a change in administration at City level, and clearly this is a generalised problem that raises more fundamental questions about the gap between legacy commitments and legacy outcomes. Essentially public monies have been used to underwrite luxury waterfront apartments with a relatively negligible proportion of affordable housing units whose impact on housing need will be miniscule.

We can see that whilst the use of the concept legacy has emerged post 2002, each city has to a greater or lesser extent included a housing legacy. The athletes' village has provided an important source of post-Games housing in each host city excluding Atlanta. The athletes' villages at Barcelona, Sydney and Beijing were developed by the private sector with some input from the public sector and they have all been converted into relatively exclusive private housing complexes after the Games. The inclusive design required for the Paralympics has made them attractive for people with disabilities and the high eco specification at Beijing, Sydney and Vancouver offers the potential to opt for 'green' living. However, the cost has excluded many residents from accessing the benefits of this housing. The Athens village was to be the most socially inclusive, however, in other respects it has not been successful. Both Vancouver and London's villages were developed post-2002 when legacy had been added to the growing expectations placed on host countries. Vancouver's athletes' village was to be a significant part of its legacy, however, over time the scheme has become more similar to other private-led models with much smaller proportions of affordable housing at significant cost to the taxpayer.

An increase in the value of properties in host cities has been evident to varying degrees across each host city. However, whilst the Olympics may have contributed to this increase it is not the key explanatory factor. Barcelona is the outlier in this regard with substantial house prices linked to the transformation of the city arising from the Olympics. In other cities such as Sydney and Athens price increases were more marked on schemes some distance from Olympic venues. Similarly, in Vancouver the huge increase in population has increased demand for properties. Therefore, any assumption that such events translate into increased property prices should be viewed with caution. On the other hand evidence from Barcelona, Beijing and Sydney suggests that housing at the athletes' village itself may benefit from above-average increases in property prices, though this has not been the case so far in Vancouver.

The homeless appear to have endured varying levels of harassment across these host cities during Games time. This was particularly marked in Atlanta, Athens and Beijing. Both Sydney and Vancouver did demonstrate some commitment to adopt good practice in this area. More generally the poor appear to have benefitted very little in terms of housing legacies to date. Moreover, the increase in land values associated with regeneration has led to secondary displacement.

Before, before moving on to explore London's legacy it is worth looking at London Docklands because many of the tensions and contradictions in this scheme are relevant to London 2012.

London Docklands

Plans for regenerating London Docklands had been developed from the late 1960s onwards. In 1981 the area was subject to what was then a new approach to urban planning marking a shift away from consensual policy making and the implementation of a market led approach to regeneration. An Urban Development Corporation, The London Docklands Development Corporation, was established and development control powers for the Docklands parts of Southwark, Newham and Tower Hamlets were transferred from the respective local authorities to an unelected quango. The London Docklands Development Corporation was answerable only to the Secretary of State. It was argued that given the area's strategic significance (it bordered the City of London) it should be developed in the 'national' rather than 'local' interest. A Thatcherite approach to regeneration was adopted in which the market, unfettered by government controls, would be the central agent of regeneration.

Plans had been drawn up by respective local authorities to use vacant land to meet local need. However, the LDDC's brief was simply to bring land and buildings into 'effective use'. The role of the agency reflected the then government's concern to promote owner occupation and reduce the role of government and indeed they were successful in this regard with owner occupation increasing from 5 per cent in 1981 to 44 per cent by 1989 (Brownill 1989). The LDDC argued it was necessary to create a balanced community by attracting a more affluent group to the area.

Between 1981 and 1998 (when the LDDC was disbanded) some 24,402 properties were built across the docklands areas, 17,789 of which were for direct sale (77 per cent of the total) and a further 722 for sale through shared ownership schemes. On the Isle of Dogs, 4,965 properties were built. The majority of these were for owner-occupation (84 per cent) with a small proportion of these for sale through shared ownership. In addition, 783 properties (16 per cent) were developed for housing associations for social rent (LDDC 1998). In Wapping and Limehouse 4,601 properties were built and more than 90 per cent of these were for owner-occupation. The London Borough of Tower Hamlets lost more than 400 homes as a result of the construction of the Limehouse Link Road and through the Right-to-Buy scheme so that the proportion of social housing available in the Borough declined from 82 per cent in 1987 to 46 per cent in 2004 (London Borough of Tower Hamlets 2005). The pattern was similar in Surrey Docks. However, the pattern of housing completions in the Royal Docks was different: Between 1981 and 1998, 6,322 units were built of which 3,652 were for private sale and a further 229 were developed for shared ownership, accounting for some 59 per cent of the total. In the Royal Docks 2,055 properties were developed by housing associations for social rent and a further 576 by the Local Authority for social rent, generating a very different tenure mix (LDDC 1998).

One explanation for the lower proportions of rented housing in Wapping and the Isle of Dogs relates to the comparatively high land values of properties given their proximity to Tower Bridge. Land in the Royal Docks was much cheaper and more affordable to housing associations wishing to develop, whereas the cost of developing a new site in Wapping or on the Isle Dogs was prohibitive as the market-led model meant that housing associations had to compete with private developers to purchase sites. Moreover developments in the Royal Docks began a little later than those close to the city and by 1988 the LDDC, following extensive public criticism of the polarised nature of development, placed a greater emphasis on meeting local need with the introduction of 'community gain' agreements, which explicitly linked developments with community benefits. The London Borough of Newham's Community Gain agreement resulted in the provision of 1,500 social housing units in the Royal Docks (Brownill 1989).

It was always a policy objective of the LDDC to present its strategy as beneficial to local people. The proportion of local people purchasing the new housing became an important point of debate, with the LDDC claiming that significant numbers of local people had purchased these properties whilst others questioned this data (LDDC 1998; GLC 1984; Docklands forum 1987). Moreover, despite the government's commitment to promote a free market approach to regeneration, attractive financial incentives were given to developers to enable them to develop sites, so that in some instances sites were sold at half their value (Brownill 1989;

Foster 1990). In return developers were expected to enhance local take-up of schemes by capping the price on a proportion of the properties at £40,000 and offering them initially to local people through local exclusion clauses.

The LDDC claimed that by 1985, 40 per cent of new properties had been purchased by local residents. However, a GLC study found that the proportion of local people buying houses decreased over time as property prices increased and as the number of £40,000 homes declined.[6] Developers suspended local exclusion clauses because so few applicants were applying (LDDC 1988; Brownill 1989; GLC 1984). The cheaper housing tended to be located in Becton with the implication that those living in Tower Hamlets would need to relocate to Becton if they wished to purchase a home (Foster 1989). There was also evidence of fraud, with local residents selling their rent books and purchasers using fake addresses, thus questioning the reliability of the data. However, local income surveys demonstrated that for the majority of residents owner-occupation was not an option. As new properties were built across Docklands the mismatch between housing need and housing supply became apparent. Reviews of housing need indicators suggested that housing waiting lists, homelessness and overcrowding continued to be major problems (Docklands Forum 1987; London Borough of Tower Hamlets 2005: London Borough of Newham 2003; London Borough of Southwark 2006). Rather than creating 'mixed/balanced' communities in areas such as Wapping and the Isle of Dogs there is considerable evidence of polarisation both in incomes and lifestyles. For example it was noted recently that:

> Tower Hamlets has evolved from a deprived borough to a deprived borough with an oasis of wealth, which is most obviously manifest in the polarisation of incomes and the missing middle that lies between ... It has proportionately more people earning less than 20,000, the greater or Inner London average and significantly more people earning more than 85,000 than the Greater London Average. (London Borough of Tower Hamlets 2010, p. 4)

The regeneration of London Docklands has been a physical success and the urban landscape has been transformed but the project has come to symbolise both a post-industrial Britain and a post-Thatcher divide between the haves and the have not's. It was through the enduring commitment of local communities to highlight these contradictions that the legacy of 'Canary Wharf' will always be identified by these inequities:

> This is an area which suffers from its image. It may have been redeveloped but it hasn't been regenerated. Side by side with housing that is available only to the richest few there are overlooked pockets of severe poverty and urban stress. (Time and Talents 1997: 3)

---

6 Land in some parts of the Docklands was selling at between 4 and 6 million per acre.

The Docklands case study is more pertinent to London 2012's housing legacy than the housing legacy of other cities, because the approach that is being applied to the Park has some strong similarities with that applied in London Docklands in that there was an implicit policy goal of attracting more affluent populations to the area coupled with subsidised opportunities for home ownership targeted at lower-income groups and what we might describe today as affordable housing options. In Docklands a range of income studies had demonstrated that even the low-cost, subsidised housing was not affordable to most of those living in the area in housing need. The area was developed in the national rather than local interest which meant that vast tracts of land were prepared at significant cost by government and marketed to developers for the construction of mainly market housing. Local need was overlooked with an assumption that there was an over-supply of Local Authority/public housing despite the significant need for it. This meant that key indicators of need such as housing waiting lists and overcrowding increased. The area was physically transformed into a desirable place but not, in the main, for existing residents.

References

ABC News (2000). *Sydney's homeless intimidated ahead of the games.* <http://www.abc.net.au/worldtoday/stories/s154590.htm> (Accessed 20 October 2012).

Ambrose, B. and Grigsby, W. (1999). *Mixed Income Housing Initiatives in Public Housing* (Pennsylvania: University of Pennsylvania).

Amnesty International (2004). *Europe and Central Asia: Summary of Amnesty International's concerns in the region Jan-June 2004* (Amnesty International).

Auburn Council Website (2012). *Community Profile Newington: Who are our residents?* <http://profile.id.com.au/Default.aspx?id=255&pg=140&gid=160&type=enum> (Accessed 23 August 2012).

Atlanta Housing Authority (2005). *Atlanta Housing Authority – 15 year Progress Report* (Atlanta: AHA).

Baim, D. (2009). Olympic Driven Urban Development, in *Olympic Cities: 2012 and the Remaking of London*, edited by Poynter, G. and Macrury, I. (Aldershot: Ashgate).

Biziouras, S.A. (2000). Enriching the legacy of Athens 2004 Olympic village, The role of IT infrastructure. Masters in City Planning Thesis (Massachusetts: MIT).

Bounds, M. and Dwyer, W. (2000). *The Olympics and Regional Movements in the Price of Residential Property: A comparative analysis of two rapid growth regions in Sydney.* Paper presented at the Sixth regional real estate conference in Sydney, January 2000.

Bristow, M. (2008). *Big Olympic Spend, but little debate.* BBC News, 31.7. <http://news.bbc.co.uk/1/hi/world/asia-pacific/7523235.stm> (Accessed 2 March 2013).

Brice, K. (2003). *The Atlanta Housing Enterprise Zone: From Concept to Revitalisation* (Atlanta: Atlanta Alliance for Community Development Investment).

British Columbia Factsheet (2010). Ministry of Housing and Social Development, *2010 Inner City Inclusivity*, February 1.

Brownill, S. (1989). *Developing London Docklands? Another Great Planning Disaster* (London: Paul Chapman).

Bula, F. (2010). First tenants move into social housing at Olympic Village. *The Globe and Mail*, 22 December 2010.

Bula (2013) Investors group acquire Olympic village apartments, *The Globe and Mail*, 20 August <http://www.theglobeandmail.com/news/british-columbia/investors-group-acquires-olympic-village-apartments/article13864833/>.

Canaves, S. (2008). *Beijing Olympic Clean Up Sends Migrants and Homeless Packing*, The Wall Street Journal, 4.8. <http://online.wsj.com/article/SB121788405566611245.html> (Accessed 2 March 2013).

Carbonel, J. (2005). *The Olympic Village, ten years on: Barcelona: the legacy of the Games, 1992–2002.* <http://olympicstudies.uab.es/pdf/wp087.pdf> (Accessed 10 October 2012).

CBC News (2011). *Olympic Villages condo prices cut up to 50%*, 10.2. <http://ca.news.yahoo.com/olympic-village-condo-prices-cut-50-20110210-175629-990.html> (Accessed 9 May 2012)

China.org.cn. (2008). *Price of Athletes Villages Flats Double.* <http://www.china.org.cn/olympics/news/2008-07/30/content_16097806.htm> (Accessed 2 March 2013).

Centre on Housing Rights and Evictions (COHRE). (2007). *Fairplay for Housing Rights, Mega Events, Olympic Games and Housing Rights* (Geneva: Geneva International Academic Network).

Centre on Housing Rights and Evictions (COHRE) (2007a). *The Impact of the Sydney Olympic Games on Housing Rights* (Switzerland: COHRE Centre on Housing Rights and Evictions).

Centre on Housing Rights and Evictions (COHRE) (2007b). The impact of the Athens Olympic Games on Housing Rights (Switzerland: COHRE Centre on Housing Rights and Evictions).

Channel Five News (1992). Techwood Residents vote on sale of Land, 26.5.1992. <http://www.youtube.com/watch?v=zo8VHtv7dC0> (Accessed 19 July 2012).

Docklands Forum (1987). *Housing in London Docklands* (London: Docklands Forum).

Economist (2007). *Beijing's Olympic Spirit: Inflated by the Olympic Spirit.* 1 March <http://www.economist.com/node/8776275> (Accessed 3 January 2012).

Ekamintheri (2012). *Olympic Stadium Opens Doors to Homeless*, February 2012. <http://www.ekathimerini.com/4dcgi/_w_articles_wsite1_1_01/02/2012_425521> (Accessed 19 May 2012).

Enchin, H. (2010) Athletes village fiasco: The city is to blame. 21 October, Vancouver Sun Staff Blogs, <http://blogs.vancouversun.com/2010/10/21/athletes-village-fiasco-the-city-is-to-blame/> (Accessed 4 August 2011).

Greater London Council (1984). *Housing and Employment in London Docklands* (London: GLC).

Globe and Mail (2010). *City demands of non profit organisations keeping Olympic Homes empty* <http:://m.theglobeandmail.com/news/british-columbia/city-demands-of-non-profit-housing-operators-keeping-olympic-village-empty/article1704748/> (Accessed 23 August 2012).

Globe and Mail (2012). *Life thrives after the games in Vancouver's Olympic Village* <http://www.theglobeandmail.com/news/british-columbia/life-thrives-after-the-games-in-vancouvers-olympic-village/article4476200/> (Accessed 3 January 2013).

Halifax Bank (2004). *House prices go for gold in Olympic Cities*, 18 October 2004 Press Release <http://www.cashquestions.com/threads/5416-House-prices-go-for-gold-in-Olympic-host-cities, going for gold> (Accessed 19 January 2012).

Heim, K. (2010). Will Vancouver meet Olympic Promise of helping the Poor? *Seattle Times* 12.1.

Hellenic Republic (2004). Embassy of Greece, 14 September 2004, *Olympic village housing to be allocated to beneficiaries in early October* <http://www.greekembassy.org/Embassy/content/en/Article.aspx?office=3&folder=200&article=14020epublic of Greece> (Accessed 3 May 2012).

Hue, S. (2010). *Homelessness doubled ahead of Vancouver Olympics Report shows* <http://www.straight.com/article-273777/vancouver/homelessness-doubles-ahead-vancouver-olympics-report-shows> (Accessed 3 May 2012).

Foster, J. (1999). *Cultures in Conflict: Worlds in Collision* (London: UCI Press).

Keating, R. (2000). Sixty and Out: Techwood homes transformed by enemies and Friends. *Journal of Urban History,* 26(3), pp. 287–304.

Ladner, P. (2010). *Vancouver Olympics: No medals for Olympic Housing Legacy*, 25 October 2010 <http://crosscut.com/2010/10/25/vancouver/20291/Vancouver-Olympics-no-medals-for-housing-legacy/> (Accessed 19 December 2012).

Lee, R. (2000). *Olympic Games Homelessness Parliamentary Debate.* Hansard Parliament of New South Wales, 22 June 2000 <http://www.parliament.nsw.gov.au/prod/parlment/hansart.nsf/V3Key/LC20000622041> (Accessed 19 October 2012).

London Borough of Southwark (2006). *Housing needs in Southwark* (London: London Borough of Southwark).

London Borough of Tower Hamlets (2010). *Tower Hamlets Local Economic Assessment 2010 Fact Sheet Volume 4: People and Places* (London: London Borough of Tower Hamlets).

London Docklands Development Corporation (1998). *Housing in the Renewed London Docklands* (London: LDDC).

Mason, G. (2011). *Olympic Village dream turns sour* <http://www.theglobeandmail.com/news/british-columbia/a-18-million-olympic-village-dream-turns-sour/article624044/> (Accessed 25 March 2011).

Markle, T. (2010). City Hall tries to run away from social housing promises at the Olympic Village, *The Mainlander*, 18 December.

Mauboles, C. (2010) Opinion: The Canadian Way, *Inside Housing*, 5 March.

Mohtes Chan, G. (2011) *House prices climb to global heights for latest Olympic Host.* Inman news, 31 May 2011 <http://www.inman.com/news/2011/05/31/housing-prices-climb-global-heights-latest-olympics-host> (Accessed 19 December 2012).

Newman, H.K. (2002). *The Atlanta Housing Authority's Olympic Legacy Programme* (Atlanta Research: Atlanta).

New York Times News Service (1996). *Atlanta homeless expect a rousting as Olympics draws near: Advocates charge city with increasing arrests*, 1 July.

Nunns, T. (2012). Greece: More than a demonstration: less than a revolt, *Red Pepper*, April.

OGI (2011). *Olympic Games Impact Study for the 2010 Olympic and Paralympic Winter Games, Report 2 of 4*.

Poynter, G. and Roberts, E. (2009). Atlanta 1996: The Centennial Games, in *Olympic Cities: London 2012 and the Remaking of London*, edited by Poynter, G. and Macrury, I. (Farnham: Ashgate).

Raco, M. (2008). Whose Gold Rush?: The Social Legacy of the Olympic Games, in *After the Goldrush: A Sustainable Olympics for London*, edited by Vigor, A., Mean, M. and Tims, C. (London: IPPR).

Time (2011). *Olympic Village Athletes Impressed Taxpayers Angry* <http://www.time.com/time/specials/packages/article/0,28804,1963484_1963490_1963439,00.html> (Accessed 3 February 2012).

Sadd, D. and Jones, I. (2008) *Implications and Issues of London 2012 for the Sites Residents* (Bournemouth: University of Bournemouth).

Sherlock, T. (2012). *Vancouver housing affordability declines in second quarter* in *Vancouver Sun*, 27 August. <http: estate/Vancouver+home+prices+continue+rise+second+quarter/7150541/story.html?utm_source=dlvr.it&utm_medium=twitter> (Accessed 13 February 2012).

Shin, H.B. (2009). Life in the shadow of mega-events: Beijing Summer Olympiad and its impact on housing, *Journal of Asian Public Policy.* 2(2): 122–41.

Shin, H.B. and Li, B. (2012). *Migrants, landlords and their uneven experiences of the Beijing Olympic Games.* CASE paper, Discussion paper, CASE/163. (Centre for Analysis of Social Exclusion: London).

Smith, H. (2004). Beggars and drug addicts disappear in Athens clean up before the games, *Guardian*, 11 August.

Smith, H. (2012). Athens 2004 Olympics: What happened after the athletes came, *Guardian*, 9 May.

Thomson, H. (2010). Councillor Wordsworth pleased with Coop Olympic Village, 5 November. <http://www.straight.com/article-356735/vancouver/cope-councillor-woodsworth-pleased-coop-olympic-village-affordable-housing-operator> (Accessed 13 May 2012).

Time and Talents (1997). *Time and Talents Newsletter* (London).

United Nations Committee on Economic, Cultural and Social Rights (2004) Concluding Observations of the committee on economic, cultural and social rights. Greece. 07.06.2004 E.C.12.1.Add 97 <http://www.unhchr.ch/tbs/doc.nsf/(Symbol)/E.C.12.1Add.97.En> (Accessed 20 May 2012)

Walsh, A. (2012). Sydney's Newington Olympic Village 12 years after the closing ceremony in *Property Observer*, 9 August. <http://www.propertyobserver.com.au/residential/sydney-s-newington-olympic-village-12-years-after-the-closing-ceremony/2012080855832> (Accessed 9 October 2012).

Watts, J. (2008). Beijing announces pre-Olympic social clean up. *Guardian*, 23 January. <http://www.guardian.co.uk/world/2008/jan/23/china.jonathanwatts> (Accessed 19 May 2012).

Zamani, A., Karavorikos, G., Kotzamanis B. and Lalenis, K. (2009). The Social Identity of the Post Olympic uses of the Olympic village settlement in Greece <http://www-sre.wu.ac.at/ersa/ersaconfs/ersa10/ERSA2010finalpaper1248.pdf> (Accessed 19 May 2012).

Chapter 2
Moving Out: Experiences of Those Decanted to Make Way for the Olympic Park

In July 2005 London won the bid to host the Olympic and Paralympic games and while much of the UK celebrated, many travellers and residents at the Clays Lane Housing Cooperative were devastated by the news and some had mixed feelings:

> We were all excited about it. We were pleased London won it. All of our families and grandchildren were raised in East London and at the same time we knew we had to move and we would rather have stayed where we were. (Traveller)

> I felt absolutely gutted. Physically sick. (Resident, Clays Lane)

What followed was a major displacement programme organised by the London Development Agency including the compulsory purchase of land and the relocation of homes and businesses. Within two years all of the residents had been decanted. This chapter presents the findings of a research study that set out to explore the experiences of these residents.

Research Study and Methodology

The research was undertaken between June 2011 and June 2012 and focused on three main themes:

1. The general management of the move with regard to availability of information, advice and support (both practical and emotional) and perceptions of choice.
2. Perceptions of housing conditions – before and after the move.
3. Perceptions of 'neighbourhood' and 'community' before and after the move.

Methodological Challenges

There was a number of methodological challenges. Initially, it was anticipated that we would undertake a mix of focus groups and one to one interviews with residents and Travellers. The research team encountered two main problems with regard to focus groups. Whilst Travellers were located as one group in

Newham, they were located across three sites in Hackney and in the case of Clays Lane across the country; therefore identifying a suitable venue that would be convenient was a problem. We did organise a focus group targeted at Newham Travellers and employed research assistants to recruit participants, however, not one single Traveller attended the group. There was also a problem of research fatigue as residents and Travellers had been contacted by a range of organisations and individuals for similar information. We therefore decided to rely more on conversations on the doorstep combined with semi-structured interviews. We interviewed ten Travellers across Newham and Hackney and gathered information from other residents through informal conversations. We also drew on published and unpublished documents related to their experience.

We also experienced difficulties recruiting residents who had previously lived at Clays Lane. We wanted to recruit as many residents as possible and wrote to authorities involved in the decanting asking if they would forward an invitation to participate. Agencies did not maintain a list and therefore this process of recruitment was not successful. We then wrote to a resident active in the former residents' association and they forwarded an email to his contacts asking for volunteers to participate in the study. Clearly this sample would have excluded many individuals, however, the interviews did provide an insight into the research questions. Once these interviews had been undertaken key themes and issues that emerged in the interviews were used as a basis for interviewing policy makers.

Contextualising the Decanting Process

Displacement is often an unfortunate but inevitable feature of regeneration and often results in the break up of longstanding communities. Across East London displacement has been an ongoing theme. This was graphically described in Young and Wilmot's study, *Family and Kinship in East London* that explored a group of residents displaced from Bethnal Green to Debden and its impact on community ties in 1957 (Willmott; Young 1957).

A number of housing and regeneration projects have led to the displacement/decanting of longstanding residents, sometimes these projects are related to the demolition of unsuitable housing, and others more specifically to regeneration. For example in 1990, 500 families were decanted to make way for the Limehouse Link Road resulting in a fracturing of communities and networks in South Poplar. The future of the Carpenters Estate in Stratford is also uncertain.

There is an emerging literature on the impact of mega-events on poor communities around the world. According to the UN, displacement and forced evictions tend to take place to facilitate urban regeneration, large scale development projects, mega events, natural disasters and climate change or are economically related. Their research has highlighted a range of problems associated with this and some of these are reflected in the findings of this study – psychological disorders, economic problems, loss of social ties, cultural and familial identity and discrimination when settling into a new community. They also suggest that forced evictions tend to affect the most vulnerable groups (UN Habitat 2004). However, there is a dearth of literature in the UK on residents' experiences once they have been decanted (Tunstall; Lupton 2010).

More generally there has been a concern within London and other major cities about a process of gentrification that has encroached on the ability of low income households to live in inner city areas and the demolition of social housing when it is now in such short supply through regeneration activities. The Expert Independent Panel that provided a number of recommended revisions to the London Plan in 2011 included a recommendation that there should be no net loss of affordable housing in regeneration areas. However, this was modified by the Mayor to stipulate that 'plans should resist the loss of housing including affordable housing unless replaced by better quality housing providing at least an equivalent floor space' and therefore disregarded the advice of its own Examination in Practice Panel (Greater London Authority 2011a, para. 2.62; Greater London Authority 2011b, p. 7).[1]

In the case of Stratford the area was presented as a derelict and dilapidated place in urgent need of change and therefore the loss of housing both at Clays Lane and on sites housing the Travellers was presented as an inevitable outcome of social progress with the promise of legacy acting as a trump card that enabled policy makers to demolish a significant source of housing in East London. Moreover, given the huge amount of land elsewhere on the park, it is hard to imagine that the demolition of housing at Clays Lane was inevitable. Raco and Tunney (2010) argue that planners and policy makers promoted a discourse that reinforced the notion that the area was a blank slate awaiting comprehensive redevelopment on land that was derelict, contaminated or degraded and in the process played down the way that land was being used at the time. During games time, media coverage continually reinforced the notion that this area had previously been an urban wasteland, ignoring the long-standing communities that simply found themselves in the way of one of Britain's largest ever regeneration projects.

Displacing/Decanting Residents at the Clays Lane Housing Cooperative

The Clays Lane Housing Cooperative was set up in 1984 and housed 450 individual tenants organised into 107 households. The cooperative was set up to house single young people in East London: There were 425 tenants living in the cooperative when London won the bid. It was at the time the second biggest purpose-built housing cooperative in Europe and catered exclusively for single adults. The accommodation comprised a mix of one-bedroom flats, bungalows, and four, six and ten-bedroom houses. The Cooperative provided a route into social housing for single people who would not have easily accessed social housing elsewhere.

---

1 The Examination in public hearings comprised an independent panel who reviewed expert evidence in 2011 in order to make recommendations about revising the London Plan.

Cooperative housing comprises a small proportion of housing in the UK at 0.6 per cent of total stock and residents living in this kind of housing tend to be more satisfied and appreciative of the mutual support that is offered and the empowering nature of the governance model (Bliss 2008).

Prior to London winning the bid there had been serious concerns raised by the Housing Corporation about the management of the estate. The Housing Corporation initiated a process whereby management and ownership of the housing Cooperative had transferred to the Waltham Forest Community Based Housing Association (a branch of Peabody). Residents had appealed against this, expressing a preference to be managed by Tenants First, a Scottish Mutual Society, however, this was rejected and in August 2005 WFCBHA took over management of the estate (Audit Commission 2005). The quality of the multi-occupancy, large houses was deemed to be below the 'decent homes' standard.[2] However, this was the case on many estates across the country.

The London Development Agency (LDA) was given responsibility for purchasing land and clearing it for the Olympics through the use of Compulsory Purchase Orders. The Clays Lane Housing Cooperative committee as an organisation objected to the Compulsory Purchase Order and a group of residents appealed against the outcome of the Compulsory Purchase Order (arguing it was in contravention of their human rights). The chair of the housing cooperative submitted an affidavit to the London Borough of Newham planning committee in September 2004 asking for a double decant with a temporary move and then a return to the park. This position was expressed in initial talks with the LDA from November 2003 onwards. However, the planning consent was not amended to include this as it was claimed it was subject to specific conditions that made this impossible (Fluid 2005).

Essentially then the residents' concerns were rejected. As the process of decanting unfolded, tensions between those managing the decant and a number of residents became fraught resulting in an appeal against the Compulsory Purchase Order on the grounds that their human rights had not been respected.[3] A CPO inquiry was set up and residents were awarded legal aid to fight their case. At the CPO inquiry residents raised concerns about a shift away from initial commitments with regard the quality of replacement housing, the necessity of the need to demolish Clays Lane as a unique co-operative housing project, the consultation process and failure to facilitate a group move. According to the head

---

2 The decent homes standard set a benchmark for improving the quality of public housing based on a range of criteria such as state of repair and facilities. Significant proportions of public housing were deemed to fall below this standard and subject to renovation. See Department of Communities and Local Government (2006) A Decent Home: Definitions for guidance and implementation – update June 2006 https://www.gov.uk/government/uploads/system/uploads/attachment_data/file/7812/138355.pdf. Accessed 9 December 2012.

3 There were 74 residents listed as objectors at the Public Inquiry, though it appeared there was some dispute as to whether all of these residents were actual residents.

of Public Law at Irwin Mitchell, acting on behalf of the residents and commenting in relation to one resident:

> He was promised he would be re-housed in equivalent if not better housing, but so far these promises have failed to materialise. He was informed he could move as part of a group in order to salvage what he could of his community but now he is being told he must accept whatever is on offer. My client now feels he is being forced to accept accommodation, however unsuitable it may be, in order to avoid being homeless and that once he is rehoused any hope of being reunited with fellow residents will diminish. (Mitchell 2005, 30 May)

However, the promise of legacy effectively acted as a trump card leading the Inspector to conclude that:

> In my consideration of the objections relating to the Clays Lane Estate, the overt sense of community and the value that many residents put on their homes and their surroundings is foremost in my mind. Their loss will be a substantial one. However, I find the anticipated benefits and the catalytic effect of the Olympic games to be a more forceful factor. (CPO Inspectors Report 2006, para. 6.2.87)

The LDA as part of its preparations for the London bid commissioned a study on residents' views and preferences with regard to moving and included 70 per cent of the 425 households. The majority of those surveyed (53 per cent) indicated they would prefer to live outside of a housing cooperative. There was a substantial minority (32.7 per cent) that would wish to remain in a cooperative or collective housing arrangement and a further (14.1 per cent) that were unsure. Therefore, there was clearly support to retain a cooperative or collective housing element, with Fluid suggesting that this may emerge as a preference for up to 200 individuals. There was also a clear preference for residents both wishing to move out of the cooperative and those wishing to live within a cooperative or collective arrangement for self contained flats as compared to shared accommodation, 84.2 per cent of residents expressed a desire to live in self-contained flats with only 8.6 per cent expressing a preference to live in shared accommodation (Fluid 2004). The Chair and a number of residents refused to participate in the Fluid Survey; therefore, the extent of support for the Cooperative or collective housing arrangement may have been higher than that indicated in the survey. In 2005 after London won the bid and Waltham Forest Community Based Housing Association took over the management of the housing they undertook another survey and residents were unhappy about this as they had already participated in the survey undertaken by Fluid which was comprehensive and more significantly failed to include a question about a collective move.

Moving Residents – Systems and Structures

The London Development Agency was responsible for establishing the relocation system and strategy. Its role was to negotiate with housing providers to ensure access to housing for Clays Lane residents and put in place a system of information, advice and support. It commissioned a number of agencies to work with them including WFCBHA which in addition to its management role on the estate was also involved in providing advice and support about re-housing options. Newham allocated a worker to assist residents applying for re-housing through the choice-based letting system. The LDA commissioned the Safer Neighbourhoods unit to provide independent advice to residents and this was available from February 2006. The Safer Neighbourhoods Unit (SNU) was selected by a tenant panel and held weekly drop-in surgeries; they also instigated the establishment of a residents' group as a vehicle for representing residents' concerns 'Clays Lane on the Move'. In January 2007, PECAN (a Christian counselling service) was employed to provide emotional support.

The LDA was responsible for developing a formal relocation strategy as part of the planning permission attached to the granting of the CPO. However, the strategy was slow to emerge and was not produced until January 2006. Residents at the inquiry expressed their disappointment as they had anticipated a strategy that would set out choices about relocation including collective moves. However, at the CPO inquiry it was implied by the Senior Manager leading the decant for the LDA that the actual strategy was less important as the detail of the relocation was emerging over time following negotiations (Rose 2006, para. 4.3.108).

There were a number of key themes that emerged in the Fluid survey that were important in developing any relocation strategy. The first related to the ability to move as a group/collective. The second related to findings in both the Fluid survey and subsequent WFCBHA survey that the preference for the majority of residents was to remain in Newham. Most social housing in Newham was owned by the Local Authority and in order for residents to be able to access this housing they would need to be given decant status by the London Borough of Newham as this ensures that residents have high priority when bidding for units. However, in order for residents at Clays Lane to be given decant status an agreement with Newham was required and it was not until July 2006 that agreement was reached and therefore by the LDA's own admission very few residents had been able to secure a move to Newham up until this point. This would clearly add to the anxiety and confusion already confronting residents and would have meant that choices were limited because of slowness in establishing crucial processes to facilitate choice against a background where residents were told that anyone who had not left the estate by July 2007 would forfeit their compensation.

The Clays Lane Housing Cooperative was home to residents with a higher proportion of disabilities than Newham as a whole. For example, the Fluid survey found that of those responding 39 (13.2 per cent) indicated they had a disability, compared to (5.5 per cent) of the UK population and 6.8 per cent of the Newham population (Fluid 2005).[4] The survey identified a range of disabilities including both medical and mental health problems that may have had an impact on relocation. According to the LDA, residents that were identified with a disability were prioritised in the immediate decant process. However, it was not until very late on in this process that a support agency was employed to offer emotional support to residents.

Replacement Housing – 'at least as good, if not better'

One key area of dissatisfaction amongst some residents arose with regard to initial commitments about the quality of replacement housing. In June 2004 residents received a letter from Mr Winterbottom, the then Director of the LDA, indicating that residents would receive housing that 'reflects their individual needs and would be at least as good if not better than existing accommodation', however, this was amended in the Fluid Survey to include 'as far as is practicable' (Fluid 2005, p. 50). Ken Livingstone, in a reply to a question from a GLA member in November 2005 stated that they were committed to Clays Lane residents being given a range of re-housing options that are expected to lead to an improvement in their current accommodation (*The Lawyer* 2007)

These commitments led to a considerable degree of disgruntlement as it was felt that there was a lack of clarity about what this actually meant and how it would translate into entitlements. How would it be measured? Did it relate to rent levels/housing costs? Size of property? More specifically would it mean that residents could move as a group? The LDA at the public inquiry asserted that the tone changed in the Fluid Survey in order to provide some clarity and rejected any claim that the initial commitment referred to rent levels. The inspector at the CPO Inquiry conceded that the initial letter and subsequent statement in the fluid report about 'reasonable practicability' appeared to be an added test and may have aroused suspicions. Understandably then, there was a perception that initial commitments were not adhered too and were effectively meaningless (Rose 2006).

Moving as a Group/Retaining a Cooperative/Collective Living Arrangement

The desire of a number of residents to move as a Cooperative or in some kind of collective arrangement emerged as a key issue from 2004 onwards. Many residents had made a positive choice to live at Clays Lane because of the group/ cooperative lifestyle. Therefore, from their perspective the ability to retain this element in some form was a key factor that needed to be facilitated through the decant process.

---

4 The comparative figures are for adults aged 16–74.

There was evidence of significant demand for a collective or group move. This was confirmed when the Clays Lane Residents' Association expressed a preference for a double decant and again in the Fluid Survey with an estimate that up to 200 residents may want to move and again at the CPO inquiry where it was estimated that some 120 residents had expressed an interest in a group move. From the perspective of these residents there had been a lack of commitment for a group or collective move evidenced in the exclusion of a specific question on a group or collective move in the WFCBHA questionnaire and in the slow response of the LDA to develop a strategy facilitating a group move. This was explored at the public inquiry into the CPO. According to the lead manager from the LDA, they had concentrated initially on individual options as this was the area for which there was most support. They confirmed that discussions about the possibility of a group move did not take place until the end of 2005 and this delay was clearly problematic given that a system to facilitate a group move would be more complex and require more time to organise than individual moves. Nevertheless the LDA assured the inspector at the CPO inquiry the LDA that there had been considerable progress in this area and that they identified a number of possible sites for a group move leading the CPO Inspector to conclude:

> To my mind there is nothing to suggest that the LDA ever set out to deny the option of a group move ... but by comparison with the individual moves it has taken longer to get off the ground. (Rose 2006, para. 6.2.52)

He concluded that he was satisfied that there had been significant progress to facilitate a group move and tenant management initiatives through the CPO (Rose 2006). However, a group move was not facilitated.

One of the key sites identified for a group/collective move was a new build development at Gallions Reach. The site was large enough to accommodate the residents with the potential for significant input from residents into the design. There were between 50 and 100 residents interested in this option. However, the location of the site was not popular with many residents, who felt the site was very isolated in comparison to Clays Lane and very close to the London City Airport. The Chair of Clays Lane Housing was keen to proceed with the site, but others were not, and at this point the larger group began to fracture.

According to one manager working independently with the residents:

> We employed a consultant in the early days to try and find properties and it was terribly disappointing, they had trouble finding anything except blocks where you wouldn't want to live ... We went on a tour and came across a site near City Airport where there was a possibility of a group move ... people were talking about it excitedly about taking part in the design of it. Now, the problem is that the city airport is sort of miles from anywhere. This was the problem; any site that could have been afforded wasn't particularly desirable.

Moreover, the CPO inspector conceded that residents would have to move twice given the time it would take to construct the site:

> Those opting for Gallions roundabout will be faced with the inconvenience and frustration of delay and a move into temporary accommodation. (Rose 2006: para. 6.2.53)

Another site that was considered for a group move was at the Nag's Head Estate in Bethnal Green that was owned by Peabody and used as short-life housing. Some residents were unhappy when they found that residents living in short-life housing on the Nag's Head Estate would be evicted in order to facilitate the group move (Inside Housing 2006).[5] Peabody confirmed that the existing residents were always aware that this was short-life housing, nevertheless 11 residents were given notice to leave in order that the housing accommodate Clays Lane residents. According to (SNU 2008) 40 residents moved as individuals to this scheme, however, there were no specific arrangements put in place to reinforce a group identity/collective arrangement.

The need to vacate the site by July 2007 placed a considerable pressure on residents and over time some of those initially committed to a group move moved on an individual basis leading to a decline in the number of people interested in a group move and a fracturing of the large group and an emergence of smaller groups interested in moving together. For example, a group of residents originally interested in moving as a larger group established a separate group of 13 people. However there was a lack of agreement over suitable sites and a more general pressure related to the stress of the move that led to the group becoming smaller and eventually disbanding. Another group of four wanted to move to the coast, however, this again never came to fruition. Two residents of this group described their frustration when they felt they were being pressured to move as individuals:

> They said we were not helping them, we said what more can we do over and above telling them where we want to live and that we want to move as a group. We went to a meeting and they said there are offers on the way for you and we were saying we don't want to look at that we are part of a group, we had to call the LDA and ask them to call the dogs off. (Former Clays Lane residents)

This group of four residents met with a housing provider on the south coast who indicated that he would be happy to re-house them together, but it would take a few years for enough properties to become available. Another suggestion by the housing provider was that a house be purchased and converted into flats, however, according to one member of the group, it was clear this was not going to be contemplated. Eventually, delays in achieving a group move meant that

---

5 *Inside Housing*, 18 August 2006.

residents moved as individuals with little time to exercise choice. This resulted in one resident having to live in a motel for two months pending preparation of their accommodation.

It was suggested by lawyers speaking on behalf of residents at the CPO inquiry that the substantial delays in realising suitable alternative group accommodation had led to 'a piecemeal relocation of residents who fear for their future and in the process has an erosive effect on the community' (Rose 2006, day 40, p. 108.)

> Towards the end of the campaign the LDA did give a lot of effort to find accommodation where people could live together and they did identify some groups of dwellings together. However, they were all wrong for the residents for whatever reason. If they had come up with a convenient location that did not require too much effort the residents may well have gone for it. (Manager involved in decant)

The failure to facilitate a group/collective move has to be understood as a serious failure on behalf of those organising the decant resulting in the fracture of a longstanding community and a failure to adequately meet their preferences. Having provided a context to the key issues arising with regard to the rehousing of residents at Clays Lane, I would like to move to consider the perceptions of residents about the rehousing process.

London Wins the Bid – Residents' Responses

We began our interviews by asking residents how they felt when they learnt that London had won the bid to host the Olympic and Paralympic Games. What was clear was that responses to this appeared to range from devastation to relief, though the majority interviewed in this survey were devastated:

> I was devastated, The Olympics wasn't a great thing for me, and I knew they wouldn't listen to us.

> The feeling was disbelief, I had lived on the estate a long time as part of a community.

> A bit sad, and then again I thought it was for the best because the housing was run down and dilapidated and it was a bit insular.

Routes into Clays Lane

We were interested to explore the reasons why individuals came to live at Clays Lane and in the main it was clear that is served as a relatively easy route into housing for single people confronted with a lack of alternatives. Residents applied to the cooperative and were interviewed by members of the cooperative the process between application and acceptance was often relatively quick. Residents moved initially into shared housing and overtime as vacancies arose they had the option of moving into different parts of the estate including bungalows or self contained flats:

> Originally, I was homeless, I was never a rough sleeper, I lived with someone, the relationship broke up we ended up crashing on lots of floors, which was fine, I was lucky I had lots of friends when I tried to stabilise my situation I looked around for housing and I found out about Clays Lane, which was the only Housing coop in London that was specifically offering accommodation for single people without a massive up front deposit.

> Access was relatively easy. I found out about it through an advice centre. They told me what a co-op was about, what I needed to do. I went through a series of interviews, from start to end it was probably about a week or two and I was living on the lane and it felt like a privilege. You know what London's like, there was no deposit to be paid or anything like that. It was amazing.

> The house interview was a bit worrying but you got to see what other people were like. The house was really dirty. You had an idea of the place by being interviewed, they were looking for someone they thought could fit in and you were looking for somewhere you thought you could fit. (Resident who lived at Clays Lane for more than ten years)

Once residents moved into Clays Lane the majority lived there for more than two years. For example, the Fluid survey indicated that 32.1 per cent had lived there for less than two years, a further 37.2 per cent for between two and five years and 30.7 per cent for more than five years. They concluded that the population was a slightly more stable population with regard to turnover than other private sector tenants living in Newham. It was clear that Clays Lane offered a relatively easy route into housing for single people.

Systems of Support to Facilitate the Decanting Process

As we have already seen a range of agencies were employed to offer support and advice to residents: These agencies had a presence on the estate. The plan was to re-house residents from the estate from January 2006 onwards. Residents interviewed for this study felt that there was a significant amount of confusion about their options, and some specifically commented on the way in what they perceived as a patronising attitude from the housing association now running the estate:

> They acted like they thought we should be grateful that we were being rehoused.
>
> There was nobody at CBHA that was that helpful because everybody gave conflicting information. It was very much about doing it for myself. In the end I went to my local MP.
>
> We had lots of meetings to make it clear about the moving, they sent to us regular letters to let us know that we are soon moving. I used to go there to speak to them but I did not find them helpful.

Up until July 2006 residents were dependent on selecting from a limited amount of stock:

> Initially they had choice based lettings and could opt for Peabody and partner organisation properties such as East Thames ... Then they had nomination rights to Newham properties. They had a double A rating which means that it is just below the highest priority, i.e. those with severe disabilities, for some people it was a once in a lifetime opportunity to have that level of choice and for some they were already registered with Choice based lettings ... They moved from the back to the front of the queue (Senior Manager, LDA).

This model then was reliant on tenants pursuing offers through the choice based lettings system and some tenants felt that it would have been more helpful if lists of available properties could be provided or matched with residents preferences. Towards the end of the process the decant team were more proactive in identifying properties. To incentivise the rehousing of residents, a joint agreement was established stipulating that where agencies rehoused a resident they would receive 1.25 nomination rights per unit in legacy housing.[6]

According to one Manager involved in decanting residents:

> Any housing association that assisted the LDA in rehousing residents would get one and a quarter nominations in the athletes' village, that hasn't been entirely ironed out and they may provide money instead, but that was the intention. We basically got them to express what they wanted, it wasn't restricted to the local area and then we found landlords. The landlords were persuaded to help. There was a huge thing around the Olympics and it was presented as their national duty to do it.

---

6 The Greater London Authority, London Development Agency, Olympic Development Authority signed a joint statement on the affordable housing legacy ensuring that those RSL's and Authorities rehousing residents would be given nomination rights for 1.25 legacy social housing units. The agreement refers to the potential that up to 50 per cent of the 9,000 units, though the actual level is likely to be much lower and this is discussed elsewhere in this book.

Residents were clearly very anxious about the move and there was a sense in which there was a lack of clarity about their entitlements with regard to the number of offers they were entitled to. There was a general perception that they were entitled to three offers and that there was an element of risk involved as they did not view three properties and make a decision about which they preferred rather they had to reject a property before receiving another offer:

> I was worried if I turned down one property, the next property might be worse, I felt like I was in a lottery gambling on the best property and it made me really anxious.

The three choices policy was dismissed by a senior manager at the LDA:

> That wasn't the case, they had as many choices as they wanted, when we got into the last month and a half if you rejected properties we said we would give you three more and that would be quits. Nobody ever had to take the third choice that never happened.

Nevertheless, it was clear that for some residents there was this anxiety and a fear that any delay in accepting properties may result in unsatisfactory compromises. Another resident expressed frustration about the lack of flexibility in approach. For example:

> I said to them I want to come back after the Olympics. They said it was very complicated, we don't think there is much desire for that. I suggested they get a piece of paper and write on the top. 'People who want to come back after the Olympics' put it in a filing cabinet and then contact them after the Olympics...I didn't make any headway and I subsequently contacted them and was told I wouldn't get priority unless I was on the housing list of my Local Authority which I am not because I have housing.

The SNU (Safer Neighbourhoods Unit) undertook a follow-up survey of residents following the decant. This survey indicated that 59 per cent were satisfied/fairly satisfied with information on housing options and 30 per cent fairly or very dissatisfied and residents were asked about their satisfaction with help and advice in finding a new home, 52 per cent indicated they were satisfied or very satisfied and 26 per cent were either fairly or very dissatisfied with help and advice in finding a new home (SNU 2008). The study also explored satisfaction with agencies. There was a small minority of residents dissatisfied with all agencies. Residents were most satisfied with SNU with 69 per cent indicating that they were satisfied or very satisfied and 9 per cent dissatisfied or very dissatisfied, followed by the WFCBHA with 55 per cent satisfied or very satisfied and 33 per cent dissatisfied or very dissatisfied. The study identified very low levels of satisfaction with the LDA with only 48 per cent stating that they were either satisfied or very satisfied and 30 per cent dissatisfied or very dissatisfied. The London Borough of Newham received the lowest ratings of any agency with only 38 per cent indicating they were satisfied or very satisfied and 41 per cent indicating they were dissatisfied or very dissatisfied. This perception of lack of support from the London Borough of Newham was a recurring theme in interviews. A number of interviewees commented positively on the support offered by their local GLA councillor.

The group of residents most dissatisfied were those that moved to private sector housing. This group contained many residents who because of their immigration status had no recourse to public funds and opted for private rented housing due to a lack of alternatives. The LDA did eventually devise a system to rehouse these residents into social housing through the establishment of a rent guarantee scheme[7] devised to incentivise RSLs to house this group. However, this was not operationalised until very late in the process i.e. February 2007.

Housing Destinations

Data was available for the destinations of 406 of the 425 residents. The majority 239 (59 per cent) residents were rehoused in Housing Association properties (mainly Peabody Properties), 88 (22 per cent) were rehoused in Local Authority properties (mainly in Newham), a further 67 (16.5 per cent) took up private sector tenancies, and 11 residents (3 per cent) moved into owner-occupation. Therefore in addition to the 450 individual tenancies lost at Clays Lane, an additional 327 social housing units were used to re-house these residents. Therefore the net loss of social housing was far in excess of the 450 tenancies lost at Clays Lane equating to 777 tenancies. Most residents remained in East London, 287 (70 per cent), a significant proportion moved elsewhere in London 91 (22 per cent) and a smaller proportion moved outside of London 28 (7 per cent) (SNU 2008).

Practical, Emotional and Financial Support Systems

Practical, emotional and financial support systems are a crucial part of any successful decant, particularly given the tight timescales. There were as we have already seen a range of individuals appointed to support residents. Nevertheless there was a clear sense that those interviewed in this study felt that practical and emotional support had been limited and in the main support had been financial:

> You got the money, they said that they would help people practically, they said they would offer it, but you knew that they were not really offering it. There was nothing, if you are going to offer someone help you have to tell them what

---

7 Residents' compensation was used as a deposit for 12 months and if residents had not fallen into rent arrears over this time the money was refunded to them.

is available. I asked them several times what practical help was available, well they said you have the money to help you, if there is something else, approach us and we will see if you can help.

They didn't give us much practical help; it was like here is the money get on with it.

The initial compensation package offered was £6,000 including £3,800 home loss (a statutory amount which increased to £4,000 on 1 September 2005) and £2,200 to pay for costs associated with moving. Residents made a case for increased compensation through the 'Clays Lane on the Move' forum and eventually the compensation package was increased to include an additional sum of £1,555 in recognition of the increased rent costs, an *ex gratia* payment of £320 for loss of viable home and community and an additional sum of £425 to pay for white goods as residents would in the main have been sharing these previously. In total residents received a total compensation package of £8,500. The additional payment was paid to all residents including those that would have moved before the enhanced package was agreed and in order to qualify for these payments residents had to have vacated their properties by July 2007 – any rent owing was deducted from this package (SNU 2008). The LDA established an arrangement with a local removal company which gave the residents a discounted rate and this was deducted from their compensation. According to one resident:

The Senior Manager leading the decant for the LDA helped with that, I said I have three days to move to X and he arranged a van for me.

The Fluid survey had identified that there were a number of vulnerable adults living at Clays Lane. Moreover, the decanting of an area with clear evidence of a strong sense of community and collective living would create its own emotional challenges. According to the LDA, both they and WFCBHA identified those who were vulnerable and had support needs early on. Towards the end of the Decant (January 2007) a Christian counselling service was employed to provide counselling support for those identified as vulnerable and this was publicised in newsletters The LDA and WFCBHA felt that the regular presence on the estate had addressed this issue:

One of the things that marked the process was that we were not distant. (Senior Manager, LDA)

I think there was a lot of emotional support. There was a lot of handholding. We understood what they were going through. Whether it was enough I don't know. (Manager, CBHA)

However, this perception was not shared by those we interviewed, with many laughing when asked about emotional support:

> There was no emotional support, we supported each other.

> We never had emotional support which is a bit sad as it would have been good for us to have moral support especially vulnerable people ... We felt that they pushed us to move and they did not think about how we felt.

One resident who had used the counselling service commented:

> I wasn't too keen at first because I am anti-religious (the agency appointed was a Christian counselling service) but I thought I will see what these people can do for me. They were useless they just came down talked to me and went off.

However, the Director of SNU who had suggested employing their services felt that Pecan provided useful support for some residents and was available to anyone who required it, both before and after the move. According to SNU's follow up survey 22 of the residents indicated that they had used the service. Of these 36 per cent indicated they were either satisfied or very satisfied and 18 per cent dissatisfied or very dissatisfied with the service (SNU 2008). There was clearly scope for more effectively developing a resident support strategy that anticipated and addressed a range of needs.

Housing Quality Before and After the Move

We explored residents' perception of housing quality and general satisfaction with housing after the move.

Satisfaction with Housing Before and After the Move

In this study it was clear that residents were happy with the quality of their housing both before and after the move. The Fluid survey (2005) reported numerous concerns with the state of repair both internally and externally. However, concerns about maintenance at Clays Lane did not emerge as significantly in this piece of research, though according to one resident:

> It was a bit patchy and sometimes the work was a bit shoddy, response times were rubbish if you were in a housing association you wouldn't have accepted that but because it was a co-op you said that's alright.

However, overall satisfaction with housing at Clays Lane appeared high, though cleanliness of common parts was an issue and for some there was a sense that housing conditions deteriorated following the decision to decant the properties:

> I was very happy, up until the end when CBHA took over, because maintenance wasn't being done any more. Any problems you had weren't being addressed, I still enjoyed living there, but it became harder. If the shower broke you knew it was not going to be fixed, unfortunately it was getting run down.

> I was completely happy with it, I had one of the best rooms for a ten person house. Sometimes it would change, I wasn't as happy it would depend who was in the house with you. There would only have to be one person in the house to disrupt it. I was on the flat list, you had to be not in rent arrears and contribute to the cooperative in some way and you could be offered a flat. I had been offered flats in the past but I had turned them down, because I was happy living in shared accommodation.

We also explored satisfaction with housing after the move. In general residents appeared happy with their new housing and this reinforced the findings of the (SNU 2008) survey which found that 73 per cent were satisfied with their new home, and 19 per cent dissatisfied. For example:

> Overall it is very nice flat; I'm quite happy and settled.

> My flat is very nice, I have a roof terrace.

> I really like it, it is in a great location and there is not so much poverty.

One resident expressed dissatisfaction with her housing and wanted to move. They had been one of the last residents to leave Clays Lane as they had hoped for a group move and therefore had to compromise:

> I like aspects of it, but I also find it a bit depressing, because there is no outside space, and it is a bit cold even in the middle of summer and it is chilly and winter. I am on two housing waiting lists but they won't rehouse me because I am not in housing need. I am continually searching for someone to swap.

Another resident reported initial problems with anti-social behaviour. However, over time these issues had been resolved and they were very happy in their accommodation. Overall then in terms of satisfaction with actual housing residents did not appear dissatisfied and were generally happy with their new accommodation.

Housing Costs – Before and After the Move

One of the most significant issues for residents following the move was an increase in housing and heating costs. The shared housing and communal living provided very affordable housing. Residents living in shared accommodation paid an inclusive sum of £44 (including utility bills) for shared accommodation and £58 per week for a self-contained flat.[8] Costs were low in part because of the communal nature of the housing and in part because the Cooperative purchased electricity and gas at wholesale prices and therefore savings were passed to residents.

Concern about a substantial increase in housing costs was one dimension of the objectors' case to the CPO inquiry. The LDA argued that the objectors' case was based on distorted data for a limited number of properties in more expensive districts. They acknowledged that there were likely to be increases but these would be modest and would depend on areas moved too. Moreover, they argued that it was likely that rents would have increased at Clays Lane following the takeover by WFCBHA (Rose 2006, para. 4.3.115). The LDA indicated that increases were likely to be between £5 and £7 per week excluding utilities and also suggest that the benefits system would cover any shortfall (Rose 2006, para. 4.3.214). However, whilst there was no specific data on the number of residents in work, the Fluid Survey indicated that many of the residents were in work and therefore it is wrong to assume that benefits would pick up this additional cost.

The survey undertaken by SNU in 2008 found that the average rent was £71 overall, £68 for those living in social rented housing in Newham and £69 for those living in Peabody accommodation in Newham. Therefore, if we compare this with the £58 cost of renting a self-contained flat we see that residents were paying an average of £13 per week more, which was substantially higher than the figures provided at the CPO inquiry by the LDA. For those in shared accommodation the gap was higher and may contribute to a poverty trap for those wishing to work. The survey concluded that housing costs was the biggest problem that residents had experienced since moving with 32 per cent indicating that living within their income was a bit of a problem and 39 per cent indicating that it was a big problem. In addition to rents, residents were paying service charges averaging £6 per week, council tax averaging £19 per week and energy and water rates. Therefore, the overall costs were significantly higher and it is clear that the additional compensation payment of £1,555 would have served as a very limited cushion.

One resident explained another financial benefit of living in the cooperative:

> At Clays Lane you could pool your money and this helped. I do that now with a friend but it was easier to do this at Clays Lane.

---

8   This was the cost in 2007.

> My rent is much higher. At the cooperative we did so much of the work that was involved in running it and this made it cheaper. As a collective we bought electricity as a group and this gave us a 10 per cent reduction.

We can conclude that the LDA underestimated the additional housing costs of residents and that many residents experienced financial difficulties after the move.

'Community' – Before and After the Move

One of the relatively unique characteristics of Clay's Lane was a sense of community. According to the (Fluid Survey 2005) this was facilitated through the cooperative management structure, the people and design:

> The communal courtyard was an integral part of the design from the beginning. the main pedestrian access routes lead through courtyards that also act as a social hub, aided by the presence of garden benches and planners. Courtyard Meetings are held here. The living rooms and kitchens of houses have large windows and are positioned on the ground floor facing the courtyards. The Coop includes a community centre, cafe and a shop. (Fluid 2005, p. 12)

However, this community was not without its tensions as bullying and poor leadership had been identified as problems in a number of reports.[9] Moreover, it was clearly more significant for some people than others, given that the majority of residents indicated a preference to move out of co-operative housing into self-contained accommodation. The lead officer with responsibility for the decant at the LDA acknowledged that there was some evidence of a mutually supportive community, but at the same time only limited support for retaining it. Moreover, he suggested social relations were based around houses rather than the Cooperative itself. However, the Fluid Survey 2005 argued that:

> What emerges very strongly from the consultation process...is the unique character of Clays Lane ... many of its qualities are greatly cherished by residents and will not be replicated elsewhere. (Fluid 2005, p. 51)

The value of living as part of a community at Clays Lane was a clear theme that emerged in this study. At the point in the interview when we began to discuss the community it was clear that this triggered painful memories and a strong sense of loss:

---

9   The Audit Commission 2004 and Fluid Survey 2005 both identify these as problems and it also emerged in the interviews.

> That was one of the joys of Clays Lane. You would sit together in the kitchen, sometimes we would cook together. We had an Indian chef, who used to cook for everybody. They could water my garden when I'm away. Having people I could rely on was a good thing.
>
> If I was skint or emotionally down there was always somewhere there. When my (X) died I got a letter from the management committee offering support that is a good example of how the place worked. I can't imagine any other housing provider doing that.
>
> If I had been at work all day and I came home and was in a bad mood I could go to my room. If you wanted to be sociable you could knock on doors or wander by the courtyard to see if someone was sitting there. There was so much support there – both on a social and practical level.
>
> There were a lot of creative people there. There were lots of musicians, artists and people like that. So, we had a good, strong community ... The structure of it made very good communities. We were all facing each other and there was a lot of to-ing and fro-ing between houses.
>
> On a summer's evening you would come home and see people sitting in the courtyard on chairs, because everyone was on the ground floor it was much easier for everyone to come out of their housing and mix together.

Two residents appeared to have settled in and formed new relationships with neighbours, for example:

> I am the secretary of the Residents' Association here. There is a gardening club, and I have been fortunate as neighbours are friendly and have offered me support. Being involved in the Tenants' Association has helped this.

On the other hand, others had not been able to find this support and it was clear that it was the breakup of the communities had a significant effect on many residents' years after the decant:

> This is a traditional east end area ... Most people are very friendly but it's not like a place you just drop in. It's not sociable like clays lane though it's friendlier than other places in London.
>
> I don't know any of my neighbours; I just hear them through the wall. It is a bit sad.
>
> I have had lots of hostility from neighbours and this is so different to the support I had at Clays Lane.

You are cut off, by the design. If I am in my kitchen I cannot see anyone. I am now less sociable and have a definite feeling of isolation.

I think I met my neighbour for the first time two weeks ago (2012). I had a plumbing problem and she invited me in. The flat is not set up to interact. Here you are closed off in your flat; once the door is shut that's it. There is no communal place, there is no meeting point and the older you get, and the less socially active you are. You spend hours stuck on your own.

I've gotten to know a few of my neighbours but it's nothing like it was at Clays Lane; I mean I'd been there for so long I practically knew everybody in the court yard. I think that it's more individualistic here.

A number of former residents had maintained a degree of contact:

In one way, the Clays Lane community has never gone away, because you can still ring people and I am connected to many people who lived at Clays Lane, and some live quite close to each other.

Marris writing in 1986 sums this up:

Eviction from the neighbourhood in which one was at home can be almost as disruptive of the meaning of life as the loss of a crucial relationship. Dispossession threatens the whole structure of attachments through which purposes are embodied, because these attachments cannot readily be re-established in an alien setting. (Marris 1986, p. 57)

Essentially then the fracturing of longstanding communities is problematic. In this instance there was substantial evidence of a strong community. Therefore, the impact of displacement for many of these residents cannot be overstated.

Moving Back to Clays Lane

Finally, we asked residents whether they would like to return to Clays Lane. Clearly this was hypothetical, but there was little appetite for returning. For example:

No, the place is completely different now and I have no interest. I liked living there because of what it was by then.

Not sure, I love the idea I still have dreams I am living in Clays lane, though my largest problem would be London and the crowds of people.

> I can't pretend that I haven't got used to my own space, and that was one of the big disadvantages of a shared space. I have quite a big flat and it is nice to be able to have books on the floor rather than stacked up on a platform.
>
> I would seriously consider it moving back if it was the same community that I left, I don't think I could start again and try to forge a brand new community.
>
> You can only go forward. For me overall it's been a positive thing the process was disastrous and the actual year or two here was difficult but I came through it and I'm happy here.

Two interviewees felt that they would like the opportunity to live in new housing at the athlete's village and one had registered for this opportunity.

Conclusion: Residents – Clays Lane Housing Cooperative

For those wishing to move into self-contained accommodation the relocation process clearly offered a route into housing that might otherwise not have been available with a considerable degree of choice over destination. Nevertheless the process of establishing relevant systems even for this group was slow and therefore residents experienced a considerable degree of anxiety about their futures given the pressure to leave the estate by July 2007 and this pressure cannot be underestimated. There was, however, a failure to realise the preferences of a significant proportion of residents who wished to move as a group/collective who had to settle for individualised housing options resulting in the fracturing of a strong community that offered social support and this was perceived as the necessary price to pay for the longer term legacy benefits that would accrue.

There was clearly a significant financial impact for most residents and whilst an enhanced financial compensation package was reached this would not have covered the additional costs and the evidence given at the CPO indicated a significant underestimate of the additional costs. More generally what was lost was a relatively unique form of affordable housing available for single people living in East London at a time when there is serious shortage of such housing.

The LDA had a job that had to be done, residents had to evicted from the site by July 2007 and systems were put in place to ensure this happened. However, there was nothing particularly exemplary or scandalous about this system or the way these residents were treated. According to a manager leading the decant on behalf of the LDA:

> I think it was a very successful process, we moved 425 people in the time we did, not to have any forced evictions. We got so many success stories I think it went very well.

However, this study tells a different story of a relatively indifferent process that sought to move residents on as quickly as possible and in the process failed to put in place a timely relocation strategy that would facilitate the needs of residents in terms of emotional support or their housing preferences or indeed to adequately assess the additional costs that residents would encounter. We turn now to two other groups decanted by the LDA.

Introduction

There were two groups of longstanding Travellers living on what we now know as the Olympic Park. There were 15 English Romany families living on the Clays Lane Travellers site in Newham and 20 Irish Traveller Families living in Hackney. The London Development Agency commissioned consultants[10] to work with Travellers to identify their preferences and produce a relocation strategy. One key problem was that relatively large sites were needed. Identifying sites that were suitable to Travellers and realisable from a planning perspective within the timescales was extremely difficult. As a consequence, a small group of Travellers in Hackney were decanted twice and in the case of the Clays Lane Travellers they were decanted to Parkway Crescent with a temporary licence with the possibility that they might be re-housed again and it was not until January 2013, more than five years later, that a permanent licence was granted.

There were not many precedents with regard to decants of this size. According to the senior manager leading the project on behalf of the LDA:

> We did a lot of work with a company called Fluid to try and find out their aspirations and what they wanted to achieve and based our strategy on that ... There were not awfully good precedents for it, We consulted with central government; the DCLG and the London Gypsy and Travellers Unit ... As a team we had some very clear principles. We wanted to engage face to face and provide independent support networks, so people had access to the best advice ... People would go from pitch to pitch at Clays Lane and Waterden Road talking to people in their own homes. It was rare that we would look to hold a meeting.

However, others indicated that there were a large number of meetings held throughout the process.

The LDA commissioned the London Gypsy and Travellers Unit (LGTU) to provide support and advice to the residents in a role similar to that undertaken by the Safer Neighbourhoods Unit in Clays Lane. In addition to this the London Borough of Hackney provided a Hackney Homes floating support service which

---

10 Fluid were employed to work with residents both at Clays Lane Housing Cooperative and Hackney Travellers.

was set up in 2007 and offered support during the final phase of the move. Each family was allocated its own support worker, more generally local councillors in Hackney were perceived as being very supportive. The Travellers' site at Clays Lane was managed by Newham and there was no specific support service available to Travellers over and above that provided by LGTU. Moreover, it was reported by a number of interviewees that the relationship between the Newham Travellers and the Local Authority was poor. According to one respondent:

> Everytime we went to meetings the council (referring to Newham council) were not there. We had to fight to get a councillor to come out.

However, both Travellers and residents at Clays Lane felt that London Assembly Member, John Biggs had offered considerable support to residents and Travellers both during and following the relocation process.

Relocation and the Compulsory Purchase Order Inquiry

Both groups of Travellers objected at the CPO inquiry. Their objections were not against the decant per se but on the lack of suitable sites being available before the proposed decant date of July 2007. According to the LDA:

> So far as the merits of the CPO are concerned, the objectors have not contended that the land is not required for the purposes for which the CPO is made, but that confirmation should be delayed until relocation sites are found. There is no obligation on the LDA to provide relocation sites as a pre-requisite to the confirmation of the CPO. The Secretary of State would be entitled to find that a compelling public interest exist, bearing in mind the benefits of the Olympic and legacy proposals, even if he concluded on the evidence that there would be no relocation sites in July 2007. If no sites were available the relevant local authorities would be obliged to re-house the gypsies and Travellers, however, the LDA considers that progress to date should provide a high degree of comfort that suitable relocation sites will be provided in time. (Rose 2006, para. 4.3.390)

The LDA argued that whilst they were asked to respect the human rights, needs and lifestyles of gypsies, this did not extend to guaranteeing sites but undertaking reasonable steps to identify suitable sites and its position, therefore, was compatible with Article 8 of the European Convention on Human rights. In that:

> It would strike a balance between the public interest and the interference with convention rights. (Rose 2006, para. 4.3.91)

The inspector leading the inquiry concluded that the removal of the sites without replacement would undermine government policy in this area and that appropriate sites should be secured before possession of the land was confirmed in the CPO:

> In my opinion as a pre-requisite the LDA need to demonstrate that they have secured appropriate sites which will accommodate the Gypsies and Travellers before it takes possession of the respective plots, and the Secretary of State should be so satisfied before confirming the order. (Para. 6.2.116)

In April 2007, residents on both sites appealed again when it was clear that plans to move them off the land were progressing before new sites were secure. However, on this occasion the judge ruled that the 'greater benefits of the Olympics outweigh the human rights of the Travellers' (LGTU 2008).

Initially, Travellers were to receive a lower level of compensation than the residents at the Clays Lane Housing Cooperative. The LDA proposed a statutory compensation fee of £2,200 to cover the associated costs of moving (*Observer* 2006). It was initially argued that they were not entitled to a statutory home loss payment as under the law this did not extend to those living on a caravan site. However, solicitors representing the Clays Lane (Newham) and Waterden Crescent (Hackney) Travellers highlighted the inequity of this in relation to those living in social housing and the LDA agreed to pay this through the provision of an 'enhanced disturbance payment' equivalent to the home loss payment.

Clays Lane (Newham) Travellers

There were 15 Traveller families at Clays Lane and they had lived there since 1972. They were relocated to a site in Major Road in 2007 with the possibility of a subsequent relocation on the Olympic Park following the games. The LDA explored three possible sites for relocation of the Clays Lane Travellers and eventually re-housed them onto a site that was not acceptable to the Travellers.

The first site considered for relocation was under a flyover on the A13 (large dual carriageway) in Becton and close to a retail site. Both the owner of a nearby site, National Amusements Limited and a representative of the Clays Lane Travellers Residents Association opposed this at the CPO inquiry. According to the residents' representative:

> It is a long way from the existing site, inaccessible other than by private car; it is remote from shops and services. It is close to a flyover, waste transfer station, a sewage treatment works, and late opening commercial uses and lies within a flood plain. (CPO Inquiry 2006, para. 4.16.5)

The Clays Lane Travellers proposed relocating to a site in Redbridge near the Preston Drive Allotments. However, this was not supported by the London Borough of Redbridge. The Travellers and the LDA then identified another site at Chobham Farm/Angel Lane. The site was very close to where they were living and the Travellers were keen to relocate here. However, there were a number of objections (including LB Newham) to this and in particular concern that a public inquiry may be required to progress the planning application thus delaying the process and therefore the LDA decided that they would not pursue this. The Travellers made a legal challenge against the decision not to progress the site, however, the courts rejected the challenge and the Chobham Farm site was not progressed but is now part of a proposal for a mixed-use development discussed in Chapter 5.

The LDA identified a third site at Major Road. The site was 400 metres from the Clays Lane site and therefore in one sense would lead to less disruption. However, its location was seen as problematic as the area was already in use as a major community facility, including a community centre, children's play area and multi-use games area. The relocation of the Travellers to this site was challenged by three local councillors who argued that it was being presented as the most suitable option, but was in fact the least suitable option, rejected by both local residents and Travellers, and was simply the last resort in a context in which time was running out to find a suitable replacement. Local residents and Clays Lane Travellers joined forces on a local campaign called 'save Major Rd Park action group'. They gained support from Lyn Brown MP and the local ward councillors. They presented a petition and representations to the planning committee in March 2007. The three councillors argued:

> Not only does it destroy valuable community, sports and recreational facilities, but it also places the relocated Travellers in a totally inappropriate position. They are to be in a boxed site surrounded by high walls, surrounded by two busy roads in what can only be described as a ghetto. They may be perceived by others as the cause of the loss of facilities and this could do untold damage to their previously good relationship with the resident community. (London Borough of Newham 2007, para. 1, 5, pp. 11–12)

Despite the huge outcry from the local community and Clays Lane Travellers, the relocation was approved by the Mayor of Newham who acknowledged that the loss of community facilities was not desirable but that the need to find an alternative site for the Travellers had become significant. Moreover, he argued funding would be made available to upgrade some playground provision close to the site, along with a contribution to pay for the Local Authority to either purchase new open space or upgrade existing social space (London Borough of Newham 2007). The Travellers' preferences were overruled.

According to one Traveller:

> They wanted to put us down the road near the pub and we liked that but after some time they changed their minds and we ended up here. No one likes it here as there was a park and local people thought that it was us taking their park from

the kids. We did not want people to hate us. We put fliers through people's doors so they would know that it's not our fault that we were moved here.

In addition to having to move to a site acceptable to neither Travellers nor residents, the former were then subjected to a number of delays related to the actual move. Both housing co-op residents and Travellers at Clays Lane were aware that the deadline for decanting their sites was July 2007, however, by September 2007, a national news report confirmed that Travellers at Clays Lane had been given ten different moving dates, none of which were realised. Between July 2007 and the final move in October they were given 13 different dates to move. According to Tracey Giles speaking on ITN News,

> First of all we get a letter from the LDA saying you are going to move on this date. It may be a day or two before that date, then we get another letter saying Newham council and Newham Homes haven't accepted the handover. (ITN News 2007)

Newham's reluctance to take over the site was explained by the failure of the LDA to produce appropriate certificates that indicated the site met health and safety regulations; this lack of cooperation between agencies seriously impacted on families. According to the Senior Manager leading the decant for the LDA:

> With hindsight it is a matter of regret that we changed the moving dates a number of times, I should have been more disciplined about when we did make the first date that I think more than anything soured our relationship. The ODA needed them out. We couldn't get Newham to inspect the site, or take handover. We gave them three or four move dates and they had packed up boxes, it is a shame that I didn't go back to the ODA, and say we need six weeks rather than two weeks. That would have been a better solution.

Residents interviewed did not feel supported by the LDA and felt that the ultimate goal was to ensure that the site was vacant to enable the Olympic project to go ahead:

> I can't complain. They were not horrible but they wanted us to move so quickly. The houses were brought in on lorries. They put the drains in when we had already moved in. It took five months to do the gardens and they promised electric gates and didn't do that.

Satisfaction with Accommodation Before and After the Move

There were mixed views about the quality of accommodation housing at the old and new sites. Some residents felt that the new site was much cleaner, whilst others felt that it was preferable to live in a more isolated location with more privacy. There was a general dissatisfaction with the high wall erected around the site:

> We feel isolated due to the wall around us; it makes us feel like we are in prison though the council did that for the purpose of protection. I wish they did it different so that we can see outside.

The Travellers interviewed generally recognised at least some advantages with regard to their new accommodation. They welcomed the input they were given into the design of kitchens and outside areas and commented on having a garden and modern facilities. There were mixed views on the heating systems with some perceiving them to be both more effective and more expensive at the new site. Two interviewees commented on the construction and size of the new accommodation:

> I wanted like a big unit together and they promised me that they will give me a big plot but they gave us little tiny sheds/plots when we came here. So I lost my big caravan. These plots are not really brick though they look like it ... The old site was built with bricks it was very solid.

Another resident also commented on the construction:

> These are not proper bricks and it's cold in winter and very expensive to maintain.

Another commented on the general delay in responding to issues:

> Everything here is in wrong place, i.e. my water leak needed to be fixed, they put in the wrong pipes for me and it took them a full year to fix it.

Other residents were more positive:

> At the old site, the shed was smaller but better than here as we had our privacy there. In terms of the caravan, it's better here as we have new accommodation compared to the old site and it is cleaner here. Here we have a garden which we did not have before. Also we have central heating and more kitchen cupboards.

> Everything is better than what we had before. It is more modern we have good kitchen facilities; nice doors with double glazing.

Community and Neighbourhood – Before and After the Move

This group of Travellers had moved as a group and therefore the sense of loss and separation encountered at Clays Lane Cooperative was not evident; there was continuity with services such as schools and GPs and generally families were together. However, there was a clear perception that they felt very much part of a community at Clays Lane and had particularly enjoyed the open space. The new site was in the middle of two busy roads and was surrounded by a large wall which reinforced a sense of separation.

> At the old site, we could take children to the BMX track to play with their bikes. We had Community Links. Children used to do painting, and different stuff. But here children have nothing to do and yet they cannot go outside because the road is dangerous.

More than one respondent felt that on the other site they had been part of a wider Clays Lane community. For example:

> We all came from the old side to here. We had a very good community. People in the flats were very good. For example, if there were a meeting those people could talk to us. But we do not know too many people around here.

There were other problems reported such as an increase in asthma as a result of being located next to a building site. This led the families to write to Olympics Minister, Tessa Jowell, highlighting the unsuitability of the site (LGTU 2009). Another respondent talked of the increased regulation that was imposed on them from the London Borough of Newham coupled with a failure to help them resolve their problems. Most residents indicated that they were generally happier on the previous site and given the choice they would return. Only one interviewee expressed a preference for the new site.

As we have already noted the Major Road (Parkway Crescent) site was not granted a permanent licence until January 2012 resulting in considerable anxiety. This has been compounded by concerns about the durability of the amenity blocks (made of prefabricated structures with a recommended life of ten years) that began to show significant sign of wear and tear after just five years. The residents are concerned that Newham Council will not maintain the site to an appropriate standard or replace the amenity blocks at an appropriate point.

At the time of relocation the LDA recognised that the Clays Lane Travellers did not want to move to Major Road and so a commitment was given to the option of a return to the Olympic Park after the games as part of the Legacy Plans. This commitment was confirmed in writing to residents of Parkway Crescent by Margaret Ford in her letter dated 8 January 2010:

> I understand before your relocation, the previous Mayor confirmed that he would be happy to support the identification of a site within the legacy development of the Olympic Park. The current Mayor has continued this support, and the new Legacy Company will now take this forward. As you know, the land comprising the Park has been dramatically altered and redeveloped. It may therefore not be possible for you to relocate to the same location as before. However, we

will do our level best in planning the Park to find you a suitable alternative ... The earliest possible date for any relocation will be mid end 2014 ... Please be assured that we are committed to working with you. (Baroness Ford, Chairman, Olympic Park Legacy Company)

Although little progress has been made since the letter from Margaret Ford in 2010, this commitment to facilitate a second move (if the residents of Parkway Crescent wish to pursue this option) is now the responsibility of the London Legacy Development Corporation who have accepted they have inherited the responsibility for it. The residents remain keen to explore the options available to them for the future.

Hackney Travellers

There were 20 Irish families living at Waterden Crescent, Hackney and they had lived there since 1993. There was a general consensus that the Hackney Travellers had been better supported than the Clays Lane (Newham) Travellers. Consultation meetings were initially held with Waterden Crescent Travellers in 2003 and Fluid were appointed to undertake research on preferences for moving. According to Fluid (2004) they did 'not particularly object to relocation' if concerns about site planning and location were addressed.

Finding sites that were acceptable to both Travellers and the LDA proved challenging. The Travellers were relocated as three distinctive groups and this separation caused a great deal of pain that was evident when we spoke to residents. The London Gypsy and Travellers Unit reported that the Local Authority and the LDA gave residents the option of splitting into smaller groups as it would be difficult to find land for such a large group, whereas the LDA indicated that the decision to move residents in smaller groups was determined by the consultation process (LGTU 2008). The Fluid survey undertaken with Travellers reported that they had expressed a preference for smaller sites with six or ten caravans and this meant that the larger group would be separated and they noted that whilst most residents expressed a willingness to be part of a larger residential development, their comments indicated a preference for smaller developments. The issue of separation was clearly very painful for residents as they had to decide which families they wanted in their group:

> That was the hardest part. I did not know and nobody knew who is going with whom. It was chaos, choosing who is going with whom.

> You felt very funny about picking and choosing you were all the same. There were a lot of families – who have three daughters and two sons they would want to go together. You had to separate from families you had been with for years it was very hard making the decision but it had to be done. People had to

stand up in meetings and say who they wanted to go with. It left an awful lot of people hurt.

At the CPO Inquiry Travellers expressed their concern that the proposal from the LDA was based on a package of sites each requiring planning permission and that there was a mismatch between the Travellers' preferences with regard to groupings and the size of the sites:

> Relocation is not simply a matter of space for a caravan, but is also about maintaining a community that the residents have established. (Rose 2006, para. 4.3.354)

It was reported to us that there had been the option of returning to the Olympic Park, however, there was caution about this:

> We had a choice to live in temporary accommodation until the Olympics was over and go back into the Olympic zone, we had that choice. We could have held back with the bungalows and gone into a temporary site with a pitch, but no one trusted the LDA that much, we were concerned that when the Olympics were over we wouldn't be given what we want, what if they said the money wasn't there.

Other preferences that emerged in the Fluid survey with regard to relocation related to for example sites being of sufficient size to accommodate the Traveller lifestyle of family and friends visiting them; to be relocated within a six mile radius of the existing site and to be located in relatively isolated locations.

> We were wary of being located in a built up area because they didn't have any land on the outskirts in open spaces, everyone would live in open spaces if they had the choice.

> We didn't want to be in a built up area, we don't like it very closed in.

Two groups of Travellers were re-located to sites within walking distance of Waterden Road. Five Traveller families were located at Wallis Road, Hackney on a site that was previously used for employment purposes. This site was perceived as desirable by Travellers as it was close to existing networks and would enable residents to continue to use social and educational services. The London Borough of Hackney objected to residents being relocated here as it was designated for employment use and there was a lack of open space. There was also opposition from local residents who signed a petition arguing against relocation to that site. The plans were modified and redesigned to include four families on that specific site and one family on an adjacent site. Seven families were relocated to St Theresa's Close, Homerton, and this appeared relatively unproblematic. The final group of eight Traveller families were relocated to Ruby Close in Homerton and this particular relocation was fraught with difficulties. In the first instance Travellers made it clear that they did not wish to relocate to this particular site as it was located in a very busy residential area. A local campaign was organised to object to the relocation of Travellers to the area. Nevertheless, the site was progressed by the LDA but was subject to delays as it had previously been used as a waste processing plant and this needed to be relocated in order to enable the site to be developed. Due to the delays, the Travellers experienced a double decant moving temporarily to Eton Manor and then in March 2009 to Ruby Close. The Travellers experienced considerable hostility when they initially moved into Ruby Close, however, a range of agencies such as the London Gypsy and Travellers Unit, the Hackney Learning Trust and the Hackney Homes floating support service worked with them to challenge this and by 2012 these initial problems had disappeared with reports of good relations with local neighbours. Clearly this group would have experienced a considerable degree of anxiety given that they had expressed a preference not to move there, the extent of local hostility and the time delay. However, one Traveller explained that the disruption from the Olympic building project meant that they were keen to move:

> It got a bit stressful at the end, because there was a lot of development going on there. Lots of lorries, you know, it was constantly, rubble and dust and everything. We were getting very frustrated and glad to leave in the end.

Both in Newham Clays lane (Newham) and Waterden Road (Hackney) Travellers felt supported by LGTU and overall, Hackney Travellers had an additional form of support as the council had a specific unit located within the authority to support Travellers.

> They were constantly at the meetings with us, a lot of Travellers were not educated and they were coming forward with big words to do with the Olympics. You were gobsmacked you didn't understand a thing they were saying, so you had them teaching us, letting us know our rights and we didn't have to jump at things.

There were mixed views with regards to the LDA. According to one Traveller:

> Before the move you could have asked for anything. However, once we had signed the papers that was it, you never saw them again.

> The London Development Agency had three or four workers and they were very good. I felt more relaxed, and they had proper plans with them. They organised everything for us, new land and it was very professional.

Designing New Homes

The Travellers were keen to input into the design of their new homes and worked closely with architects and the LDA on design issues. The LDA were also committed to facilitating resident involvement on design issues. Traveller families had the option of a bungalow (with room for a touring caravan), a more traditional pitch with an amenity block and a hard-standing for a mobile home and touring caravan. The choice of bungalows was a proposal that came from the Travellers themselves (modelled from a scheme in Ireland). In addition to this the LDA held a series of meetings to discuss the form and layouts of the site and the configuration of the group houses and amenity blocks.

There was a consensus that a considerable degree of choice and input with regard to the design of the new homes:

> We got to design everything, like the colour of the bricks on the walls and I did a lot of the design myself. They're all similar from the outside, but each one is individual on the inside.

> We had a choice of the layout. We wanted everything on the one level that is why we picked the bungalow.

> They're all similar from the outside, but each one is individual. The family over there they chose the old traditional way – a chalet.

> They spent a lot of time going out and measuring units, sitting down with the Travellers working out how they would arrange them it was a massive jigsaw puzzle trying to fit them all in with the fire regs. (Lead officer, Decant LDA)

Satisfaction with Housing Before and After the Move

We were interested to explore perceptions of housing quality before and after the move. There was a consensus that whilst they were satisfied with their housing conditions before the move they also recognised that housing conditions had improved following relocation:

> I have better facilities.

> It is all modern.

> We did not have facilities like a sitting room before, so it is better.

> Everything here is better than that at the old site of Waterden road, better shower, accommodation and everything. I do not miss anything there. It's like a new life here.

But they also felt compromised as the previous site was spacious and enabled Traveller families to extend in response to changing circumstances. For example, if a young person married they could move into another caravan on the site and retain extended family connections. From the perspective of other agencies, the Waterden Road site was already overcrowded and any additional caravans would have been in breach of health and safety regulations. However, the long term impact of the lack of sites and sites large enough to accommodate growth is clearly a significant problem for the retention of 'Traveller communities as many have moved into "settled" accommodation due to lack of alternatives'. Another issue specific to the Travellers that had moved to Ruby Close was that the location and design of the site meant that from the outside it did not look like Traveller accommodation and therefore they had to some extent compromised their Traveller identity.

Community and Wider Neighbourhood Before and After the Move

The Travellers spoke positively about the 'community' before and after the move and whilst they acknowledged the pain of the separation they appeared to be have come to terms with this and contact was retained as all sites were in relative close proximity and therefore they visited each other enabling the retention of these important links. They were also able to continue to use the same school and health services. The site at Waterden Road was isolated and this isolation was perceived positively. Moreover, there was a sense that it was less crowded with more open space and residents recalled the benefits of being in a larger community, though overall appeared happy to stay where they were:

> Everyone was friends, so it was a lot of families. You could go around and chat to anybody. I miss that. But there were too many families and the kids would always be fighting and I think it is better now on a smaller site.

> I miss the lifestyle. We're more like 'settled' people now. It was much easier over there. I miss my friends most, going out at the weekends … always seeing someone. Everyone stuck together, if anybody dies, god forbid, they would all be very good support. It was good like that.

> The children miss their friends, we miss our community but we are happy now, we cannot swap for the big site because it was too big as a group, too many children and too hard to control.

Moreover, those residents who had initially been anxious about living in a residential area reported that over time they had developed good relations with their new neighbours. We asked residents whether they would like to return to the old site and most reported feeling settled where they were, though one respondent indicated that they would move back to the old site.

Concluding Thoughts – Travellers Relocation

The two groups of Travellers shared some common experiences such as considerable anxiety about finding suitable sites, uncertainty and delays in moving. The LDA had commissioned research to identify the preferences of Travellers, however, these preferences were ultimately disregarded and two groups of Travellers were forced to move to sites unacceptable to them and where there were serious concerns about hostility in the immediate neighbourhood. The Hackney Travellers had to separate into smaller groups causing them considerable anxiety.

Both groups of Travellers had input into the design of sites and specific units, however, Travellers in Hackney appeared to be more satisfied with their new housing. The presence of an additional source of support in Hackney was important in securing more satisfactory outcomes with Travellers talking positively about a range of agencies supporting them ranging from Hackney Homes through to the Hackney learning Trust and the London Gypsy and Travellers Unit. Travellers in Newham on the other hand, felt unsupported by their Local Authority and indeed their relationship appeared to be conflictual rather than supportive.

What is clear is that both residents living at the Clays Lane Housing Cooperative and residents living on Traveller sites found themselves in the way of a prestigious national project. Anxiety about the need to complete the project on time meant that there was a relatively short time period between London winning the games and the final decant (two years). The need to expedite the project meant that both sets of residents had to respond to a very tight and highly pressurised timetable which created added pressure and led to less desirable outcomes. In retrospect the project was completed well ahead of time and it is a pity that more time was not given to at least ensuring the most positive outcomes. The perceived or alleged legacy benefits to the whole area acted as a trump card enabling policy makers to move Travellers off the site before new permanent sites were ready irrespective of their rights.

References

Audit Commission (2005). *Clays Lane Housing Cooperative – Inspectors Report* (HMSO: London).

Bliss, N.E. (2008). *Independent Commission on Cooperative and Mutual Housing* (Manchester: Independent Commission on Cooperative and Mutual Housing).

COHRE (2007). *Fairplay for Housing Rights, Mega Events, Olympic Games and Housing Rights* (Geneva: Geneva International Academic Network).
Fluid (2004). *Waterden Road Travellers: Residents Survey Report for the London Development Agency* (London: Fluid).
Fluid (2005). *Clays Lane Housing Cooperative Residents Survey Report for the London Development Agency* (London: Fluid).
Greater London Authority (2011a). *The London Plan 2011*, 22 July. (London: GLA).
Greater London Authority (2011b). *EIP (Examination in Public) Panel Report and Mayoral Responses*, 22 July (London: GLA).
Mitchell, I. (2006). *Unique Housing development under threat as the games comes to town* (London: Irwin Mitchell Press Release).
Inside Housing (2006). *Tenants make way for Clays Lane Evictee*, 18 August.
ITN News (2007). London 2012 Olympic Travellers: Clays Lane Travellers eviction postponed for tenth time, 25 September. <http://www.itnsource.com/shotlist/ITN/2007/09/25/T25090733/?v=2> (Accessed 9 June 2012).
London Borough of Newham (2007). Report to the Mayor: Major Road Open Space, 28 February 2007.
London Gypsy and Traveller Unit (2008). <http://www.lgtu.org.uk/olympic-site-relocation.php> (Accessed 13 March 2013).
Marris, P. (1986). *Loss and Change* (London: Routledge).
Mitchell, I. (2005). *Olympic victims are considering appeal after high court decision to quash CPO order – Press release,* 25 May (London: Irwin Mitchell).
Rose, D.M.H. (2006). *London Development Agency (Lower Lea Valley, Olympic and Legacy) CPO 2005, Inspectors Report* (London: Department of Trade and Industry Compulsory Purchase Order, Public Inquiry).
Safer Neighbourhoods Unit (2008). Moving on from Clays Lane: Survey of Former Tenants – Final report, May.
The Lawyer (2007) Irwin Mitchell to appeal high court ruling on Olympic Village evictions, 4 June.
Tunstall, R. and Lupton, R. (2010). *Mixed Communities Evidence Review* (London: Department of Communities and Local Government).
UN Habitat (2004). Report of the Special Rapporteur on Housing on Adequate Housing E/CN.4/2004/48, UN Switzerland.
Wilmot, P. and Young, M. (1957). *Family and Kinship In East London, 1st edn* (London: Penguin).

A Note on the Carpenters Estate

Many people may remember that when London won the bid to host the Olympic and Paralympic games, a number of film crews headed for the Carpenters Estate to film residents living in this deprived part of Stratford adjacent to the planned stadium, Village and Aquatics Centre. It was residents in places such as the Carpenters Estate that would be the beneficiaries of the Olympic legacy (or at least this was what was thought): seven years later, in the year that London hosted the games, plans were progressed for a total decant of the Carpenters Estate to enable the construction of a new campus for University College London.

The Worshipful Company of Carpenters had originally bought the land in the nineteenth century to develop it for industrial purposes. The Company had a commitment to the wider welfare of its workers and built housing, a school and established a social club for workers and residents. An estimated two thirds of housing was either destroyed or badly damaged during the war. In the 1960s the London Borough of Newham issued a Compulsory Purchase Order (CPO) on much of the land and buildings and constructed a new housing estate comprising 700 units, including three tower blocks, low rise blocks and houses. The Carpenters Company continued its connection to the estate by supporting the Carpenters and Docklands Centre. Over time a proportion of these units were sold through the right to buy. In 1997 the Estate became a Tenant Management Organisation enabling the residents to sit on the board and shape decision making. The TMO comprised a mix of tenants, leaseholders and freeholders (Dunn et al. 2010).

Over time the three high rise blocks had fallen into disrepair and it was estimated that it would cost at least £25 million to refurbish them. In 2004 it was agreed to decant and demolish the first tower block and sell the land using the proceeds to refurbish the other two tower blocks. A master plan was drawn up for the two blocks and the remaining estate. In 2006/7 the GLA and London Borough of Newham explored options for refurbishing the estate but this was viewed as too expensive. Many of the residents in Lund and Dennison Point were leaseholders and would be individually liable for the cost of the works estimated at £120,000 (each property was valued at £110,000). Alternative options were explored such as refurbishment of kitchens and bathrooms though it was argued this would not have resolved the external issues. In 2009 it was agreed to decant the remaining two tower blocks and one low rise building with a view to refurbishing the latter two blocks, however, it was again argued that the cost was prohibitive. Those residents who wished to stay would have to be decanted and then return to the estate, however, the majority (59 per cent) indicated they would rather move permanently (Dunn et al. 2010).

The Stratford Metropolitan Master Plan was approved in 2010 and in February 2011 a specific document was produced setting out a range of potential options ranging from no change through to fundamental transformation with appraisals based on residents' perspectives, London Borough of Newham perspectives and the financial implications of the different options. The preferred option was a phased redevelopment as a residential neighbourhood with improved integration to the surrounding area and a park and its integration with option G which included commercial, educational or other uses in the final phase dependent on the market. However, there was clearly a lack of ownership or commitment from local residents who had not supported any of the options as there was a desire to leave things as they were – though of all the options this received most support from residents (London Borough of Newham 2011; Watt et al. 2013).

Research undertaken by (Barata et al. 2013) highlighted the way in which residents at the Carpenters Estate had been subject to almost ten years of consultation on a number of successive master plans and had become frustrated with what they perceived to be tokenistic consulting on pre-determined plans as compared to a genuine opportunity to shape their futures. They argue that this has resulted in a democratic deficit with residents increasingly unwilling to participate in formal political processes or community self-help and who have little trust in local government, antagonism with elected representatives and suspicion of official information.

Moreover, despite a preference to redevelop the estate as a residential neighbourhood, in November 2011 it became clear that a more wholesale redevelopment of the site into a university campus was being considered. The London Borough of Newham signed a memorandum with UCL on the basis that they would talk exclusively to them about regeneration and in October 2012 approved plans for the construction of a new UCL campus in Stratford which would result in the demolition of the existing Carpenters Estate and the possibility of some housing (though specific details were not available). The Tenants Management Organisation representing the tenants opposed the plans and argued for the retention of the estate and a Campaign to Save the Carpenters Estate was formed by a group of local residents who formed alliances with UCL students and Academics (Minton 2012).

At the Cabinet meeting where the plans were approved residents organised a protest and made representations. A representative from the Resident Steering Group noted that:

> Proposals from UCL could be accommodated on other prime sites in Newham that were vacant, and that neither UCL nor the Council had undertaken proper consultation with the TMO. He stated that the Carpenters Estate had been a TMO since the 1990s and had been acknowledged by the Mayor as a "beacon of how an estate should be and that the residents wished to stay" (Mr Fabikan, Carpenters TMO Residents Steering Group)

The minutes of the Cabinet meeting recorded that several Members were surprised at claims with regard to the alleged lack of consultation referred to by the RSG given a chronological record of meetings and resident engagement undertaken by Council officers and UCL. However, Mr Bird, who was employed to provide independent advice to residents, argued that consultation was limited in scope and that residents were not consulted on the plans per se with alternatives or potential compromises, but simply on matters of detail such as whether they would want to vacate properties early etc., and as Minton has implied, such approaches to consultation are common and simply reinforce pre-determined decisions, whilst at the same time providing an illusion of democracy and due process (Minton 2012).

Plans for UCL to relocate to Stratford were rationalised to staff and international stakeholders in a bulletin as 'Olympic legacy, scale, value and affordability', therefore we can see that whilst not part of the Olympic legacy this is a project associated with the accelerated regeneration of the area and its attractiveness following substantial public investment, improvements in transport accessibility and ongoing affordability in a London context (University College London 2011).

The number of occupied units on the Carpenters Estate had been declining over the years as a result of a number of decants: In 2009 there were 685 units occupied on the estate including 514 (73 per cent) who were social renting, 98 (14 per cent) leaseholders and 93 (13 per cent) freeholders. By 2012 less than half of this number remained and as of September 2012, 318 homes were still occupied including 156 (50 per cent) who were social renting, 66 (21 per cent) leaseholders and 96 (30 per cent) freeholders (London Borough of Newham 2012).

The London Borough of Newham produced a residents' charter setting out a range of commitments with regard to re-housing for tenants; leaseholders and freeholders. The residents living in the three tower blocks and one low rise block had been given decant status and this means that they were given high priority through the choice-based letting system. Following the decision to progress plans with UCL, the council met with those additional residents that were likely to be affected setting out their options. However, as plans were still under negotiation the decant was not formalised. In May 2013, UCL withdrew plans for the redevelopment of the Carpenters Estate and therefore those residents scheduled to be decanted as a result of the UCL project could remain, though they had clearly experienced considerable anxiety. The London Borough of Newham has indicated that it will continue to explore options for the estate and therefore the residents continue to remain in a relatively uncertain position.

If the decant had proceeded as planned the Residents Charter would have underpinned their choices. Under the charter residents are able to choose to be re-housed either with the council (and if they are under-occupying they can continue to under-occupy their property i.e. have more bedrooms than they need), or they can choose to move into housing association property but in this instance they would not be able to under-occupy their property. They are eligible for statutory home loss payments – there are two sets of payments for leaseholders and freeholders. Those who have lived in their property for the last year will be entitled to the market value of the property plus 10 per cent, in addition to other costs such as stamp duty, if they have not lived there for the last year then the sum is reduced to 7.5 per cent and does not cover stamp duty but does cover associated legal costs. Leaseholders are also entitled to lease swap to another Newham Council property or purchase an equity share of another council property of higher value. East Village does provide the opportunity for residents to opt to remain in Stratford and a number of events have been held with Carpenters Residents to publicise the properties to them. Leaseholders are also eligible for equity shares in Triathlon's homes within East Village, however, the value of properties at East Village are likely to be substantially higher than their existing homes and those opting to rent at East Village will also be subject to higher rental costs and it is likely that, as was the case on the Carpenters Estate, residents will experience an increase in housing costs. The Resident's Charter argues that:

> The council is in any case committed to the general principle that no tenant should be worse off as a result of the rehousing process. This is an important commitment in respect of paying compensation for the reasonable costs of being rehoused. The council will discuss with each tenant needing to be decanted their individual, reasonable costs of removal at the time of being rehoused and agree a schedule of costs with each household.

In a sense we can see that Newham Council, in using the term 'no tenant should be worse off', are making a pledge similar to that made to residents at the Clays Lane Housing Cooperative about being 'better off'. How will it be measured?

If the UCL campus plans had progressed as planned then there would have been the net loss of further social housing in an area of great need. Additional social housing units would have been needed to re-house these residents, contributing to an additional loss of housing and the demolition of the last council estate on this side of Stratford High Street exacerbating the the potential for gentrification. An alternative strategy for renovating the Estate may have been achieved through levering resources through the planning gain system on the many developments taking place across Stratford. Carpenters Estate has essentially been disinvested over a number of years whilst surrounded by substantial government investment in the area.

What is interesting is that the Carpenters Estate, like Clays Lane Housing Cooperative, has/had a strong sense of community with a recent piece of research identifying it as a model community with regard to sustainable communities. For example, Watt (2013) reviewed a number of tenant surveys with local residents and identifies a number of themes including a desire to stay on the estate and a strong attachment to community and concluded that:

> Many London estates such as the Carpenters are characterised by routine neighbourliness, local social capital and positive place identity as well as by wage labour, often low paid and insecure alongside unemployment.

Similarly, Barata et al. argue that:

> In many ways Carpenters has epitomised this kind of active and connected community. Residents are active in volunteering, take part and organise community events ... key informants and residents consider the friendliness and safety of the estate as unique in both Newham and London. (Barata et al. 2013)

These strengths need to be built on by policy makers who seek to expand social housing opportunities and opportunities for local residents in the spirit of original Olympic legacy pledges whilst also ensuring the economic development of the area and clearly both are possible. The Relocation of UCL to the Carpenters Estate generated a concerted campaign of opposition both from UCL students, staff and local residents. Their decision to withdraw was explained in commercial terms though clearly a victory for campaigners. At the time of writing UCL are in discussions about locating their campus on the Park and indeed a more joined up approach would have steered UCL to this vacant land in the first place avoiding months of uncertainty experienced by local residents and the potential loss of social housing (BBC News: Financial Times 2013).

In the meantime there continues to be a lack of certainty for residents on the estate. Ironically recent policy changes with regard empty properties has resulted in a loss of subsidy on empty properties and as a consequence the London Borough of Newham are now seeking to tender housing in the decanted Tower blocks as short life housing. A more long term solution rests in ensuring investment in the refurbishment of the Estate providing a much needed source of 'affordable housing' that capitalises on the strengths of existing communities.

References

Barata, D., Brayford, S., Ju Hong, J., Eze John, P. and Jesus Montero, M. (2013). Meaningful participation, in *Regeneration and Well Being in East London: Stories from the Carpenter's Estate*, edited by Frediano, A., Butcher, S. and Watt, P. (London: The Bartlett Planning Development Unit).

BBC News (2013) University Colege, Olympic Campus Scheme collapses 8th May. First accessed 4 July 2013 at http://www.bbc.co.uk/news/uk-england-london-22446437.

Dunn, P., Glaessl, D., Magnusson, C. and Vardhan, Y. (2010). *Carpenter's Estate: Common Ground* (London: The Cities Programme, London School of Economics).

Financial Times (2013) UK's Olympic Park wants £1 billion UCL Project, 8 May, First accessed 6 June 2013 at http://www.ft.com/cms/s/0/e61b115c-b7ea-11e2-9f1a-00144feabdc0.html#axzz2h8JcnZir.

London Borough of Newham (2011). *Stratford Metropolitan Masterplan –* Supporting Document Carpenters Estate Options Appraisal.

London Borough of Newham (2012). *Cabinet Report Item 4 Carpenters Estate*, 25 October.
Minton, A. (2012). *Ground Control: Fear and Happiness in the 21st Century.* (London: Penguin).
TPAS (Tenant Participant Advisory Service) (2012). Report to the Residents Steering Group Meeting, Tuesday 14 August 2012. Survey Findings of Research undertaken on the Carpenters Estate Low Rise Properties, pp. 1–4.
University College London (2011). UCL to explore plans for an additional campus in Newham, 23 November.
University College London.(2012). Stratford Proposition.
Watt, P. (2013). It's not for us: Regeneration, the 2012 Olympics and the Gentrification of East London, *City*, 17(1): 99–118.

Chapter 3
London Housing Legacy: An Overview

This chapter provides a context for legacy in London. We explore trends in house prices both for sale and rent in East London and policies and treatment of homeless groups in the lead up to and during the Olympic and Paralympic Games. We explore key indicators of housing need – inequality and social deprivation in the four 'Legacy'[1] boroughs – as these were central drivers underpinning the rationale for hosting the games in East London. Finally, we examine the shifting governance of legacy and the 'convergence' agenda.

Housing and London 2012

Trends in Property Prices – an Olympic Effect?

As we have seen in earlier chapters, previous host cities have experienced house price inflation to varying degrees with Barcelona having the most marked increases linked to hosting the Olympic and Paralympic games. However, it was also clear that it is problematic to assume a direct causal link between hosting the games and an increase in property values. Price increases varied with the most substantial increases in areas some distance from Olympic Venues and explained, more generally, by the demand for housing in those cities. In London there has been much hype about anticipated property value rises, however, there is little evidence of significant increases in value in the areas closest to the Olympic Park.

The London property market as a whole has continued to perform well with above inflation price increases despite the recession. There has been an increased demand for property in part due to an influx of foreign capital seeking safer places to invest. Research undertaken by the Institute of Public Policy Research identified a significant increase in the number of overseas buyers purchasing properties in the most expensive parts of London with foreign purchasers spending £3.7 billion on property in London in 2010 and £5.2 billion in 2011. In the main demand is in prime areas such as Westminster and Kensington and Chelsea, with a knock

---

1 There were six official Olympic Host boroughs i.e. Newham, Hackney, Tower Hamlets, Waltham Forest, Greenwich and Barking and Dagenham. The London Legacy Development Corporation excludes Barking and Dagenham and Greenwich from its remit and focuses on those boroughs in which legacy activity related to the Park and its surrounding area are anticipated. Therefore we have limited our focus to these four boroughs which we will refer to as 'Legacy' boroughs.

on effect on surrounding areas (IPPR 2012). The *Financial Times* commissioned Knight Frank to undertake research on trends in house prices and concluded that there are a number of distinctive sub property markets in the London area and varying house price trends with some areas experiencing relatively low demand (Hammond 2012). Research undertaken by Assetz, a property and financial services group, explored house price increases in 145 postal codes in London up to 2011. It noted that whilst Central London continues to be the best performing region this is uneven and observed that seven of the areas close to the Olympic Park are ranked in the bottom 20 for property price increases (Smith 2011).

A number of studies have indicated similar findings that despite initial speculation of substantial house price increases in the Stratford area this has not materialised. Lloyds TSB have undertaken research on the impact of London hosting the games on property prices in fourteen East London Postal districts. It found that property prices increased at an average of 33 per cent across this period between 2005 and 2012. Lloyds TSB identified particularly high increases in Homerton (59 per cent) and Dalston (53 per cent) but much lower increases in Stratford (14 per cent) and neighbouring Plaistow (6 per cent) (Lloyds 2012). Most recent data up to March 2013 indicated a 2.49 per cent increase in Stratford on the previous 12 months compared to a 4.44 per cent increase for London as a whole (Zoopla 2013).

Rightmove explored trends in the six Olympic boroughs between 2005 and 2012. Their research indicated that only two of the boroughs performed above the London average of 60 per cent for the period – Hackney (69 per cent) and Tower Hamlets (79 per cent) with the remainder failing to keep track with growth in the capital generally. More generally price increases relate to specific features of these areas such as the docklands effect in Tower Hamlets and the gentrification of parts of Hackney, such as Shoreditch and London Fields (Rightmove 2012). Moreover, the gap between property prices in Stratford and Greater London has remained constant. In 2001 house prices in Stratford were 35 per cent below the Greater London average, this reduced to 22 per cent in 2005 when London won the bid and widened again to 35 per cent in 2012 (Goodley, Bowers 2012).

Despite the relatively modest increase in house prices, affordability remains a problem. Newham has the lowest median earnings of any authority in London and the largest number of residents on incomes below £15,000 (18.9 per cent). Newham's income-to-house price ratio[2] is 6.1 and though this is low in the London context it confirms that affordability continues to be a key issue. The London Borough of Hackney had the third lowest median income of any London authority and the third highest proportion of residents earning below £15,000 (17.1 per cent) and an earnings to house price ratio of 7.9. The London Borough of Tower Hamlets had the seventh lowest median income and the fourth highest number of residents on incomes below £15,000 (15.9 per cent) and an earnings-

---

2   Ratios are calculated by dividing the average house price by median earnings in the borough.

to-price ratio of 6.4. The London Borough of Waltham Forest had the tenth lowest median income and the tenth highest proportion of residents on incomes of £15,000 or below and an earnings-to-house price ratio of 6.4. Overall we can see that residents in the boroughs tend to have lower earnings and incomes which make home ownership problematic and a dependence on social housing more likely. Residents in Social housing fare particularly badly and tend to have lower incomes than those in other tenures and it is these tenants that are often most in need of housing (London.gov.uk 2012a).

Rental Price Trends and Speculation

Rental values have been rising both in London and across England and Wales and whilst house prices have not risen in those areas closest to the Olympic Park, there has been a substantial increase in rental values and a growth more generally of the private rented sector in these areas. Rental values in London increased by 9 per cent between March 2011 and 2012, which was significantly higher than increases in other parts of the country with many regions experiencing negative growth (Find a Property 2012). Rental values in three of the 'Legacy' boroughs are amongst the most expensive in the country and rental prices in areas such as Stratford have increased much more than property prices, making it an attractive place for buy to let investors. Research from Shelter in 2011 indicated that four of the six Olympic boroughs had some of the highest rental values for a two-bedroom property in England. Tower Hamlets was ranked the sixth most expensive area; followed by Hackney in 7th place and Newham in 26th place. Shelter explored the issue of affordability comparing the median income with the median rent. All four boroughs were 'very unaffordable' as defined by Shelter's measure. For example, in Hackney median income was 70 per cent of median rent and ranked the 6th least affordable area in the country, in Tower Hamlets median income was 67 per cent of median rent and ranked 7th least affordable, Newham's median income was 55 per cent of rent and ranked the 15th least affordable area in England and Waltham Forest was ranked 27th with a median income of 50 per cent of median rent. In England only 8 per cent of authorities are defined as 'very unaffordable' using Shelter's measure (Reynolds 2011). Data from the Mayor's Office indicated that rents in Stratford are significantly higher than in Newham generally, though significantly below the average for Greater London (London.gov.uk 2012b).[3]

---

3 Rents in the lower quartile are £202 per week in Newham, £219 per week in Stratford and £254 in Greater London. Rents in the median quartile are 219.00 in Newham, £254.00 in Stratford and £280.00 in Greater London. Rents per week on properties in the upper quartile ranged from 255.00 in the London Borough of Newham, £279.00 in Stratford and £360.00 in Greater London. The data covers the period in the year up to July 2012 (London.gov.uk 2012).

Homelessness and London 2012

In other host cities there has been evidence of increased victimisation of the homeless during the games. However, a more complex picture emerges in London. There were two key homelessness concerns that emerged in other cities one linked to landlords trying to maximise income during the games period by either increasing rents or evicting tenants in order to house visitors during the event and the other related to the potential victimisation of the homeless during the games.

Increased Evictions

There was evidence that there has been an increase in rents and evictions in the months leading up to Olympic and Paralympic Games. Shelter established additional advice services in Hackney, Newham and Tower Hamlets ahead of the Games and confirmed that they had received many more enquiries from people living in Olympic boroughs concerned that they had been faced with substantial rent increases and threats of eviction, with additional premiums added for the Olympic period (Twinch 2012). Landlords added clauses to leases specifying that residents could not remain in the property during the Games, a problem that was compounded for residents as prices had also increased across the area making it difficult to for them to stay (NBC 2012). According to Cityzen, an agent letting property in the area, around one third of the 400 landlords in Stratford would be serving notices on their tenants to move out because of the Games (Cited in Collinson, *Guardian* 2012). The Housing Minister Grant Shapps, speaking on BBC Television, indicated that illegal evictions could result in imprisonment (BBC 2012a). However, current housing law makes it relatively easy to evict tenants therefore it was not so much that the actions were unlawful but that they had negative consequences for local residents. The focus on capital gains in the residential sector is a key benefit associated with hosting the Olympics. Newham, in particular, has seen a substantial growth in the private rented 'buy-to-let' sector in recent years and in the lead up to the games a range of agencies emerged advertising the potential gains that could be made from renting out a property in the area during the games. It is, therefore, unsurprising that this problem emerged.

Street Homelessness

In London, targets were set in the years leading up to the games to eradicate street homelessness. The initial strategy 'No One Left Out' was proposed in 2008 by the then Labour administration and followed through by the subsequent administration under the leadership of Boris Johnson. The Mayor's Office established a delivery board comprising voluntary and statutory agencies to focus specifically on eradicating street homelessness. Their strategy was underpinned by a policy of 'No Second Night Out':

> No one living on the streets and no one new to the streets of London should sleep out for a second night out. (Broadway 2012, p. 2)

An initial pilot project was established in April 2011 focussing on ten London boroughs and this was then formalised as best practice across the whole of London from June 2012. The focus was specifically on new rough sleepers with the intention of providing a swifter service of advice and support and a reconnection with family and supports systems in their local areas. The 'No Second Night' Strategy was adopted at national level in August 2012 indicating that its commitments will extend beyond the games.

In addition to the 'No Second Night' Strategy, local authorities introduced a number of mechanisms and strategies to respond to a potential increase in street homelessness during the games. For example, the eight London authorities that constitute the East London partnership purchased additional emergency bed spaces and outreach workers. One London Authority purchased some of its additional space outside of London due to a shortage of bed spaces with the intention of moving the homeless back when space became available. Nevertheless, a homeless charity in Colchester claimed that there had been an increase in homelessness in their area with homeless people moved on from London though this was disputed by the Metropolitan Police and Community Organisers (Cox 2012).

There were clearly concerns, based on the experience of previous host cities, that a street cleaning exercise would take place to present a positive image during the games. Homeless Link, a charity that has worked with the homeless over many years, countered these claims three months ahead of the games:

> We have been contacted several times about reports that, in some areas of London, rough sleepers are being encouraged to "move on" in preparation for the Olympics. We would be highly concerned if this was taking place but, as far we know, the only activities underway are part of the long-term strategy to end rough sleeping in London. In other words services are working to get new and long-term rough sleepers off the streets and into accommodation but this should be happening whether or not the Olympics were taking place. (Homeless Link 2012)

However, there was clearly a desire from some quarters to implement this kind of action. The Cardiff Retail partnership in Wales requested that the Police make use of the 1824 Vagrancy Act to imprison the homeless during the Olympics in Cardiff. However, this met with swift opposition and a Facebook campaign encouraging people to show solidarity with the homeless by sleeping out for one night (Wales Online 2012).

On a more positive note, the homeless were included in the cultural Olympiad for the first time. A one-night festival was held at the Royal Opera House in July 2012 comprising 300 performers who had experienced homelessness at some point and entitled 'With One Voice'. A petition was presented to Jacques Rogge,

Table 3.1   Rough sleeping in the 'Legacy' boroughs

Name of Borough	2009/10	2010/11	2011/12
Hackney	63	57	81
Newham	18	38	79
Tower Hamlets	149	156	256
Waltham Forest	30	26	46

Source: Broadway (2012): *Street to Home Annual Report* – based on number of people seen sleeping rough by outreach or buildings based service teams during the year.

President of the IOC, requesting that homeless people be given a platform in future Olympic and Paralympic Games (May Young 2012).

Unsurprisingly given a raft of welfare reforms and a much harsher economic climate, street homelessness has been on the increase both in the 'Legacy' boroughs and in London more generally in recent years. In 2011–12 about 5,700 people were counted as sleeping rough on the streets of London for at least on one night throughout the year, a rise of 43 per cent from the previous year and almost double that in 2003. Just over a quarter of rough sleepers were from Central and East European countries and between 2010–2011 there was a significant increase in UK nationals sleeping rough (London Poverty Profile 2012).

We can see from Table 3.1 that rough sleeping is a particularly pronounced problem in Tower Hamlets and Hackney and has become more significant in Newham in recent years. Anecdotal evidence suggests this increase, particularly in Newham, is due to a number of workers moving to the area on short term contracts to work on Olympic-related construction projects and then once the work is completed they have found themselves without sufficient income to pay their rent.

Moreover, even if efforts have been taken to ensure that the homeless are not pushed out of the city during the games the impact of housing benefit reforms, resulting in a cap on Local Housing Allowances, has meant that people living in more expensive areas on housing benefit have been re-housed either in cheaper parts of London or in different parts of the country and following the Games (BBC News 2012b).

Housing Need and Poverty in the 'Legacy' Boroughs

A review of a range of indicators reveals the extent of poverty in the 'Legacy' boroughs. In Waltham Forest 33 per cent of children live in poverty[4] increasing to 39 per cent in Newham, 40 per cent in Hackney and 53 per cent in Tower

---

4   The measure used was where the household income was below 60 per cent median income and families were in receipt of at least one benefit.

Hamlets; this compares with a London Average of just over 30 per cent and a national average of just over 20 per cent (Leeser 2011).

Indicators on income also suggest proportionately more residents are in low paid employment. Newham and Waltham Forest have some of the highest levels of the population on low pay (defined as the London Living Wage 7.85 per hour) in London with more than 19.5 per cent of the population earning low pay rising to 25 per cent in Newham. The proportion of the population on low pay in Hackney is also high and is in excess of 18 per cent of the population. There are much lower numbers of the population in Tower Hamlets on low pay. However, here there is a greater degree of polarisation between those in work and those on benefits. Tower Hamlets and Newham have the highest levels of worklessness in London closely followed by Waltham Forest. Hackney on the other hand has seen declining levels of unemployment over recent years and this may be explained by a wealthier working population moving into the owner occupied and private rented sector (New Policy Institute 2012).

The Index of Multiple Deprivation (IMD) uses a combination of measures such as unemployment; income; health; overcrowding; and educational qualifications to ascertain the extent of disadvantage at an area level. The Legacy boroughs have disproportionately high levels of deprivation as compared with other authorities in London and at a national level. Hackney and Newham are the two most deprived areas in the country on three of six measures used and Tower Hamlets is in the top three for two of the measures used (there are 354 authorities in the country). All four boroughs are ranked in the bottom eight of 32 local authorities in London (Leeser 2011).

The situation confronting the 'Legacy' boroughs may be summed up as follows:

> Despite their proximity to key areas of wealth generation in central London, the six Olympic Host boroughs show many of the signs of economic deprivation, with low employment rates and high unemployment, a preponderance of people in lower skilled jobs, and relatively low earnings. Even ... in Canary Wharf, there is a big disconnect between the jobs located in the area and the jobs undertaken by those living in the area as many of the highest value-added jobs in central London are taken by commuters. (Oxford Economics 2010, p. 7)

Housing Tenure

At a national level the most significant changes in housing tenure between 2001 and 2011 was the demise of owner occupation and the rise of the Private rented sector. The Private Rented Sector increased from 12 per cent to 19 per cent across this period with owner occupation falling from 69 per cent to 64 per cent with only marginal changes in the proportion social renting down from 19 to 18 per cent. In London owner-occupation fell from 56.5 per cent to 49.5 per cent, private renting grew from 15 per cent to over a quarter and the Social rented sector and the social

Table 3.2   Housing tenure in the 'Legacy' boroughs' 2001 and 2011 census

Legacy borough	Owner occupied	Social rent	Private rent	Total number of households
Hackney 2001 census	27,613 (32%)	43,699 (51%)	13,370 (16%)	86,042
Hackney 2011 census	24,179 (24%)	44,430 (44%)	29,499 (30%)	101,690
Newham 2001 census	40,048 (44%)	33,505 (37%)	16,385 (18%)	91,821
Newham 2011 census	33,822 (34%)	30,092 (30%)	34,570 (34%)	101,519
Tower Hamlets 2001 census	22,742 (29%)	41,236 (53%)	13,105 (17%)	78,530
Tower Hamlets 2011 census	24,552 (24%)	40,106 (40%)	32,964 (33%)	101,257
Waltham Forest 2001 census	52,918 (59%)	21,393 (24%)	14,086 (16%)	89,788
Waltham Forest 2011 census	48,361 (50%)	21,376 (22%)	25,102 (26%)	96,861

Source: Office for National Statistics (2013).

rented sector declined from 25.4 to 24.1 per cent (GLA Intelligence Unit 2012; OSCI 2012).

The table above explores housing trends with regard to tenure in the four 'Legacy' boroughs. We can see that in each of these authorities there has been a considerable increase in households between 2001 and 2011. Some of this increase may be explained by the conversion of houses into flats and HMO (Houses in Multiple Occupation) There has also been a considerable amount of new build activity particularly in Tower Hamlets, Newham and Hackney that would also account for this trend. We can see from this table that owner occupation has declined in all four boroughs as a proportion and percentage of properties, with the exception of Tower Hamlets where there has been a net increase in terms of numbers but a decline as a percentage of housing. Newham, Tower Hamlets and Waltham Forest have seen a net fall in social rented housing with this fall being most marked in Newham and is significant given the extent of need in the area. The most significant change has been in the rise of the private rented sector which has more than doubled in net terms in Hackney, Newham and Tower Hamlets and ranges from 26 per cent in Waltham Forest, 30 per cent in Hackney, 33 per cent in Tower Hamlets and 34 per cent in Newham. Clearly the growth of Houses in Multiple Occupation (HMO) will account for some of this, However, much of

Table 3.3   Overcrowding in the 'Legacy' boroughs

Overcrowding	Position in country with regard to extent of overcrowding (2011 census)	Proportion of residents living in overcrowded conditions (2011 census)
Newham	1st	25.4%
Tower Hamlets	3rd	16.8%
Hackney	6th	15.6%
Waltham Forest	7th	15.6%

Definition of overcrowding: *Households with at least one bedroom less than required to accommodate those that live there.*

the new housing built for owner occupation in these areas is quite often privately rented.

Overcrowding

The problem of overcrowding is a significant problem. The 2011 census indicated that overcrowding in England was 4.8 per cent. Overcrowding is a substantial problem in London generally and provides a good indicator of housing need. London is the most overcrowded region in the country with an average 11 per cent of the population living in overcrowded conditions (Office for National Statistics 2011).

The four 'Legacy' boroughs have disproportionately high levels of overcrowding and this is indicative of the extensive housing need. We can see from this data that overcrowding is particularly problematic in all 'Legacy' boroughs and particularly marked in Newham, in fact all four 'Legacy' authorities are ranked in the top seven for overcrowding in the country. There has not been a statistical breakdown of the relationship between housing tenure and overcrowding at the time of writing. However, each Local Authority has attempted to estimate this as part of its strategic needs assessment. Newham estimated that overcrowding ranged from 12.5 per cent in the owner-occupied sector, 16.2 per cent in social rent and 23.3 per cent in the private rented sector. In Tower Hamlets it was estimated that overcrowding ranged from 14.7 per cent in the private rented sector, 26.6 per cent in the social rented sector, 13.4 per cent for those in the owner-occupied sector with a mortgage, falling to around 7.5 per cent for owner-occupiers without a mortgage. In Waltham Forest levels of overcrowding ranged from 7.9 per cent in the owner-occupied sector, 8.1 per cent in the social rented sector and 17.6 per cent in the private rented sector. Moreover, they identified a trend for more

Table 3.4 Housing waiting lists in 'Legacy' boroughs 2009–2011 and proportion of population on housing waiting lists

Local Authority	2009	2010	2011	% of population on waiting list
Hackney	11,461	11,956	13,423	14.6
Newham	28,649	31,851	32,045	34.9
Tower Hamlets	19,681	22,707	23,128	23.6
Waltham Forest	14,341	15,624	16,153	17.6

Source: Department of Communities and Local Government, 2012.

rooms to be used as bedrooms that are not designed for this purpose. In Hackney it was estimated that levels of overcrowding ranged from 5 per cent in the owner-occupied sector, 12 per cent in the social rented sector and 10 per cent in the private rented sector. We can conclude then that overcrowding is a prominent problem in both the social rented and private rented sector and less of a problem for owner-occupiers in all four 'Legacy' authorities, though even within these sectors the levels of overcrowding exceeds the average for England as a whole.

Overcrowding is also a key factor in why people want to move. For example in Newham residents who wanted to move were asked why this was so and more than 40 per cent wanted to move because their house was too small. Similarly, in Hackney of the more than 17,000 living in unsuitable housing more than half of this was explained by overcrowding (London Borough of Tower Hamlets 2010; London Borough of Hackney 2010; London Borough of Newham 2010; London Borough of Waltham Forest 2011).

Housing Waiting Lists

The proportion of the population of each Local Authority/borough on the housing waiting list provides a very good indicator of housing need. In England 8 per cent of the population are on Housing Waiting lists and in London the figure increases to 11 per cent of the population.

The table above indicates that the demand for social housing has continued to grow in all four 'Legacy' boroughs. We can see that Newham and Tower Hamlets have 34.9 per cent and 23.6 per cent respectively of their population on housing waiting lists and this is the highest of any authority/borough in the country (Department of Communities and Local Government 2012). Whilst

Table 3.5   New affordable homes and homes for social rent in 'Legacy' boroughs

LA numbers of affordable housing and social rent	2007–8	2008–9	2009–10	2010–11	2011–12	Total
Hackney affordable	1020	990	1260	690	1020	4,980
Hackney social rent	270	390	610	370	610	2,250 (45% of all affordable housing)
Newham affordable	1180	570	700	580	810	3,840
Newham social rent	830	170	260	310	510	2,080 (54% of affordable housing)
Tower Hamlet affordable	1380	1250	1990	1430	1800	7,850
Tower Hamlets social rent	700	550	1260	820	1430	4,760 (61% of affordable housing)
Waltham Forest affordable	200	560	250	460	630	2,100
Waltham Forest social rent	130	470	150	280	440	1,470 (70% of affordable housing)
Total affordable housing units						18,770

Source: Additional affordable dwellings by Local Authority; Table 1008 and additional social rent dwellings by Local Authority; Table 1006 downloaded at HCA <https://www.gov.uk/government/statistical-data-sets/live-tables-on-affordable-housing-supply> HCA New build homes for social rent; Table 1006 new build housing by Local Authority.

Hackney and Waltham Forest have lower levels of housing need in comparison to Tower Hamlets and Newham, demand is also higher than the London average.

New Affordable Homes in the 'Legacy' Boroughs

The Barker Review of Housing published in 2004 highlighted the systematic failure to build affordable homes and as a result of this review there was a policy shift towards the construction of more affordable homes achieved in part through the use of Section 106 planning gain agreements coupled with increased requirements for affordable housing in the London Plan 2004.[5]

We can see that there has been a considerable amount of new build affordable housing built between 2007 and 2012. This new-build activity does not necessarily correlate with need as we can see that more affordable housing was built in Hackney despite the greater need for it in Newham. Moreover, the term affordable housing refers in this instance to two categories of housing including intermediate housing such as shared ownership and discounted rent and social rent.

There is a huge need for social housing for rent in the 'Legacy' authorities and this was recognised in the first London Plan which stipulated that 70 per cent of affordable homes should be for social rent and would have guided policy when these schemes were approved. However, as we can see, proportions of affordable housing for social rent ranged from 45 per cent in Hackney through to 70 per cent in Waltham Forest. The replacement of the 'social rent' model with the 'affordable rent' model coupled with cuts to housing grants has made it increasingly difficult to deliver genuinely affordable housing for rent and we explore this in more detail in Chapter 6.

Satisfaction with Area

A survey about place undertaken by the Department of Communities and Local Government in 2008 found that residents in the 'Legacy' boroughs were much less likely to be satisfied with their neighbourhood than in other areas of London. Residents in Newham, closely followed by Waltham Forest, were less likely to be satisfied than residents in any other authority in London. Residents in Tower Hamlets were the fifth least satisfied in London. Levels of satisfaction were closer to average levels for Hackney. There was also a much greater concern about anti-social behaviour. Across London 26.2 per cent of residents felt that anti-social behaviour was a problem. However, this increased significantly in all four 'Legacy' boroughs i.e. 47.9 per cent of residents in Newham, 45.9 per cent in Tower Hamlets, 36.5 per cent in Waltham Forest and 37.6 per cent in Hackney felt this was a problem (Skanlon, Travers, Whitehead 2010). Clearly perceptions of place will need to be addressed in order for places such as Newham to attract an aspirational middle class.

---

5   In 2003 housebuilding by RSL's had fallen to its lowest level since 1990 with just 12,820 units being built in the country. Between 2006 and 2011 numbers of new build housing completed by Housing Associations began to rise and reached its highest point in 2011 with 25,880 units completed. Completions in the private rented sector declined across this period from 154,210 in 2007 to 86,500 in 2011. Source table 244 house dwellings completed by Tenure England Source: http://www.homesandcommunities.co.uk/sites/default/files/aboutus/national_housing_statistics_june_2012_tables_rev1.pdfdownloaded 2 January 2013.

In summary, we have established there are high levels of deprivation and housing need in the Host boroughs along with lower incomes indicating an urgent need for new affordable housing in the main for social rent.

The Shifting Governance of 'Legacy'

In this section we review the range of agencies established to oversee the Olympic and Paralympic Games and its associated legacy and legacy plans. What becomes clear is that there have already been significant shifts in the governance machinery and key players within this. Those originally appointed to lead the 'legacy' agenda are no longer in post, creating a significant risk that the commitment to reducing social deprivation and improving housing conditions, commitments central to the original bid, will be diluted. We also consider the raft of plans and reports that have been published with regard to legacy including the 'convergence' agenda developed by local authorities.

> London's bid was built on a special Olympic Vision. That vision of an Olympic games would not only be a celebration of sport but a force for regeneration. The games will transform one of the poorest and deprived areas of London. They will create thousands of jobs and homes. (Hansard 2005)

In 2008, Laura Keogh from King's College London was commissioned by the Department of Communities and Local government to flesh out in more detail the concept of legacy:

> The creation of a desirable socially diverse and balanced new areas providing a housing legacy for London ... A model for Social Inclusion bringing communities together ... A high quality environment for neighbouring mixed communities ... Catalyst for Economic and Social Regeneration around the Park. (Keogh 2009, p. 10)

London's approach to legacy is relatively unique in that it established an infrastructure to secure legacy in the pre-event phase, however, there have been huge changes in central and local government policy across the period which is likely to have a significant impact on initial ambitions for housing legacy.

London's bid was developed by a Labour government and a Labour-controlled Greater London Authority with Ken Livingstone keen to present hosting the games much more as an urban regeneration project than a sporting event. However, in 2008 Labour lost control of the GLA and in 2010 the Government. Commitments to using the Games as a catalyst for the transformation of East London continued, with the Mayor/GLA assuming a central role in securing a long term legacy.

London's Mayor has played a central role in governance. The Mayor was co-Chair of the Olympic board which supervised the work to prepare for the Games; a signatory of the Host City Contract, which enshrined the commitments made by London to the International Olympic Committee; a funder of the ODA; a founder member and shareholder of the London Organising Committee of the Olympic and Paralympic Games (LOCOG) and the Olympic Park Legacy Company (OPLC); Chair of the Olympic Park Regeneration Steering Group and has responsibility for coordinating a wide range of legacy work related to sports participation, education, employment and skills and volunteering and the establishment of the London Legacy Development Corporation which now leads on legacy (GLA 2012).

The key government agency with responsibility for the games was the Department of Culture, Media and Sport and it established a specific Government Olympic Executive to oversee the games, along with a number of other agencies. Each host city has an organising committee for the Olympic and Paralympic Games: LOCOG (London Organising Committee for the Olympic and Paralympic Games) was established specifically to prepare and stage the Games, including the opening and closing ceremonies, funded mainly from the private sector and is a private company. The ODA (Olympic Development Authority) was a public body established by the London Olympic and Paralympic Games Act 2006. The ODA consists of representatives from the public and private sectors and initially worked with the LDA, Transport for London, LTGDC and the five designated Olympic local authorities. The ODA was given planning powers for the Olympic Park area and had the task of Compulsory Purchasing and clearing land. It was responsible for the construction of permanent and temporary structures, the development and implementation of a transport strategy and ensuring the project set new standards for sustainable development. The ODA also had responsibility for securing the use of these new venues after the games. The Nation and Regions Group was set up to ensure that the whole of the UK benefited from the games and comprised representatives from different regions and nations across the UK. An Olympic Board was also established comprising the London Mayor, the Sports Minister, the Chair of the British Olympic Association and Chair of LOCOG and met monthly. A London 2012 Equality and Diversity Forum was also established with the intention of promoting equality and monitoring progress with regard national and regional equality commitments for the games. The Olympic Park Regeneration Steering Group was set up in 2007 to provide views on planning and developing new neighbourhoods, services and businesses and to ensure political oversight of the project.

The London Development Agency was established in 2000 by the GLA to work on economic development issues across borough boundaries and played a lead role with regard to Compulsory Purchase Orders and the decanting of residents and businesses at the Olympic Park, working closely with the Olympic Development Authority. The LDA was initially tasked with developing a Legacy Masterplan Framework for the area which was subsequently developed by the Olympic Park Legacy Company in the form of a revised Masterplan for the Lower Lea Valley. In 2008 with the election of a new Mayor there was an overhaul of responsibilities. The LDA's role was amended and the Olympic Park

Legacy Company was established in 2009 and key staff transferred from the LDA to the OPLC (Olympic Park Legacy Company). In March 2012 the LDA was abolished as part of the policy trend towards localism.

The London Thames Gateway Development Corporation was the agency with lead responsibility for the Lower Lea Valley area surrounding the park from 2005 up until the establishment of the London Legacy Development Corporation in 2012. In 2007 the five boroughs partnership board (Host Boroughs Unit) articulated the views of initially five and then six Host boroughs and produced the Strategic Regeneration Framework/Convergence Framework discussed below. The problematic nature of the wide array of agencies involved in governance in comparison with other major regeneration schemes was noted in February 2010 by the London Assembly's Economic Development, Culture, Sports and Tourism Committee:

> There are a large number of different bodies responsible for the Games legacy in East London. While complexity is not in itself necessarily a problem, and is perhaps inevitable given the wide range of legacy goals and the layers of government involved, this complexity must not result in a situation where it is unclear who is leading delivery of particular legacy goals and who they are accountable too. (GLA 2010a, para. 1.6, p. 22)

Both the Host boroughs and the London Assembly have exerted pressure to ensure that legacy ambitions are realised. For example in 2010 the GLA published a report on legacy and concluded:

> So far only a minority of jobs have gone to local people, and the number of apprenticeships offered on the Olympic Park is dismal. It is still unclear whether local people will get their fair share of the new housing compared with affluent incomers. More ambitious targets must be set and enforced. (Dee Doocey, Chair of Economic Development, Culture, Sport and Tourism Committee, GLA 2010a, p. 7)

The LDA proposed the establishment of an agency with a specific legacy brief in 2008. In May 2009 The Olympic Park Legacy Company was established by the Mayor of London and the government to ensure long-term planning, development and maintenance of the Queen Elizabeth Park, including its transformation and re-opening following the games. The LDA transferred land including the Olympic Park and the Three Mills Estate owned by the LDA to the OPLC along with some staff. A new Chair, Baroness Ford (a Labour peer) and Director, Andrew Altmann, were appointed to lead the organisation. The OPLC was perceived as a welcome step forward with an agency with a clear focus on long term legacy. The strategic aims of the company were to:

> Deliver social, economic and environmental benefits for East London; to deliver a return on public investment in the park and to optimise the sustainability and the success of the park and its venues. (Parliament.co.uk 2011)

In February 2012 it was confirmed that the London Legacy Mayoral Development Corporation would be established and Baroness Ford announced she would be stepping down after the games, and shortly after, Andrew Altmann announced that he too would be stepping down. The former chair of Transport for London Daniel Moylan replaced Baroness Ford in June 2012, however, his appointment was short lived and in September 2012 it was confirmed that Daniel Moylan would be stepping down as Chair and replaced on an interim basis by Boris Johnson. Some staff from the OPLC transferred to the LLDC. There were a number of key changes: powers that transferred to the LLMDC, including Development Control powers for the areas, previously shared by the London Thames Gateway Development Corporation and the Olympic Development Authority and plan making powers for the area. The rationale for passing plan making powers to the LLMDC was linked to concerns about the potential for inconsistent planning objectives arising from four different authorities and to enable them to have control over the Community Infrastructure. This was strongly opposed by local authorities. One issue that emerged in the consultation was a perceived overemphasis on physical regeneration and the Mayor conceded that this was a problem and affirmed his commitment to the social dimensions of legacy central to the initial bid and strongly underlined in work begun by the Olympic Park Legacy Company to ensure a lasting legacy. The consultation document stressed the need to develop constructive relationships with the four 'Legacy' boroughs and included recognition of the need to learn important lessons from previous bodies such as the London Docklands Development Corporation.

The land included in the LLMDC includes the Olympic Village and associated development sites owned by London Continental Railway and the ODA; the Stratford City Development including the Westfield Shopping Centre and Chobham Farm; Hackney Wick and Fish Island; Pudding Mill Lane and Sugar House Lane; Three Mills and Mill Meads; Bromley by Bow North and the Carpenters Estate and land owned by the OPLC and the Lea Valley Regional Park Authority including Eton Manor (GLA 2011).

The role of the London Legacy Mayoral Development Corporation has been defined as:

> To promote and deliver physical, social, economic and environmental regeneration in the Olympic Park and surrounding area, in particular by maximising the legacy of the Olympic and Paralympic Games, by securing high-quality sustainable development and investment, ensuring the long-term success of the facilities and assets within its direct control and supporting and promoting the aim of convergence. (GLA 2011, p. 7)

At a central government level the Cabinet office has an Olympic and Paralympic Legacy Unit working with relevant agencies across the country to focus on a wide range of legacy related issues ranging from transforming perceptions of disabled people in Society through to East London Regeneration. To date then we can see that London has been relatively unique in terms of trying to plan for legacy from 2005 onwards. However, those charged with leading on legacy both within individual agencies and the agencies themselves have changed and therefore it is fair to conclude that there has been a lack of continuity which is not conducive to legacy. Frustration about a perceived lack of focus on those early commitments led the five Host boroughs[6] to develop their own strategy on convergence.

Convergence Agenda

In a similar vein to Vancouver's Inclusivity statement The five Host boroughs established a policy agenda around 'convergence' aimed at realising legacy commitments and partly in response to a perception that the government had failed to focus sufficiently on legacy. In October 2009 the five Host boroughs set out an Olympic Strategic Regeneration framework with indicators and actions across a wide number of areas aimed at ensuring that a legacy of lasting social and economic benefits would be realised. In particular the policy objective was to ensure that the life chances of those in the five Host boroughs converged with the rest of London through focussing improved joint working and targeting resources on these issues.

> The common theme which runs through all of these actions is the determination to create the most enduring legacy of 2012 in the communities of the Host boroughs and to do that by ensuring that over the next 20 years the residents of the Host boroughs will come to enjoy the same life chances as other Londoners. (Host boroughs 2011, p. 2)

The convergence agenda was subsequently endorsed by the wider legacy community in documents such as the replacement London Plan, planning documents of the respective authorities and in government plans.[7] The boroughs argued that the document was produced because of the failure of the government to act on legacy. The intention was to provide a strategic direction to realise the policy commitments made around legacy aimed at reducing social deprivation and ensuring that the environment is transformed in the interests of all of its residents.

---

6 The five Host boroughs include Greenwich which hosted two temporary Olympic venues. However, these venues were not linked to legacy in any broader sense as they were temporary.

7 In December 2010 the Department of Culture Media and Sport published a document Plans for the Legacy from the 2012 Olympic and Paralympic Games endorsing the objectives.

The 2009 framework committed itself to improvements across seven key areas. In 2011 a review of progress was undertaken and the strategy revised. There was an acknowledgement that progress has been made in relation to 12 of the indicators including educational attainment, additional housing units, life expectancy for men and employment rates, a worsening situation on two indicators and no change on five indicators including those on median earnings, children living in families on benefits and working-age families with no qualification.

In 2011 the plan was amended and a convergence action plan 2011–2015 was produced in response to the changing policy context and in particular cuts to public expenditure and the reform of the housing benefit system and its implications for the demographics of London with an anticipated shift eastwards of people dependent on housing benefit. Barking and Dagenham was also included as a Host borough in the revised plan. The seven key indicators were revised to three interconnected themes; creating wealth and reducing poverty, supporting healthier lifestyles and developing successful neighbourhoods. The developing successful neighbourhoods theme included commitments related to crime reduction, neighbourhood/public realm improvement, service improvements and housing. There were three key objectives around housing: These included building new homes and reducing overcrowding. The target for housing was 50,000 homes in the six boroughs of which 12,000 would be affordable by 2015. There had been progress on this target since 2009 with 13,000 new homes including 4,300 affordable homes built in 2009/10 in the Host boroughs, and therefore the target was revised to a further 38,000 homes including 7,700 affordable homes by 2015. Other indicators include retrofitting to achieve low carbon homes and reduce fuel poverty and the development of a joint working methodology to tackle overcrowding. Another key target related to neighbourhoods was the development of new city districts with a range of accessible and high quality facilities linked to the development of new health and educational facilities at the Olympic Park (Host Boroughs Units 2011).

The work on convergence provides an opportunity to focus on these issues and measure and monitor progress and has over time been incorporated into legacy planning frameworks, however, there are no specific budgets linked to achieving these outcomes, and it could, therefore, be perceived as a 'wish list' rather than a viable strategy for the reduction of deprivation in east London.

Conclusion

We began this chapter by exploring the wider housing legacy impacts that have emerged in previous host cities, such as rising house and rental prices and evictions along with victimisation of the homeless. In London there are a number of distinguishing features in this regard. Firstly, whilst London has experienced a significant increase in the value of properties in recent years Newham, the host borough, has experienced a relatively negligible increase in values across this period. Moreover, it has been suggested that house price increases in areas such Docklands and Homerton need to be understood as a result of the regeneration of these specific areas as opposed to the London 2012 project. Secondly, rental values have increased in 'Legacy' boroughs reflecting a national upward trend in rental values and the demand for rental properties more generally. There was evidence of significant price inflation in the period leading up to the Games and it remains to be seen whether the significant infrastructure investment in the area and improved transport infrastructure leads to sustained price increases over time or whether this was a blip in long term trends. There was also evidence of investors capitalising on the games and evicting long term residents. Lastly, the Mayor's Office used the Games as an incentive to eradicate rough sleeping and there was limited evidence of the victimisation of homeless that has been experienced elsewhere (despite calls for it in Cardiff). Ironically, reforms to the housing benefit system meant that many families were forced to leave London and their local connections, whilst London simultaneously prepared to host the world.

We then moved on to consider the extent of income and housing deprivation in the four 'Legacy' boroughs. The analysis demonstrated the urgent need for 'affordable housing' with both Tower Hamlets and Newham having the largest proportion of residents in housing need in the country. We then reviewed the ever changing range of individuals and agencies that have been tasked with legacy and the implications of this for focussing on those goals of inclusion and deprivation reduction central to the original bid. The establishment of one agency (LLMDC) does provide the potential for a more coherent and consistent approach to legacy. This agency will have to ensure that it manages the political and financial tensions that will arise from the competing agendas of the local authorities and the Mayor with regard to the nature and actual form of legacy. Most significantly it will have to square the circle in a climate of fiscal austerity of securing legacy with a negligible budget. It is to these legacy plans that we now turn.

References

BBC News (2012a). London 2012: *Shapps Olympic eviction jail warning* <http://www.bbc.co.uk/news/uk-politics-17993170>. (Accessed 27 September).
BBC News (2012b). *Social cleansing benefit cap row* <http://www.bbc.co.uk/news/uk-politics-17821018> (Accessed 24 April).
BBC News (2012c). BBC Sports News, *New Legacy Chief Shatters Political Consensus* <http://www.bbc.co.uk/blogs/adrianwarner/2012/05/_conservative_councillor_danie.html> (Accessed 10 May).
Broadway (2012). *Street to Home Bulletin 2011/12* <http://www.bbc.co.uk/news/uk-politics-17993170>, <http://www.broadwaylondon.org/CHAIN/Reports/S2H%20bulletin_201112.pdf> (Accessed 10 May)
Collinson, P. (2012). The East End tenants facing eviction during the Olympics, *Guardian*, 18 May.

Cox, J. (2012). Are Olympics making Colchester's homeless problem worse, *Daily Gazette*, 7 August <http://www.essexcountystandard.co.uk/news/ecsnews/9860349.print/ (Accessed 27 August).

Daily Mail Online (2012). Tenants living near the site face last minute eviction as Landlords cash in on the games, *Daily Mail*, 8 May.

Department of Communities and Local Government (2011). *English Housing Survey 2010–11* (London: DCLG).

Department of Communities and Local Government (2012). Table 60: *Number of households on housing waiting List by district, 1997–2011* <http://www.communities.gov.uk/housing/housingresearch/housingstatistics/housingstatisticsby/rentslettings/livetables/> (Accessed 29 September 2012).

Find a property (2012). <http://www.findaproperty.com/rental-index.aspxt> (Accessed 5 September 2012).

Greater London Authority (2010). *Legacy Limited: A Review of the Olympic Legacy Park Company's Role*, February (London: GLA).

Greater London Authority (2011). Olympic Park Legacy Corporation, proposals by the Mayor of London for Public Consultation, February (London: GLA).

Greater London Authority Intelligence Unit (2012). *2011 Census Snapshot: Housing* (London: GLA).

Goodley, S. and Bowers, S. (2012). Dinner party talk of Olympics house-price rises is idle chatter, *Guardian*, 15 June.

Hammond, S. (2012). London House prices diverge sharply, *Financial Times*, 6 June.

Homeless Link. (2012). *100 days to go: Rough sleepers and the Olympics* <http://homeless.org.uk/news/100-days-go-rough-sleeping-and-olympics>.

Host Boroughs Unit (2011). *Convergence Framework and Action Plan 2011–2015* (Host Boroughs Unit: London).

Keogh, L. (2009). *London 2012 Olympic Legacies: Conceptualising Legacy: The Role of Communities and Local Government and the Regeneration of East London* (London: DCLG).

Leeser, R. (2011). *Focus on 2011: Poverty: The Hidden City* (London: Greater London Authority).

Lloyds TSB (2012). Press Release, *East End House prices up over 800 per month since Olympic win*, 27 February 2012.

London.gov.uk (2012a). *Focus on London: Income and spending at home* <http://data.london.gov.uk/visualisations/charts/fol10_income_spending/tableau_chart_Income.html> (Accessed 27 September 2012).

London.gov.uk (2012b). *London rent map* <http://www.london.gov.uk/rents/london/social.jsp> (Accessed 27 September 2012).

London Borough of Barking and Dagenham (2007). *Housing Strategy 2007–10* (London: LBBD).

London Borough of Hackney (2010). *Better Homes, Places and Opportunities*; Hackney's Housing Strategy, 15 February 2010 (London: LBH).

London Borough of Newham (2010). *Newham Strategic Housing Market Assessment 2010* (London: LBN).
London Borough of Newham (2012). *Newham Joint Strategic Needs Assessment* (London: Newham).
London Borough of Tower Hamlets (2010). *Report of the Scrutiny Review Working Group on the Private Rented Sector* (London: LBTH).
London Borough of Tower Hamlets (2010a). *London Borough of Tower Hamlets Housing Strategy Summary 2010 update* (London Borough of Tower Hamlets: London).
London Borough of Waltham Forest (2007). *Waltham Forest Housing Needs and Market Survey* (London; Waltham Forest).
London Borough of Waltham Forest (2012). Appendix One, Strategic Market Housing and Needs Assessment, April 2012.
London Borough of Waltham Forest (2012a). Statistics about the borough (Housing) <http://www.walthamforest.gov.uk/Pages/Services/Statistics-economic-information-and-analysis.aspx?l1=100004&l2=200079> (Accessed 8 October 2012).
London Poverty Profile (2012). Rough Sleeping in London <http://www.londonspovertyprofile.org.uk/indicators/topics/housing-and-homelessness/rough-sleeping-in-london/> (Accessed 17 September 2012).
IPPR (Institute for Public Policy Research) (2012). *London's housing market – the new global Reserve Currency*, 13 March <http://www.ippr.org/?p=711&option=com_wordpress&Itemid=17> (Accessed 5 October 2012).
May Young, R. (2012). *Petition calls for homeless to be represented at future Olympics*, <http://www.civilsociety.co.uk/governance/news/content/13085/petition_calls_for_homeless_to_be_represented_at_future_olympics> (Accessed 3 December 2012).
Mean, M., Vigor, A. and Tims, C. (2004). *After the Gold Rush: A Sustainable Olympics for London* (London: IPPR).
More than the Games Website (2010). *Five Olympic boroughs criticise government over legacy plans 15 October 2010* <http://www.morethanthegames.co.uk/summer-sports/158231-five-olympic-host-boroughs-criticise-government-over-legacy-plans> (Accessed 19 August 2013).
NBC (2012). *Olympic Housing Crunch: London Landlords evict tenants to gouge tourists* <worldnews.nbcnews.com/_.../10288441-olympic-housing-crunch-london-landlords-evict-tenants-to-gouge-tourists?> (Accessed 19 August 2012).
New Policy Institute (2012). *London's Poverty Profile* <http://www.londonspovertyprofile.org.uk/indicators/topics/work-and-worklessness/unemployment-by-borough/>. (Accessed 29 September 2012).
Office for National Statistics (2012). *Statistical Bulletin 2011: Key Statistics For England and Wales, Rooms, Bedrooms and Central Heating*, 11 December.

Office for National Statistics (2013). *Neighbourhood Statistics: Tenure Households Census 2001 and 2011* <http://neighbourhood.statistics.gov.uk/dissemination/LeadTableView.do?a=3&b=6275294&c=Waltham+Forest&d=13&e=7&g=6338537&i=1001x1003x1004&m=0&r=1&s=1363113536945&enc=1&dsFamilyId=2505Newham2011 census 101,519 total)> (Accessed 3 March 2013).

OSCI (Oxford consultants for Social Inclusion) (2012). *Changes to housing tenure: Evidence from the 2011 Census*, December 2012.

Oxford Economics (2010). *Six host boroughs Strategic Regeneration Framework*, Oxford Economics, November 2010 <http://www.hackney.gov.uk/Assets/Documents/oxford-economics-host_boroughs-final_report-nov10.pdf> (Accessed 5 September 2012).

Parliament.co.uk (2011). *Public Accounts Committee: Written evidence from the Olympic Park Legacy Company*, 7 December 2011 <http://www.publications.parliament.uk/pa/cm201012/cmselect/cmpubacc/1716/1716we03.htm> (Accessed 7 October 2012).

Regeneration Planning and Property Directive (2010). *Newham London: Local Economic Assessment 2010 to 2027* (London: LBN)

Reynolds, L. (2011). *Private Rent Watch* 1: (London: Shelter).

Rightmove blog (2012). *Main Olympic borough of Newham still awaiting housing legacy* August 22 December <http://www.rightmove.co.uk/news/articles/property-news/main-olympic-borough-of-newham-still-awaiting-%E2%80%98house-price-legacy%E2%80%99> (Accessed 19 November 2012).

Smith, R. (2011). London Olympics fails to provide house price Boost, *Guardian* 27 July 2011.

Skanlon, K., Travers, T. and Whitehead, C. (2010) *Population churn and its impact on socio-economic convergence in the five London 2012 host boroughs* (London: DCLG).

Twinch, E. (2012). Charity warns of pre-olympic evictions, *Inside Housing*, 8 May 2012.

Wales Online (2012). *Mass Sleep out protest against calls to Clear Cardiff's homeless for the Olympics*, 25 July 2012.

Watt, P. (2013). It's not for us: Regeneration, the 2012 Olympics and the Gentrification of East London, in *City*, 17(1): 99–118.

West, R. (2012) Olympics helps push London rents to record highs, *Financial Times*, 20 July 2012, p. 91.

Zoopla (2013). *House prices in E15 and House prices in London* <http://www.zoopla.co.uk/house-prices/browse/london/?q=London&search_source=nav> (Accessed: 3 March 2013).

Chapter 4

The Shifting Terrain of Housing Legacy Plans

In this chapter we explore the shifting terrain of housing legacy plans for the park. It is argued that there are four layers that need to be explored and unravelled in order to make sense of the housing legacy. The wider regeneration of the Lower Lea Valley; the Legacies Community Scheme for the Queen Elizabeth (Olympic) Park; the Athletes' Village (East Village) and plans more generally for Stratford City. In this chapter we explore plans for the Lower Lea Valley and the Legacy Communities Scheme for the Queen Elizabeth Park and in the following chapter we assess plans for the Athletes' Village and Stratford City. A central rationale for unsettling and decanting populations in East London as we saw in Chapter 2, was very much linked to the huge housing benefits that would accrue particularly with regard to additional affordable housing for East London residents. However, it would seem that claims about levels of affordable housing reflected an ambition rather than a realistic plan. Claims of substantial benefits were speculative based on the possibilities for new housing given the availability of land as compared to actual plans and budgets to finance this development. Over time there has been a downward shift with regard to the expected number of affordable housing units and a re-prioritisation of subsidised housing away from those in greatest need towards those perceived as being more deserving. In 2005 when London won the bid a commitment to providing substantial proportions of affordable housing for the benefit of those already living in East London was a clear objective:

> The regeneration will create 30,000 to 40,000 new homes in the area. It will be a catalyst for investment that will create new, quality housing – much of which will be affordable housing available to key workers such as nurses or teachers. (Lord Coe 2007)

> It was all a bit back of the envelope. There was a piece of land and we thought we could build this many houses on there. It was a piece of paper to wave at the IOC to establish the principle that we were having the games here. Some people got too bogged down in the detail. (Legacy Borough Councillor)

Ken Livingstone claimed that:

> Not only can we look forward to a great games in 2012 but also to a new era for East London with 21st-century transport links, a huge increase in the number of affordable homes built in the new area and thousands of new jobs. (Ken

Livingstone, then mayor of London, 24 July 2007, London 2012 legacy vision presented to IOC)

Perhaps one of the most compelling statements was set out in the candidature file and claimed that:

> The most enduring legacy of the Olympics will be the regeneration of an entire community for the direct benefit of everyone that lives there. It will become a model for social inclusion. (London Candidate File 2004, p. 19)

> The Olympic Park will provide local people with significant improvements in health and well-being, education, skills and training, job opportunities, cultural entitlements, housing, social integration and the environment. Importantly, the Olympic Village will become a new, desirable and sustainable residential community with 3,600 new housing units. (London Candidate file 2004, p. 23)

A persuasive case then was established as to why hosting the Olympics would give rise to an inclusive transformation for people living in East London. Nevertheless, commitments to housing beyond the Games were vague. David Higgins for example when asked about housing legacy in a House of Commons Media and Sports Committee noted that plans for affordable housing were being drawn up and that the Lower Lea Valley Framework anticipated about 40,000 homes across the Lower Lea Valley (House of Commons, Culture, Media and Sports Committee 2007). Similarly, discussion at the Compulsory Purchase Order Inquiry whilst keen to stress the housing benefits that would accrue to local people were not specific about actual levels of affordable housing. Plans were more specific about the Athletes' Village and as we shall see these plans were substantially modified after 2005.

The Regeneration of the Lower Lea Valley

> One of the unique features of the London 2012 bid was its commitment to deliver a lasting legacy in terms of regeneration benefits and in particular speed up the process of regeneration leading to the construction of a water city in the Lower Lea Valley comprising some 30,000–40,000 new homes. (GLA 2006)

The accelerated regeneration of the Lower Lea Valley was stated as a key legacy benefit. The planning consent attached to the 2004 Olympic and Legacy Planning Permission required the establishment of a Lower Lea Valley Regeneration Strategy demonstrating how the games might act as a catalyst for the regeneration of the wider Lower Lea Valley Area and replaced a previous plan produced in 2004. The Strategy was commissioned by the LDA and was published in January 2007 and became the Mayor of London's Strategic Planning Framework for the Lower Lea Valley[1] intended to:

> ...transform the LLV to become a vibrant, high quality, sustainable and mixed use district that is fully integrated into the urban fabric of London and is set within an unrivalled landscape that contains new high quality parkland and a unique network of waterways. (Greater London Authority/London Development Agency 2007, p. 5)

The framework set out a plan for the delivery of between 30,000 to 40,000 new homes, with a specific emphasis on family housing indicating a requirement of 44 per cent family housing (with scope for discretion) where possible, achieved through the release of former industrial land. The Lower Lea Valley Plan produced in 2004 anticipated 6,000 homes by 2016 and the revised plan estimated that up to 20,000 could be built across the same period. Unsurprisingly, the planning framework reflected the GLA approach to planning at that time emphasised in planning frameworks such as the first London Plan published in 2004. For example, the LLV plan sets out a commitment to provide 50 per cent affordable housing in line with the London Plan. As is the case with many planning frameworks this plan provided scope for discretion based on a consideration of remediation costs, borough plans, market conditions, etc. Principles for inclusive design were also included. For example there was a stipulation that 10 per cent of housing should be built to wheelchair standards; 100 per cent Lifetime homes along with the production of an access statement setting out how inclusivity had been incorporated into the design. Other principles included building at relatively high densities in areas well served for transport to ensure a critical mass in terms of population to ensure the provision of services and a focus on sustainability reinforced through the requirement to meet certain eco standards.

The London Thames Gateway Development Corporation (LTGDC)[2] was identified as the agency responsible for leading on the Lower Lea Valley Plan. The agency was established in 2005 with the intention of regenerating an area designated within the London Thames Gateway and including parts

---

1 The two documents were the Lower Lea Valley Area Opportunity Planning Framework and the Lower Lea Valley Vision.

2 As a result of the Localism Bill, the LTGDC will be transferring its assets and staff to the Mayoral Development Corporation and the GLA in the course of 2012. As it explains 'After the successful stewardship of planning and development activity in east London since 2005 which has secured over £6 billion of private sector investment along with planning consents with the potential to deliver over 18,000 homes and 15,000 jobs, LTGDC will transfer all its development assets and staff to the MDC and the GLA in April 2012 and will transfer its planning responsibilities for the Lower Lea Valley to the new Mayoral Development Corporation and the relevant local authorities in October 2012.' http://ltgdc.org.uk/ltgdc-news/ltgdc-asset-transfer-set-to-boost-mayor-of-london-regeneration-coffers-2/.

of five East London boroughs (it was responsible for planning applications with more than 50 units or 2,500 metres of floor space). Much of this land has since passed to the London Legacy Development Corporation, with other parts returning to the respective boroughs. In Chapter 6 we include a case study of planning applications on Stratford High Street demonstrating the significant gap between stated requirements in the Lower Lea Valley Plan and actual outcomes particularly with regard to the provision of affordable housing.

As has been noted a key factor shaping the principles of the Lower Lea Valley Plan was the London Plan. However, over time the London Plan has been substantially revised. The first London Plan was produced in 2004, updated in 2009 and further revised in 2011 and 2013. The Plan provides an overview and policy direction for a range of issues including housing and takes into account central government policy/ The initial Plan provided local authorities with guidance and support for developing their own housing provision and targets for house building; these are now captured in the Local Development Frameworks (LDF) compiled by each Local Authority. In 2007 the Greater London Authority was given additional powers with regard to housing including the need to publish a statutory London Housing Strategy and the first housing strategy was published in 2010 and in 2012 the Mayor was given responsibility for the investment powers and responsibilities of the Homes and Community Agency as part of the Localism bill. Therefore, the GLA has more authority for housing than they did in 2004 when the first plan was published.

In 2008, Boris Johnson replaced Ken Livingstone as Mayor and the London Plan was revised. A number of revisions have meant that the current London Plan (2013) is substantially different from the First Plan. There is a continued emphasis on the urgent need for housing generally and affordable housing and a recognition that the 'Legacy' boroughs will make a significant contribution to new housing development between 2011 and 2021, with Tower Hamlets anticipated to provide the highest proportion of housing of any London Borough at 28,500 and Newham the third highest at 25,000. Targets for Hackney and Waltham Forest are lower at 11,600 and 7,600 respectively (Greater London Authority 2004; Greater London Authority 2012). One clear departure relates to proportions of affordable housing required. Boris Johnson adopted a target of 13,200 equating to 41 per cent affordable homes per year, significantly lower than the 50 per cent target and GLA estimates of need that indicate a need for 18,200 homes per year, however, it is argued that the shift is based on a realistic appraisal of the likelihood of delivering it. Another difference relates to the balance of social/affordable rent and intermediate housing products. The first London Plan stressed the need for 70 per cent of all new housing to be for social rent with a smaller proportion 30 per cent for intermediate housing in recognition of the extensive need for social housing. The 2012 guidance has amended this to 60:40 justified by the need to enable people to get on the housing ladder and securing a more balanced mix of tenures through the provision of intermediate housing (2012, para. 4.3.8). Income eligibility has also been extended up to 74,200 for those wishing to purchase three bedroom properties or more.

However, these differences are relatively minor in comparison to the replacement of the 'social rent' model with the so called 'affordable rent' model. This change was introduced following the 2010 Spending Review as a way of cutting housing subsidy and policy has evolved over time. The Affordable Rent model replaced target rent[3] and was based on the notion that rents should be linked to market levels. It was assumed that this new funding model would facilitate the further subsidy of new 'affordable housing both in terms of increased income for RSLs but also new schemes would have to adhere to this model in order to receive subsidy.

A number of reports have highlighted particular problems of adopting this model in a London context where house prices are already very high (See for example Heywood 2013; Harrison et al. 2013). Policy responses have evolved over time with authorities such as Islington committing themselves to retaining the Social Rent model arguing that it would simply not be possible to deliver affordable housing in Islington using this model. However, in 2013 the Mayor introduced an amendment to the Plan to ensure that local authorities would not be able to set their own affordable rent levels as part of their Local Development Frameworks despite advice from an Independent Inspector that without such freedoms much of Inner London would become unaffordable and would threaten the policy objective of mixed communities (Inside Housing 2013).

A recent study confirmed that it was particularly difficult to deliver family housing under this model in more expensive parts of London and that this problem was exacerbated by the introduction of a cap on housing benefit initially affecting tenants in the private rented sector and overtime families living in larger properties under the Affordable Rent model. The study identified a shift in development towards the East and Outer London Boroughs and noted that much of the new 'Affordable Rent' provision was through the conversion of 'Social Rented' tenancies into 'Affordable Rent Model' tenancies resulting in an increase in housing costs and reliance on housing benefits (Heywood 2013).

We can see then that there is a significant gap between London Plan 2005 and the current London Plan reflecting the changed national context of 2013. The inclusive rhetoric of 2004 has been replaced and the rights of low income individuals and households to live in more expensive parts of London increasingly questioned. Moreover, what we now describe as 'affordable housing' is a very different product to that which we referred to in 2005. Ironically it may be relatively easy to deliver affordable housing units in London with rent levels at 80 per cent of market rents, though clearly the beneficiaries will be those in higher paid employment.

The London Plan also sets out guidelines with regard to negotiating affordable housing on individual private schemes and advises that development

---

3 Social rents are target rents determined through a national rent regime.

should be encouraged, not restrained and take into consideration factors such as site viability and the need to ensure 'mixed/balanced' communities (GLA 2012). Therefore, these caveats open up the possibility of a significant deviation from initial more ambitious plans for substantial proportions of affordable housing to be built. Overall then at a policy level there has been a lowering of expectations with regard to the provision of 'affordable housing and affordable housing for rent'. The London Plan continues to identify important contribution that the Games has to play in transforming East London and achieving convergence with the rest of London.

There has also been specific Olympic Legacy Supplementary Guidance produced in 2012 that pertains to this area and supersedes the guidance of the Lower Lea Valley Opportunity Area Framework and reflects much of what is in the revised London Plan such as the need to ensure mixed communities, the likelihood that the majority of housing built will be based on the affordable rent model and the need for family housing across all tenures as a mechanism for creating balanced communities and reducing population churn. The guidance also sets out a strong commitment to 'convergence'.

The commitment to family housing is interesting. We know that there is a huge demand for affordable family housing for rent, however, it is less clear that there is a significant demand for market based family housing. Research undertaken previously in Thames Gateway demonstrated that there is a risk where there is low demand for family housing that it will be purchased as buy-to-let housing with multiple tenants (Bernstock 2008). At the time of writing the London Legacy Development Corporation in its role as planning authority was drawing up its own Local Plan to underpin planning decisions scheduled for adoption in October 2014. Up until that time the London Plan, the core strategies and area action plans of the four 'Legacy' boroughs and the Olympic Legacy Supplementary Planning Guidance are likely to underpin decision making.

Overall then we see a continued commitment to family housing across all tenures and a dilution of commitments to affordable housing in formal planning documents. The issue of inclusive design was incorporated into the London Plan in 2004 and has been reflected in all subsequent planning documents with a commitment to 100 per cent lifetime homes[4] and most recent guidance stresses a commitment to lifetime neighbourhoods. The other theme that is reflected in more recent plans is a commitment to achieve convergence between the East London boroughs and the rest of London. However, as the case study below shows this may simply be achieved by bringing in a more affluent wealthier population.

---

4 Lifetime homes establish a design standard that enables from the offset or with minimum adjustments that meet the existing and changing needs of individuals. Lifetime Neighbourhoods is an evolving concept but translates the notion of inclusion and accessibility into the design and practices of the wider neighbourhood.

Sugar House Lane – Ikea/Land Prop Developments – A Case Study

Sugar House Lane is a key site identified for redevelopment in the Lower Lea Valley plan and Stratford Metropolitan Masterplan and is located on the southern fringe of the Olympic Park, (just off Stratford High Street). The LDA purchased 9.34 acres of Land at Sugar House Lane in 2004 as part of its Lower Lea Valley Land Assembly Programme. In 2008 the London Development Agency, London Thames Gateway Development Corporation and the London Borough of Newham commissioned a master-plan for the area with the intention of creating a mixed-use development whilst retaining the heritage dimensions of the site. The area was declared a conservation area in 2008 protecting many of the older industrial buildings. In 2010 the LDA transferred land to the Olympic Park Legacy Company (OPLC) including the land at Sugar House Lane.

In 2009, Landprop, the property arm of InterIkea, purchased 12.9 acres of land in Sugar House Lane and approached the OPLC with a view to purchasing its share. In October 2011 the OPLC sold its interest to Landprop. The justification for selling the land was linked to the benefits of an early capital receipt, building market confidence and to enable them to focus on core activities in the Park. However, the OPLC were aware that selling off the land at this time might lead to adverse publicity with regard to disposing of assets, and potential values that might accrue when planning permission was granted. An overage agreement was included to capture some of this value (ODD 2011).

It was originally anticipated in 2010 that the development would include around 35 per cent affordable housing and this was clearly positive given the extent of housing need in the area. In 2012 planning permission was granted for a hybrid development including residential, business, hotel, retail and community uses. The scheme includes 1,192 units including 10 per cent wheelchair accessible and 40 per cent family housing. However, affordable housing levels fell far short of initial expectations with the scheme including only 10 per cent affordable housing on a habitable room basis increasing to 15 per cent if subsidy becomes available. The mix of this small proportion of affordable housing includes 50 per cent (60 units) for affordable rent and 50 per cent (60) intermediate units which will be available on a discounted sale basis. Therefore, even this small amount of housing is likely to be accessible only to those on higher incomes.

Agencies such as the OPLC (Olympic Park Legacy Company) and London Thames Gateway Development Corporation had significant leverage in this particular scheme given that the former owned the land and the latter had development control powers enabling them to shape the scheme to reflect the original policy intention of using the opportunities generated by the accelerated regeneration to benefit existing residents living in unsuitable housing. As we will see in Chapter 6 this deviation from original policy is not limited to this scheme but is evident across a number of schemes in the area. On the other hand, according to one Councillor:

> We have lots of schemes agreed in the borough with 35 per cent affordable housing, but they aren't getting built. So we won't get the affordable housing. This scheme includes 10 per cent affordable housing, but it is one of the best quality schemes I have seen. They have considered how to make the best use of the waterways, how to preserve the streetscapes, this will get built. We could have levelled the area to the ground and build lots of flats but we would have lost out on quality.

More generally what we might broadly describe as the 'mixed communities' agenda has shaped policy approaches to urban regeneration both across the country, in East London and at the Olympic Park. It is not possible to explore the complexity of the 'mixed communities' debate, however, there are a number of salient themes that have become central to debates about urban regeneration. Tunstall and Lupton (2010) have undertaken a wide ranging review of the literature in this area and suggest that it has been informed in part by debates from the US about spatial concentrations of poverty that led to the demolition of many public sector housing projects and their replacement with 'mixed communities' schemes. Indeed the Olympic legacy programme in Atlanta was underpinned by such an approach.

It is assumed that for those living in areas of concentrated poverty, there are additional impacts over and above poverty that shape attitudes to work and worklessness. Moreover, housing tenure and in particular public/social housing is implicated in contributing to concentrations of poverty. The 'mixed communities' agenda was a central plank of 'New Labour' Urban regeneration policy and many of its assumptions continue to shape policy making. One central assumption is that large concentrations of social housing should be avoided and therefore there is a perception that where neighbourhoods contain a large proportion of social housing, arguments can be made to increase proportions of 'market housing' irrespective of the extent of housing need in those areas as a vehicle for 'rebalancing' populations and as we have seen this approach has been applied in the context of Stratford. On the other hand private developers are also encouraged to contribute to the creation of 'mixed communities' by including a significant proportion of onsite affordable housing and this is an approach that has underpinned assumptions about affordable housing delivery linked to legacy. This is significant because it means that whilst at one level there is a commitment to ensuring that regeneration should benefit the people of East London, concerns about social mix may justify limitations on the proportion of affordable housing built. Interestingly, Tunstall and Lupton's review indicates the limited benefits of the 'mixed communities' agenda. For others it is simply backdoor gentrification (Tunstall, Lupton 2010; Bridge, Butler, Lees 2011).

Stratford Metropolitan Masterplan

In 2011 the London Borough of Newham published a Stratford Metropolitan Masterplan in an attempt to provide a more integrated and coherent framework for the area in response to a perception that a number of separate and relatively disjointed large-scale developments on an unprecedented scale were taking place in Stratford that needed to be more fully integrated into a plan and connected to existing communities to ensure access to new homes and employment opportunities. The plan included a development framework setting out the main direction for the area, a planning framework and an implementation framework

There are three main aspirations/themes that run through the plans including the creation of stable and balanced communities where people want to stay throughout their lives, Stratford as London's third city after Westminster and the City offering business, education and the arts and an alternative, diverse and innovate economy that builds on local strengths and creates ladders of opportunity. There are four key projects that are discussed elsewhere in this book linked to Newham realising the Plan including Sugar House Lane, Carpenters Estate, Chobham Farm and Stratford Old Town (Southern Quadrant).

The Plan identifies a number of key problems such as high levels of deprivation, high population churn and a preference from local residents for more family housing in 'mixed communities'. In recognition of the large number of tall towers comprising mainly one- and two-bedroom flats built along Stratford High Street there is a stipulation that further tall buildings will be limited and a greater number of family housing, including a mix of houses, mews houses and maisonettes, located in mixed communities. Indeed it is these mixed communities, comprising private and intermediate housing, that it is argued will enable the funding of affordable housing for rent with an indicative figure of 35 per cent affordable housing to be included in all phases of development and located in tenure blind neighbourhoods with Sugar House Lane and Chobham Farm identified as providing 'aspirational housing' (London Borough of Newham 2011a; London Borough of Newham 2011b). However, as we have seen in the case of Sugar House Lane and the Carpenters Estate there has been a significant deviation from the plan and this is similarly the case at Chobham Farm (see Chapter 5) which again highlight the gap between plan and outcome.

The Legacy Communities Scheme – Queen Elizabeth Park

As soon as London won the bid to host the games there was an awareness of the need to develop a Masterplan framework for the park in legacy. One of the key tasks undertaken by the Olympic Park Legacy Company was to produce a Masterplan framework for the park as it moved from Games to post-Games mode. The OPLC first published a Masterplan in 2010 based on an extensive consultation exercise undertaken in 2009. The Plan made clear that the legacy must be marked by inspirational and ambitious architecture and housing that met local needs including the urgent need for family housing. According to Baroness Ford, chair of the OPLC at the time:

> They wanted to see more family homes and homes with front and back private gardens. We have responded by putting them at the heart of our plans, making up around 40 per cent of the 11,000 new homes that will be built. These homes will combine tradition and innovation in modern versions of London's Georgian and Victorian Squares and terraces, as well as riverside properties stretching along the banks of the Park's rejuvenated waterways. We believe regeneration depends on better access to jobs and training, better housing choice and balanced, stable communities. (Baroness Ford 2010)

In 2011 the OPLC produced a Legacy Communities Scheme (LCS) and submitted it to the Olympic Development Authority for approval. A substantial process of consultation, negotiation and modification took place and in June 2012 it was approved by the Olympic Development Authority. Again there was a clear departure between this plan and the earlier plan.

The Olympic Park Legacy Company has since been replaced by the London Legacy Development Corporation. The London Legacy Development Corporation are in a powerful position to shape the plans as they own the land and have plan making powers and at the time of writing Mayor Boris Johnson is chairing the organisation. They have the freehold of the estate; responsibility for common parts of the estate and are able to procure and deliver site wide infrastructure requirements. They are also able to control the supply of land by releasing over time a number of 'parcels of land'. The LCS anticipate that initial developments will be undertaken via joint venture agreements. The one very serious challenge that the LLDC has is that it has very limited resources to realise the plan and this is discussed below.

The LCS sets out a future direction for the park and anticipates the development of five new neighbourhoods between 2013 and 2031 capitalising on the infrastructure linked to hosting the Olympic Games such as international sporting facilities, parkland, excellent transport connectivity, health facilities and new schools.

The LCS does not specify a particular number of units but instead suggests that, based on floor space, up to 6,870 units could be built across nine Planning Delivery Zones. The plan for the park includes a range of uses though it is essentially 'residential led' and there has been some concern raised about a perceived overemphasis on housing over other crucial dimensions of regeneration such as employment. For example, the London Borough of Newham's response was that:

> Essentially the scheme was a large housing estate divided into separate plots which failed to excite or enthuse. (OPLC 2012, p. 201)

There are five new neighbourhoods planned as part of the Legacy Communities Scheme: Chobham Manor, (PDZ6), Marshgate Wharf (PDZ1 and PDZ2), Sweetwater (PDZ4), East Wick (PDZ5) and Pudding Mill Lane (PDZ8 and 12). It is anticipated that the bulk of residential development will take place in phase 3 between 2022 and 2031.[5]

Chobham Manor

One of the sites earmarked for early development is (Chobman Manor) PDZ6, adjacent to the Athletes' Village and located in the London Borough of Newham. The Olympic Park Legacy Company invited interested parties to put forward proposals develop the first plot of land at the park. Three bids were shortlisted with Taylor Wimpey and London and Quadrant finally selected. The scheme is scheduled for completion in 2014 and will comprise 870 units which will be mainly family housing (84 per cent) including a mix of mews; terraced housing and stacked maisonettes built around tree lined avenues). The scheme will include 25 units that will meet stringent sustainability criteria.

Affordable housing will comprise 28 per cent (244 units) of the scheme divided between 30 per cent (73) social rented, 30 per cent (73) affordable rent and 40 per cent (98) intermediate housing. This lower level of affordable housing was rationalised by the policy intention of achieving mixed communities in the context that the neighbouring development at the Athletes' Village already included 49 per cent affordable housing and ignoring the fact that there are six plots of land that may be developed mainly for market housing as part of that development (see Chapter 5). Once again as we can see of this new housing only 30 per cent will be at target rents with the remainder considerably higher. A Community Land Trust may be set up as part of the affordable housing on this site.

The site is intended to attract families who will benefit from its location near to the new 'Chobham Manor' academy, two new nurseries and a local health centre. The scheme, located on the North of the Park, is intended to connect with existing areas of Hackney Wick and Leyton. Housing is also being developed at neighbouring Chobham Farm as part of the Stratford City Development discussed in the next chapter.

East Wick

East Wick (PDZ5) is to be a new neighbourhood to be created in the area surrounding the International Broadcasting Centre/Media Production Centre in Hackney. Plans for the area include a mix of commercial, community and residential uses

---

5 It is anticipated that 266,789 metres^2 of floor space will be developed between 2015 and 2021 and 375,028 metres^2 between 2022 and 2031.

along with a canal-side park adjacent to the River Lea and a new park edge with adjacent housing with the intention of creating an area similar to Highbury Fields. Anticipated residential uses include a mix of high and lower density housing with significant scope for employment led activities arising from the IBC/MPC site. It is estimated that up to 887 homes can be built on this site with 43 per cent of this being affordable housing and will include a mix of terraced houses, mews houses and stacked maisonettes along with apartments. This area is anticipated to include a predominance of family housing (up to 61 per cent) including significant proportions of social housing for families. Residential development is scheduled for Phase two (2015–2021) and Phase three (2022–2031).

Marshgate Wharf

Marshgate Wharf (PDZ1 and 2) is located in the London Borough of Newham and includes the area surrounding the Aquatics Centre, Orbit and the Stadium and is adjacent to the International Quarter and the Carpenters Estate. It is bounded by major roads, railways and a river. PDZ1 is intended to be the major visitor destination in the Park with the intention of creating an atmosphere similar to that in the Southbank. A mix of uses are proposed including cafes, bars, retail, leisure, residential and hotel uses intended to compliment rather than compete with Westfield. Retail provision is also included in PDZ2 at the junction of the Orbit and the Stadium. Residential development in PDZ1 is scheduled for phase two (2015–2021). It is anticipated that up to 1687 units could be build in PDZ1 with just under 20 per cent of these being affordable including 15 per cent family housing. Residential development in PDZ1 will have the highest density across the scheme and will include a mix of buildings ranging in height from 8–20 storeys. Residential development for PDZ2 is scheduled in Phase three (2022–2031) and anticipates that up to 878 units could be built including 35 per cent affordable housing and 24 per cent family housing. Housing in PDZ2 will be slightly lower density than in PDZ1 with blocks ranging in height from 6–10 storeys. However, the use of the Stadium may have a bearing on residential developments surrounding it.

According to one councillor:

> I raised the point that putting a housing estate too close to a stadium could be a mistake as it may sterilise what you do at the stadium or create an environment that isn't too pleasant for the people.

Sweetwater

The Sweetwater (PDZ4) is located in Tower Hamlets and comprises the area known as Fish Island East. Plans include a new school, playing fields, businesses and a new local park along with up to 651 housing units including 48 per cent affordable housing and 61 per cent family housing. The area will include canal-side open space on to the Lea Navigation and will border the Olympic Park. There are seven sites within this area with varying levels of density dependent on their specific location. In the main it is anticipated that housing will be relatively low density family housing including terraced housing, stacked maisonettes and terraced apartments. The plan indicates that initial site preparation and construction will take place in 2013–14 and occupation in 2015. Two new bridges are proposed as part of this development to ensure connectivity with existing parts of Tower Hamlets.

Pudding Mill

The Pudding Mill (PDZ8 and 12) neighbourhood is located in the London Borough of Newham and is intended to become a new mixed-use neighbourhood combining employment and residential uses and a new secondary school scheduled for phase three between 2022 and 2031. PDZ8 is located on the Western side of the Olympic Park and comprises four discrete plots of land, including a site on Warton Road which is the main access route from Stratford High Street to Westfield Shopping Centre and areas bounded by the Cooks Industrial area. PDZ12 is on the Southern Side of Stratford High Street and is at the south eastern edge of the Olympic Park. PDZ8 will include the largest amount of employment floor space of the site 35,969 m^2 out of a total of 46,139 m^2 and will also contribute a significant amount of residential housing with up to 1,311 units including some sheltered housing. PDZ 8 includes up to 42 per cent affordable housing and 35 per cent family housing. According to the LCS the intention is to mediate between the high density housing of Stratford High Street and the industrial heritage and current character of the area.

PDZ12 is located on the south side of Stratford High Street and comprises two plots of land. It is anticipated that housing will comprise a mix of terraced houses, stacked maisonettes and terraced apartments including some high rise accommodation adjacent to Stratford High Street. It is anticipated that up to 398 units could be built in PDZ 12 including 53 per cent affordable housing and 46 per cent family housing.

Affordable Housing Across the Site

The Masterplan produced in 2010 indicated that between 35 and 40 per cent would be affordable. The LCS on the other hand sets a target of 35 per cent affordable housing whilst at the same time introducing a new 'minimum' of 20 per cent affordable housing across the site:

> Each PDZ will be the subject of a viability assessment and if the agreed benchmark values are not met the target position for affordable housing provision in the

relevant PDZ will be subject to a minimum provision of affordable housing per PDZ and a site wide minimum of 20 per cent. (OPLC 2012, para. 59, p. 251)

The LCS also provides a breakdown of types of affordable housing and incorporates the new 'affordable rent' model. The breakdown of affordable housing is anticipated as 30 per cent affordable housing for social rent having a target rent of no more than 40 per cent of market rent, 40 per cent 'intermediate rent' aimed at households on median income in the Host boroughs and 30 per cent affordable rent (defined as 80 per cent of market rent for one bedroom properties, 70 per cent for two bedroom properties, 60 per cent for three bedroom properties and 50 per cent for four bedroom properties). Overall then within the scheme we can see a significant range in affordable housing options with social housing for rent comprising a relatively small proportion of overall numbers i.e. 710 of 6,878 units. There is an agreement here providing some assurance that at least a proportion of this housing will be for social rent though given current trends this must also be uncertain and therefore actual levels of social rented housing may be even lower.

The context of 2013 is of course very different to 2005. There are four key changes that are likely to significantly impact on affordable housing provision. In the first instance there have been substantial cuts to affordable housing in the capital. The Mayor's housing budget for 2011–2015 was cut from £3.7 billion for the period 2008–2011 to £1.7 billion for the period 2011–2015 (Johnson 2012). Secondly as has previously been discussed there has been a policy shift from 'social rent' to 'affordable rent'. Thirdly the changed economic context and the lack of funding for affordable housing has enabled developers to negotiate lower levels of affordable housing and renegotiate existing agreements creating the potential for a 'race to the bottom' with regard to levels of affordable housing provision and this is illustrated in Chapter 6. Finally the introduction of Universal Credit (places a cap on overall benefits) may impact on affordability of family housing provided by Registered Social Landlords in more expensive parts of the capital (Centre for Economic and Social Inclusion 2011).

More generally debates about entitlements to housing have become much more significant across this period. For example, in October 2012 the London Borough of Newham revised its allocations policy to favour residents in employment and the Mayor of London has also announced a new housing covenant underpinned by the notion that individuals and families who contribute to the success of the capital will be supported into low-cost and good quality homes through the development of intermediate housing schemes again underpinned by the trend to support people in employment, reinforcing the notion that policies should be based on behavioural rather than need based criteria. This means that policies are seeking to discriminate and reinforce notions of 'deserving' and 'undeserving' poor and target resources at those deemed 'deserving'. This is a key policy shift and a return to previous policy eras when public housing tended to favour better-off sections of the poor. This approach was challenged in 1969 by the

Cullingworth Report which reviewed allocation policies and highlighted the discriminatory nature of this approach recommending that housing be targeted at those in greatest need. This led to a reorientation of policy to focus on those in greatest need. The problem was that the focus on need coincided with substantial cuts to new public house building and the sale of significant proportions of stock through Right to Buy Policies and therefore residents eligible for public/social housing were increasingly more likely to be disadvantaged (Lee, Murie 1997). Therefore this trend towards using behavioural criteria to prioritise resources is simply another way of managing an excessive shortage of supply and is likely to lead to a further weakening of the housing position of the most disadvantaged and paradoxically a justification to build less housing to meet their needs.

The other inherent tension relates to the need for the LLDC to recoup costs from the sale of land to cover the costs of the games. Debts are outstanding to the national lottery, the Government and the GLA and this is another reason why it is proposed that a degree of flexibility about actual levels of affordable housing is required:

> The applicants proposed approach to the development appraisal is to fix the S106 financial contributions and include a 'collar and cap' arrangement for the affordable housing to enable a degree of flexibility to be factored into the affordable housing provision to take account of future property market and financial considerations. (OPLC 2012, para. 8, p. 436)

In other words, the sale of land will be a central driving factor in decision making and the need to repay debts will mean that compromises may be made to square the tension between initial promise and current debts. An agreement was put in place in 2007 when the government had to lend an additional £675 million more than initially agreed that they would repay up to £675 million from the sale of land at the Olympic Park (National Audit Office 2013, p. 8).

Family Housing

The commitment to family housing evident in the original Masterplan is reflected in this plan with levels of family housing ranging from 15 per cent in PDZ1 to 84 per cent in PDZ 6. The level of family housing provided will be subject to viability testing and therefore 42 per cent remains a maximum intention. According to the Executive Director of Real Estate, Olympic Park Legacy Company, 'It is a good regeneration strategy, but it is also quite a smart property play, because you have the product differentiation of family homes of which there are very few being built in London' (cited in Branson 2012). However, the emphasis on family housing for sale does appear to be at odds with current demand. The LCS scheme anticipates 40 per cent of the market housing, 63 per cent of the 'affordable rent' and 63 per cent of the 'social rented' housing to be family housing. A much smaller proportion of intermediate units are anticipated as 'family housing' i.e. 16 per cent of this tenure. The East London Housing Partnership has questioned whether there is in fact a demand for market family housing and more generally a number of policy makers have questioned whether current models of housing finance will enable the provision of affordable family provision on the park.

According to one senior manager involved in developing the Legacies Communities Scheme:

> We are aware that it will be difficult to develop affordable family housing on the park with the new rent model. On the other hand, this is a twenty five year project and it is likely that over time approaches to housing finance will change. (Senior Manager)

Realising the Plan

The Plan is of course just that. It is a way of imagining how land might be developed and used between 2013 and 2031 and demonstrating commitments to legacy. Even judged on these terms it lacks a certain imagination that one might expect given its national and international significance. However, what is clear is that when we began our journey from host bid to plan there has been considerable slippage in the original policy intentions to use regeneration to address disadvantage.

As we have seen there are challenges for RSLs in terms of delivering affordable housing on the park and there are also issues for private developers. Developers themselves will need to capitalise projects in order to develop them and they may encounter problems where despite significant infrastructure development there are concerns of a relative over supply of housing in relation to demand evident in the relatively lacklustre performance of the Stratford housing market to date. Some developers are cautious about investing in housing schemes in the park:

> We didn't want to bid for Chobham Manor because we were concerned that there would be too much housing hitting the market at one time.

Moreover, with banks reluctant to lend it was the availability of housing association grants that assisted with the capitalisation of these schemes. These grants guaranteed sale of a proportion of properties effectively underwriting part of the scheme and reducing the risk for private developers. However, cuts to housing budgets mean that this funding mechanism is no longer available. Clearly private developers will have an interest in developing those parts of the park where risk is minimal and again this may impact on legacy ambitions. Registered Social Landlords clearly have an important role to play in developing and delivering much of this housing, however, they are facing very real funding challenges and may simply develop schemes at the park to cross subsidise their activities elsewhere as compared to providing significant proportions of affordable housing.

Then there is the tension itself for the LLDC to recoup money from the sale of land which may lead to short term gain as opposed to realising the very important legacy benefits anticipated when London won the bid in 2005. In many ways the current economic climate opens up possibilities to use the area as a test bed for alternative housing finance models that might lead to more socially inclusive outcomes. However, the pressure to repay debts cannot be underestimated. More importantly there is the budget itself – whilst the justification for an ever-growing budget was legacy, the bulk of the budget has been spent on stadia and remediation with very little left to realise the actual legacy and therefore it is the remediation itself that may be the most significant legacy.

> We've had thirty years worth of infrastructure. You don't get that opportunity very often. Even building the new sewer through the Park, you start with the discharge of raw sewage into the river Lea. The removal of the overhead power-lines. We used to bring developers to this site and they'd say 'it's a really good but shame about the power-lines'. That's a very expensive thing to get removed. It was very expensive, but it was only in the Olympic Games that we could do that. They are the boring bits of infrastructure which aren't sexy, aren't translated easily into housing numbers, or even jobs, but they make a site useable. That's the legacy already that will enable stuff to happen in the future, but at less of a cost. (Legacy Borough Councillor)

Moreover, as we have already seen there is a gap more generally between plans and planning requirements linked to plans based on assessments of needs and policy goals and final outcomes that are the result of negotiations with developers. Essentially, there is no shortage of planning documents but the real challenge is to follow these through into tangible outcomes that do attempt to square the circle between housing need and housing outcome.

References

Baroness Ford. (2010). *BBC News Living on the Olympics Park will Dream Become Reality* – Thinkpiece, 5 December 2010 <http://www.bbc.co.uk/news/uk-11842550> (Accessed 3 September 2012).

Bernstock, P. (2008). *Neighbourhood Watch: Building New Communities, Learning Lessons from the Thames Gateway* (London: Shelter).

Branson, A. (2012). The Elusive Finishing Line, *Planning*, 27 July.

Bridge, G., Butler, T. and Lees, L. (eds) (2011). *Mixed Communities: Gentrification by Stealth* (London: Policy Press).

Centre for Economic and Social Inclusion (2011). *Making Work Pay in London under Universal Credit* (London: Centre for Economic and Social Inclusion).

Coe, S. (2007). It's ludicrous to claim the Olympics will lead to evictions and Poverty, *Guardian*, 15 June.

Cullingworth Report (1969) *Council Housing: Purposes, Procedures and Policies* (HMSO: London)

Greater London Authority (2004a). *Lower Lea Valley Plan* (London: Greater London Authority).

Greater London Authority (2004b). *An Inspiring Legacy: A Great Future after a Great Games* (London: Greater London Authority).

Greater London Authority (2004c). *The London Plan: Spatial Development Strategy for Greater London* (London: Greater London Authority).

Greater London Authority (2006). *Draft Lower Lea Valley Opportunity Framework* (London: Greater London Authority).

Greater London Authority/London Development Agency (2007). *Lower lea Valley Opportunity Area Planning Framework* (London: Greater London Authority).

Greater London Authority (2008). *Five Legacy Commitments* (London: GLA).

Greater London Authority (2011). *Plot N06, Zone 5, Stratford City*, Planning Application No 10 90560 OUMODA, 12 January 2011.

Greater London Authority (2012a). *Housing Supplementary Planning Guidance:* November 2012: London Plan 2011 Implementation Framework (London: GLA).

Harrison, B., Wilson, J. and Johnson, J. (2013) *Challenges to Affordable Housing in London and Implications for Delivery* (York: JRF).

Heywood, A. (2013) The Affordable Rent Model in London: Delivery, Viability, Potential (London: Future of London <http://futureoflondon.org.uk/futureoflondon/wp-content/uploads/downloads/2013/06/The-Affordable-Rent-Model-in-London-Delivery-Viability-Potential.pdf> (Accessed 9 October).

House of Commons Media, Culture and Sports Committee (2007). *London 2012 Olympic Games and Paralympic Games: Funding and Legacy*: Second Report of Session 2006–7, Volume 1, 17 January 2007 (London: HMSO).

House of Commons Media, Culture and Sports Committee (2010). *Olympic Games and Paralympic Games Legacy*, 3 March 2010.

Inside Housing (2013) Vote on Affordable Rent Model Branded Historic Opportunity, 3 September.

Johnson, D. (2012). London Assembly Member Press Release – *Mayor failing on only two solutions to housing bill,* 22 October 2012 <http://www.london.gov.uk/media/press_releases_assembly_member/news-darren-johnson-am-mayor-failing-only-two-solutions-housing-benefit-bill>.

Lee, P. and Murie, A. (1997) *Poverty, Housing Tenure and Social Exclusion* (York: Joseph Rowntree Foundation).

London Candidate File (2004) *Volume 1, Theme 1 Concept and Legacy* (London Candidate File: London).

London Borough of Newham (2011a). Stratford Metropolitan Masterplan Executive Summary, February (London: London Borough of Newham).

London Borough of Newham (2011b). Stratford Metropolitan Masterplan – Housing Options (London: London Borough of Newham).

National Audit Office (2012). The London 2012 Olympic and Paralympic Games – Post Games Review (London: NAO).

Olympic Development Directorate (2011). ODD31 Disposal of Lane at Sugar House Lane (London: ODA).

Olympic Park Legacy Company (2011). *Legacy Communities Scheme* (London: OPLC).

Olympic Park Legacy Company (2012). *Legacy Communities Scheme: Regulation 22: Response and Additional Information Submission; Addendum, Housing and Social Infrastructure Statement* (London: OPLC).

Tunstall, R. and Lupton, R. (2010). *Mixed Communities: Evidence Review*, (London: DCLG).

Chapter 5
From Athletes' Village to East Village

In this chapter we explore the development of the athletes' village and its transformation into East Village. East Village will be occupied from September 2013 onwards. The athletes' village has had a turbulent history to date and for some is an exercise in double counting. When London won the bid planning permission had already been granted for more than 5,000 homes as part of the Stratford City development and it was anticipated that the development of the athletes' village would be additional to that already planned for Stratford City. The 2004 Olympic, Paralympic and Legacy Transformation Planning applications stated:

> Up to 4,600 homes will be built for the Olympic Village and will be converted post games. (GLA 2004, p. 618)

In 2007 there were substantial revisions to the scheme. The revised scheme essentially integrated part of the athletes' village with the Stratford City project enabling the utilisation of existing planning consents as part of this project.[1] The integration of these two schemes raised questions about the net gain in terms of housing that could be linked to legacy.

According to the ODA in response to a Freedom of Information question with regard to this:

> Whilst it is correct to say this housing would have been built anyway, it is called legacy housing because but for the games, this housing would not have been built by 2012 but rather would have taken a much longer time to build. The fact that the Games has sped up the building of these units makes the housing, especially because of the timing of its delivery, Legacy housing. (ODA response to Freedom of Information question, August 2008)

It was anticipated that the scheme would be both private sector financed and delivered (as was the case in other host cities) and would deliver a mix of private housing for sale and would include 30 per cent 'affordable' housing for rent and sale. The scheme would be built to house athletes during the games and after the games would be converted into 4,200 housing units as part of a new district. However, a mixture of excessive density and financial problems led to the scheme being reduced initially to 3,300 units and then to 2,800. These cuts were, in the

---

1 See Olympic, Paralympic and Legacy Transformation Planning Applications, Vol 1 Planning Explanatory Statement OLY/GLB/ACC/DOC/EXP/01 – Feb. 2007.

main, to the private sector market sale component of the village with the affordable housing element reducing marginally and therefore, whilst the actual number of affordable units declined marginally from 1,400 to 1,379, the proportion of affordable housing increased from 30 to 49 per cent.

In order to square the circle between a lower number of units and the needs of the athletes, kitchens were excluded and this meant that after the games a retrofit was needed to modify the units and convert bedrooms to kitchens.

Financing the Athletes' Village

The Olympic Development Authority underwent a competitive tendering process to select a developer to construct the athletes' village in 2007. Two bids reached the shortlist: one bid comprised French giant Bouygues and Barratt Homes and the other a consortium including Lend Lease, East Thames Housing and First Base (an urban development and investment agency focussing on transforming urban spaces and building communities). The Lend Lease consortium won the bid and at that time it was reported that 4,200 units would be built at the athletes' village including 30 per cent affordable housing.[2] Lend Lease had expertise in this area as they had constructed the Sydney village and East Thames had a long history of delivering social housing in this area. Concerns were raised about the selection of Lend Lease as the Chief Executive of the Olympic Development Authority, David Higgins was previously chief executive of Lend Lease, nevertheless, assurances were given that a transparent process had been undertaken in awarding this very significant contract.

Construction of the village began in May 2008 and as part of the initial agreement Lend Lease were to provide £450 million in private finance towards the £1 billion project. Lend Lease very quickly reported problems with regard to capitalising the project indicating that they had not been able to access the necessary finance. According to then chair of the ODA, 'people were struggling to put an end value to the project because of the uncertainties of the housing market'. Lend Lease and a banking consortium did present a solution, however, according to a press release from the Department of Culture, Media and Sport the Government decided to intervene as it felt that the offer was not in the long-term interests of the taxpayer (Hawkes 2009). The Government provided the finance for the project and Lend Lease became the contractor. Therefore, any risks associated with the project became public rather than private risks. The Government agreed to provide up to £400 million as a contingency fund to ensure the construction of the scheme.

---

2 When Lend Lease won the contract to develop the athletes' village it was confirmed that 4,200 units would be built at the athletes' village and converted after the Games. (See for example Planning, 5.3.2007 Lend Lease set to win Stratford City Contract).

According to Tessa Jowell, then Minister for the Olympic and Paralympic games:

> By funding the entire project the village will become publicly owned and the public purse will receive substantial returns from sales. (Jowell quoted in Hawkes 2009)

It is important to note that a substantial list of planning obligations that would have been the responsibility of Lend Lease were transferred to the ODA therefore increasing the cost to the public purse even further.

Initially it had been anticipated that First Base and East Thames would take on the affordable element of the scheme. However, there were concerns here too about potential risks involved. In 2009 it was announced that Triathlon Homes would be formed and would purchase the affordable element of the scheme through a pre-sales agreement. Triathlon Homes is a consortium including East Thames, First Base and Southern Homes, therefore the inclusion of an additional partner enabled any risks to be more evenly spread. They entered into a pre-purchase agreement with the Olympic Development Authority for a total sum of £268 million financed via a £110 million grant from the Housing and Communities Agency, a £63 million loan from Barclays Bank and a £95 million loan from the European Investment Bank. Triathlon purchased 1,379 properties and therefore the affordable element of the scheme increased to 49 per cent of the scheme though as has already been stated overall numbers declined. Essentially the balance of public and private had shifted to include a greater proportion of affordable housing and this clearly has to be understood as a way of capitalising the project rather than any change in opinion with regard to appropriate levels of affordable housing (Olympic Development Authority 2009).[3]

Selling the Other Half of the Village

In September 2010 the ODA invited private sector organisations to submit proposals for the long term management and purchase of the remaining 1,439 homes at the athletes' village, six further development plots with the potential to build between 2,000 and 2,500 homes and substantial parkland. In December 2010 the ODA announced a short list of nine private sector organisations or consortia who were invited to submit detailed proposals. This list included Delancey and Qatari Diar; Dorrington Pinnacle Capital; Galliard Homes; Grainger PLC and Moorfield Group; Hutchison Whampoa Limited; Le Frak Organisation; Aviva PLC and JP Morgan; London Stamford Property PLC, David Wilson and Sir

---

3 The initial scheme included 30 per cent affordable housing out of a total of 4200 units equated to 1400 affordable units and the revised scheme included 1379 units.

Robert McAlpine; The Wellcome Trust; and The William Pears Group and Urban Splash.

In April 2011 this short-list was reduced to three including a joint partnership between Delancey and Qatari Diar,[4] Hutchison Whampoa and the Wellcome Trust. Delancey and Qatari Diar went on to win the bid. The Wellcome Trust proposals for the village were far-reaching, transformative and congruent with legacy plans aimed at fundamental transformation of East London and also wider plans for creating a tech city in East London. Their proposal was to manage the whole of the Olympic Park as a single entity with a strong focus on employment through the creation of up to 7,000 new high-tech jobs located in a Life Sciences Innovation Centre acting as a global hub for research and innovation in health, technology and sport, with two universities (UCL and Loughborough) establishing campuses within the centre. The Wellcome Trust is the only agency outside of government with a triple AAA credit rating and therefore offered huge stability:

> Our vision is predicated on the premise that the whole of the Olympic Park is substantially bigger than the sum of its parts. At the heart of our proposal is the creation of an iconic hub – the Life Sciences Innovation Centre. This would be the anchor to support jobs, create new businesses, and enable us to develop residential accommodation across the Park to provide homes for the workers and others who want to live there. It could become the Silicon Valley of Europe.
> (Wellcome Trust 2011)

The Trust's proposal was dependent on them being able to purchase the freehold for the park (including the Stadium and the Aquatics Centre) in addition to the athletes' village for £1 billion. Therefore whilst they had been shortlisted by the ODA (who owned the athletes' village) their plans were dependent on much of the land owned by the OPLC and such a proposal had not been put out to tender, and therefore there would be a responsibility for this to happen, and this was seen as problematic in terms of delaying the process of confirming the future of the athletes' village at the Park. Moreover Wellcome planned to sell the housing at the village to capitalise the project and this raised concerns about the emergence of lots of individual buy-to-let investors purchasing properties on the Park.

Responses to the proposal were mixed, some saw this as a significant undervaluation of assets and others felt that it offered the opportunity to create a substantial legacy which was both economically and architecturally sound. Others saw it as a high risk strategy which would impact on the tendering process already begun at the athletes' village.

---

4   Delancey is a real estate investment company with a property portfolio in retail, residential and commercial developments; Qatari Diar is a real estate developer owning assets in more than 20 countries; Hutchinson Whampoa a Hong Kong Listed International Conglomerate with a range of interests and Wellcome Trust is a UK health charity.

According to one local councillor:

> It was a transformative bid. We thought it was a really good idea because it was economics and jobs based. But I think the treasury are in love with having numbers now to feed into spending reviews in three years, six years etc. The Welcome Trust proposals were over a much longer period of time.

In August 2011 it was announced that Qatari Diar and Delancey were the successful bidders and QDD Athletes Village UK Limited was formed. QDD purchased the properties and six additional plots for £557 million. This immediately opened up a considerable degree of controversy as this meant that the government had not recouped its £1 billion outlay, even when factoring in monies paid by Triathlon Homes and this raised questions about the extent to which this had been a good deal for the tax payer. The similarities here with Vancouver are evident with significant public sector investment and potential loss.

QDD's plans for the village include the establishment of the UK's first private Management Investment Fund. According to a senior Manager at QDD:

> Qatari were approached by Delancey to see if they were interested in a joint venture as they were established large scale investors in Europe. Delancey effectively collects together private investors and for this project this comprises 50 per cent and is known as DV4. There are not many people who would do half a billion pounds plus on their own.

Their plans are based on establishing the first UK Private Management Investment fund in light of the growth in the private rented sector:

> What has tended to happen is that the private rented sector has grown considerably but it tends to be individual investors. People have been waiting for an opportunity that provides the potential for a more long term investment. We always saw this as a rental product. (Manager, QDD)

QDD also have six development plots with outline consent for a further 2,000 homes that relate to those units initially planned as part of the athletes' village and not developed:

> We are looking at them in more detail at the moment to satisfy ourselves that the proposals for which consent has been granted are ones that think will work from a practical point of view, One of the plots has outline consent for a fifty storey block of flats. This creates building challenges so we are looking at whether a tower of that size is appropriate. We do not want to build 2,000 properties that will have an adverse impact on the existing 1,400 units. We were never going to build all of the plots at the same time it was always intended to be phased. (Manager, QDD)

Moreover, there is a tension here that reveals the lack of commitment to affordable housing by a key agency involved in Olympic and Paralympic Regeneration. In 2010 the ODA submitted a planning application *vis-à-vis* an organisation, Stratford Village Holdings, to construct 448 market units on one of these six plots of land, arguing that this would help to dilute the concentration of affordable housing across Stratford City though this rationale was later rejected by the GLA (Greater London Authority 2011).

Designing the Athletes' Village

Considerable expertise was invested in the design of the village. Seventeen architects were employed to ensure a varied, as opposed to monolithic, streetscape. The scheme is based on principles of high density living offset through good design such as high quality public realm. The village is made up of 11 separate plots each including seven blocks ranging from eight to 12 storeys in height, built around courtyards. Three of the seven blocks are nine- and ten-storey high and face onto primary roads. The remaining four blocks comprise a mix of *triplex* three- and four-bedroom houses on the ground floor with one- and two-bedroom properties located above. The housing has active street frontages, regular front doors and front gardens and parking is located underground beneath raised gardens. Winter gardens are located between the plots with the intention of creating a sense of space. What is clear is that considerable effort and expertise has been invested in the design of the scheme:

> Here the quality of finish and attention to detail are exemplary. Many studies have been drawn up over recent years showing how to make high density housing work – and the village has had the rulebook thrown at it. Ten of the twenty seven hectares it covers are given over to communal space, closed courtyards equipped with much needed play areas and handsomely landscaped gardens. (Smith Institute 2012, p. 19)

However, they go on to acknowledge that it may not attract 'love at first sight'. The village was reviewed by a number of journalists in the Summer of 2012 and these reviews were mixed. According to one journalist:

> There's a coherence about the way the buildings flow, they're individually designed, and a long way from the grey uniform tower blocks I've come across elsewhere. Portland and Cotswold stone colours mix with more industrial concrete greys and darker tones, broken up in places by wooden accents and dotted with many balconies – some in opaque green and others in clear glass. (Farquhar 2012)

Similarly, Moore writing in the *Observer* notes that there is a lot of strength with regard to design and planning including infrastructure such as quality of build and planning with facilities and services such as health clinics and schools in place and an attempt to model the scheme on Maida Vale and parts of Victorian west London where the interior of blocks include shared gardens. Moore also raises concerns:

> It also has to be said that the village is a tad forbidding not even very villagey at all. Their construction technology is essentially that of those much criticised estates of the 1960s and of the East German Plattenbau, though it is hoped with higher specifications. (Moore 2012)

Aesthetically then the village has strengths and potential challenges arising from the high density nature of the scheme.

From Athletes' Village to 'East Village'

The athletes' village was renamed East Village by QDD and Triathlon Homes with the intention of creating a unique identity as part of its marketing strategy. There are a number of unique features to the village. For example, most new housing schemes are developed in stages whereas this scheme will release nearly 3,000 properties at one time, the socio-economic mix of residents and tenure i.e. the scheme includes the first substantial private rental scheme owned by a private management investment fund of its kind to have been developed following the deregulation of the private rented sector in 1988.

It took one year for the physical conversion of the athletes' village into East Village. The contractor Lend Lease undertook a 'retrofit' which involved adding kitchens, identifying and fixing any damage and adding a final coat of emulsion paint. However, this is a relatively minor challenge in comparison with allocating and renting properties within a relatively short time scale.

Urban regeneration projects in the UK tend to be characterised by developing and releasing small proportions of properties over a period of time with early sales providing financial resources to fund subsequent phases of development. Therefore, the release of nearly 3,000 properties in a small, relatively untested geographical area where demand is unknown remains a key challenge with no equivalent precedents to draw upon. The aspiration of the ODA was to hand over all properties between September 2013 and early 2014. However, an agreement was reached providing a cap on the number of properties released in any week.

> From August 2013 we get some very large handovers ... When you actually just start working through the number of vertical movements up and down the block, in the lifts, the anticipated cubic capacity of packaging, and the like, it really brings home the challenge. (Senior Manager, Triathlon Homes)

> I think the scale is a challenge, 1,400 over a short period of time to find enough people as we don't want to have empty flats three years down the line, we want to have them occupied as quickly as possible. (Senior Manager, QDD)

Types of Housing at East Village

There will be at least five housing tenure/types at East Village. Triathlon Homes contains 100 per cent affordable housing and this includes four distinctive 'affordable housing' products. The scheme is based on a planning consent that predates the introduction of the Affordable Rent model and therefore target/social rents have been applied to this scheme.

> This is regularly held out to be the last bastion of social-rented housing in inner London because this was ultimately funded under the former programme and pre-dates the introduction of affordable rent. (Senior Manager, Triathlon Homes)

The largest proportion of affordable housing at East Village is for social rent and this will mean that the level of subsidy is greater and rent cheaper, ensuring that it is affordable to lower-income families. There will be 675 units available for social rent at East Village equating to 49 per cent of all affordable housing and 24 per cent of all housing at East Village. However, the cost of these units even based on the formula of target or social rents will be higher than average and may exclude those in work on low incomes. The average social rent per week at East Village is anticipated to be £138 or £598 per calendar month. In addition to this residents will pay a service charge of £22 per week or £96 per calendar month and at the time of writing efforts were still being taken to reduce this further. Rents are higher than average in part because a proportion of the service charge has been added into the rent.[5] Interest in the social housing has been high with 17,000 registering an interest in the units (Newham Recorder 2013). Residents have the right to acquire these properties and therefore it is possible that over time some of these units will convert to market housing.

A further 356 units will be let as part of an intermediate rent scheme. These units are similar to the new 'affordable rent' model in that residents pay 20 per cent below market rent. One bed apartments rented as part of this scheme will cost £910, two bedroom properties £1244 and three bedroom properties £1688 per calendar month (Inside Housing 2013). Residents need to demonstrate that they

---

5   The Department of Communities and Local Government provided information on data for large Private Registered Providers in London for March 2012 which indicated that the average RSL rent in London was £103.62. Large Private Registered Providers are registered parents of group structures and/or own at least 1,000 bedspaces. Information was also available for average Local Authority rents in London for 2011–12. The average Local Authority social rent was £89.17 per week.

have a good credit history, can afford the rent and pay a deposit and a month's rent upfront. Intermediate rent comprises 26 per cent of all affordable housing and 13 per cent of all housing at East Village. Intermediate rent is targeted at residents who may not be eligible for social rented housing but are eligible for this type of housing as a result of earning below a certain level or working in specific occupations. A further 348 homes are available for shared-ownership comprising 20 per cent of all affordable housing and 10 per cent of the total scheme. Shared-ownership housing offers residents the opportunity to purchase a proportion of their property and pay rent on the remainder. They are able to staircase up to 100 per cent and over time these units may convert to 'market' housing. It is anticipated that the cost of purchasing through shared-ownership at the village will be £857 per month, initial indications again are that demand is very high with 6,000 registrations of interest (Whathouse 2013).

The scheme also includes a small proportion of shared equity housing (79) units and this enables residents to purchase up to 75 per cent of the property. They do not pay rent on the remaining share and the property remains affordable.

Overall then we can see that there is a relatively extensive affordable housing offer. However, at least half of these units will be targeted at those on higher incomes and it is possible that over time the shared-ownership units will become market housing as residents staircase to 100 per cent and some of the social rented units may also convert through the right to acquire/buy to market housing.

The QDD and Triathlon apartments are located in specific blocks though they will share large communal courtyard gardens and the intention is that, viewed externally, the scheme will be tenure blind. However, there is differentiation within the units in terms of specification:

> We are very close to now agreeing kitchen packages for tenures and, whilst one kitchen might have a slightly different colour palette, and they might have slightly different work-tops, generally they all have the same carcass and they are all very robust. I can genuinely put my hand on my heart and say these are amongst some of the highest – if not the highest – spec units, that I've been working on. Certainly that's the case in the social-rented units.

A New Community/Community Development

When the village is fully occupied it will comprise a significant new community of at least 6,000 individuals in 2,800 properties and what is perceived as the wider offer will be a central selling point for the village.

> East Village may be London's newest neighbourhood, yet you'll think it had been here for years. Lush wetlands, fully grown trees and fabulous fauna and flora. Local independent shops, cafes and bars, and Westfield Stratford City, just a short stroll away. Outstanding free schooling for all ages at Chobham

Academy, a community centre and an advanced medical clinic. Not forgetting the obvious – world class sporting facilities right on your doorstep. (East Village Website: Accessed 31 December 2012)

As a newly-established district, East Village has a number of advantages as compared to other new schemes, where infrastructure investment may take several years to come to fruition (Bernstock 2008). In particular the scheme benefits from outstanding transport connections, a new school, health centre, proximity to parklands and Westfield Shopping Centre and more generally the scale of the development offers the capacity for community development:

> One of the attractions about the village when you are talking about nearly 3000 homes being created is the engagement with residents. You can provide significant opportunities for participation in activities with other residents in the village. You may have a village darts team or a Pilates Class. We will be the catalyst so that people have the opportunity to learn about all of the things that are happening in Stratford at the moment. We don't want this to be run as a Butlins Holiday camp by organising everyone, but we want to give them the opportunity to know what they could do and let other people know about them. (Senior Manager, QDD)

More generally what is perceived as the wider community offer will be essential if the village is to attract residents from across the socio-economic spectrum to live there. The approach to community development will be tenure blind. However, there are likely to be conflicting interpretations of extent and nature of community development between Triathlon and QDD:

> There is an emphasis on ensuring that community development caters for residents across the whole development. What we don't want is for residents in the premium market rent to look upon it as something which has no benefit to them, something which they associate with the people in the affordable housing. We are doing quite a bit of work looking at how we can make that offer attractive to the residents in the market-facing tenures as well as those in the more traditional affordable homes. (Manager, Triathlon Homes)

There are a number of initiatives in development such as open-air cinema screenings, a community radio station, a time bank, employment support, and gardening (growing) projects and whilst community development is a key dimension of any new scheme, the scope of this scheme makes it both more significant and opens up more possibilities. According to a senior manager at East Thames Homes:

> We will be doing the same kinds of things we do on all of our developments but the branding might be different so that volunteering might be renamed 'Timebank' to be attractive to all interested parties.

The Community Development Strategy envisages stages of support related to moving in; where people are familiar with their surroundings and are enjoying their home and then a steady state with an assumption that if community development has been undertaken appropriately the role of professional community workers will be redundant with the 'community' leading on subsequent developments.

Triathlon are focussing significant energy into ensuring employment opportunities for village residents:

> We are talking to workplace at Newham in terms of employment. We have had dialogue with High profile Olympic and Paralympic Sponsors. We are saying to them, you were active and high-profile in terms of supporting the Olympics and the Paralympics, but what about longer term, what's your commitment to the legacy? We recognise they can't ring-fence job opportunities but what they have said is (in reference to National Recruitment Agency) "look, if there is anything coming in in the E15, E20 area, then rest assured we will be sign-posting these opportunities to Triathlon Homes." So there's a mechanism in place.

A new school is also a central feature of the wider community offer with the intention of acting as a magnet across the socio-economic spectrum. The Chobham Academy located in East Village opened in September 2013 and caters for children from 3–18. It has been built to a high specification and includes a fully-equipped theatre and dance studios, extensive sports facilities including tennis courts, a state-of-the-art gymnasium and all-weather football facilities along with access to the Aquatics Centre and stadia.

The school has three private sponsors including Lend Lease, Lord Harris of Peckham, who established the Harris Federation and will manage the school, and Nigel Hugill (previously chair of Lend Lease and instrumental in initiating the Stratford City project). The school has a performing arts specialism and intends to capitalise on its proximity to local arts providers such as Theatre Royal. The sixth form offers both a traditional academic and a Performing Arts pathway.

Residents at East Village will have high priority with regard to the allocation of school places. However, as the school opens in September 2013 it is likely that earlier intakes will be drawn from a wider catchment as the majority of residents will not yet be living at the village. Herein lies a tension as it is seen as crucial both in serving the village and establishing a community. However, if most pupils come from outside this may make this more problematic and may also mean that people moving in to the village are unable to access a place at the school and therefore may have to travel outside for school:

> We have worked tirelessly trying to ensure that the admissions programme for the school, and the handover programme for the Village fit. One of our earlier concerns was that, based on the initial programme that was presented we could end up with a school that is going to open in September 2013 which is going

to be largely full of eligible people, but households not living on East Village. (Senior Manager)

However, another manager suggested that the gap between residents arriving and the school opening will mean that residents living nearby will be able to access the school and ensure a mix between existing and new residents.

The S106 agreement stipulated that a Community Development Trust should be established at East Village: The Olympic Development Authority are required to pay £1 million towards this, however, this money will not be spent but invested and any interest used to generate a fund. Its stated core principles are:

> The long term sustainability of an area in its widest sense with its economy, its environment, its facilities and the services and the 'spirit' of its community. (London Legacy Development Corporation 2012a, p. 2)

The intention is for it to be community-based and accountable to its management, working in partnership with the community, private and public sectors. The purpose of the CDT is to carry out economically, social or environmental projects and to raise income to fund this. The plan is for the board to evolve over time as the village becomes occupied with initial representation from Chobham Academy, Triathlon Homes, QDD, the ODA and London Legacy Development Corporation and over time the inclusion of residents (London Legacy Development Corporation 2012a).

East Village will have a community centre providing a place to meet. However, one area that has been overlooked is a space for prayer/worship. A significant amount of resources are being invested in Community Development at East Village and in addition to the work being undertaken by QDD and Triathlon, there are a number of other community development initiatives being led by agencies such as the Local Authority and the London Legacy Development Corporation:
According to one manager:

> There are so many different groups doing community development work in this area, but we need a much more joined up and coherent approach that focuses energy and resources.

Governance/Management at East Village

The scale of East Village and the range of tenures and partners involved has meant that governance and management structures have been given considerable attention in order to avoid the kinds of problems found on other developments where a range of agencies are involved. QDD is the freeholder for the site and responsible for the management of the site. As freeholder they are responsible for common parts, such as lifts, courtyards and undercroft parking. QDD have employed an estate management company to undertake this task and service charges collected from all residents will be used to pay for this service. Triathlon is responsible for tenant management issues and repairs in the actual apartments that they own. From the perspective of both Triathlon Homes and QDD there is a mutual benefit in the reality that most properties will be rented rather than sold:

> QDD's business plan does not predicate on open-market sale. They are certainly not in it to make a quick buck, cut and run; they are very much in this for the long-haul which from our perspective – and I should imagine from the ODA's perspective – is music to their ears. (Manager, Triathlon Homes)

> You would think by the way we were approaching this that we were partners in it anyway, all discussion we have with Triathlon is on the basis that we both have expertise in property management. The issues with the estate management company are basically the same for Triathlon homes as they are for QDD in terms of the people we want to employ and the quality we want to deliver. (Manager, QDD)

QDD have the larger share of accommodation 51 per cent: 49 per cent and this will be reflected in governance structures and they are also the freeholder. Initial structures are designed to include representation from those renting and buying and this has had to be reworked in response to QDD's plans to lease the majority of their properties. It is anticipated that the East Village Management Committee will be managed for a transition period by QDD, Triathlon and the East Village Management Company and then, over time, handed over to residents from different blocks with representation provided through a Residents' Forum across all tenures. The robustness of these mechanisms will be crucial to ensuring the establishment of a successful 'mixed community'.

In addition to the Estate Management Company both Triathlon and QDD will have onsite offices and therefore each set of residents will report concerns to a specific office managed by either QDD or Triathlon:

> The scale gives us the opportunity to manage our properties ourselves. We will ensure a high level of management in addition to that we will be setting up our own management operation and vetting operation on site for our direct tenants. It enables us to provide a good level of service but also to get to know the people who are renting our homes. That sort of relationship is important in ensuring that you are not the distant managing agent that turns up when there is a problem. You are there on site. You bump into people. That is a significant advantage in providing the quality of management that renting needs, as management is often cited with people dissatisfied with private renting.

When the village was developed it included only one estate management office for Triathlon Homes and this means that a temporary structure will need to be established for QDD residents. There is the potential for confusion with regard to the varying responsibilities of different agencies and therefore whilst QDD and Triathlon residents will report faults to different offices, officers within these offices will identify those responsible for solving the particular problems.

However, the management task will be even more significant given the high density nature of the scheme. Professor Peter Hall highlighted this issue on a visit to East Village:

> I think that the question of lifestyle is very important. We are not, perhaps, as controlled or civilised in our lifestyles as many continental European communities. In Germany and France, there are quite strict regulations about what you're allowed to do in residential areas. I think they accept those sorts of restrictions because they have a long tradition of living together at rather high densities. If you're going to get a lot of fairly young people together, you're going to need a combination of good sound insulation and an element of social control – no crazy parties in the central square areas at 1 am. (Hall 2012)

The need for regulation of resident behaviour is acknowledged by both Triathlon and QDD, however, agencies may have different perspectives on levels and systems of control and these may manifest themselves over time. At the time of writing there was a debate about pets, with QDD more willing to enable residents to own pets, perceived as an important part of village life, compared to Triathlon who anticipated this to be a potential management problem.

Residents buying or renting Triathlon properties will be interviewed prior to moving in and will have to sign a good neighbour agreement setting out expectations related to a range of issues such as noise management, no washing on balconies as well as other behavioural expectations. It is envisaged that there will be a strong management presence on the estate reinforcing these rules where appropriate.

High Quality Public Realm and Service Charges at East Village

High quality public realm is a feature of East Village with the intention of offsetting high density living through the use of high quality landscape creating a sense of space.

According to one manager:

> The public realm is unparalleled. Up until November (2011) the site was a series of buildings sitting in a construction site. Over a very short space of time, it succeeded in knitting all of these buildings together and generally softening the environment but longer term, in ensuring that the very high level of landscaping is maintained. There are implications for the management company and the home owner.

In other words, the high quality public realm has to be paid for and this comes at a significant cost. An agreement in the initial S106 agreement provided some protection from high service charges through a requirement that linked service charges to the RPI index. In November 2012, staff at Triathlon were urgently trying to square the circle between high quality public realm and affordable service charges and it has since been agreed that a proportion of the service charge has been included in the rent for those in the social and intermediate rent properties. Those in shared ownership will pay the full service charge as an additional cost. One senior manager from Triathlon Homes conceded that current levels were above that of other developments and posed a risk in terms of ensuring access for low income households and there had been considerable energy invested in ensuring affordability.

Who Will Live at the Village?

A scheme of this significance and scale has led to a considerable degree of attention to issues of who will live at the village at a range of levels. In a parliamentary debate Andrew Altmann (then Director of OLPC) and Baroness Ford (the Chair of OPLC) indicated that they had been both concerned with and involved in discussions about who would live on the park, exploring issues ranging from nominations through to sales on the park and implications if multiple purchasers were involved. Clearly the sale of the market properties to QDD eases some of the concerns about multiple buy to let landlords buying up flats at the village. According to Andrew Altmann:

> It has been an issue very much of concern to our board because we recognise how important it is going to be for setting the overall tone. It is going to be the first neighbourhood. (Culture Media and Sports Committee 2010: Evidence 9)

The attractiveness of the offer and the market will determine who chooses to rent premium market rent housing with QDD. A more complex allocations process will apply to the affordable housing. QDD initially planned to sell a small proportion of properties and rent the majority. However, in December 2012 the indications were that all properties would be marketed for rent. One of the biggest challenges facing QDD is the amount of rental property that will become available at one point in time in a relatively untested area with regard to demand and the impact of empty properties if take-up is lower than expected. It has been noted elsewhere that there has been a very limited increase in the value of properties for sale in this area and a more positive increase in the rental sector. In September 2013 QDD were marketing their properties under the banner Get Living London. At that time one bed properties were being marketed for £1344 pcm and two beds were being marketed for £1603 per calender month with a sales agent reporting high demand. QDD are keen to attract residents on longer leases and rentals are available on one, two or three year tenancies.

Allocations of the 'social rented housing' are more complex. In December 2011 the Allocation Policy for the 675 social rented units was confirmed. The London Borough of Newham has allocation rights to 50 per cent or 348 of the social rented properties; Barking and Dagenham, Hackney, Havering, Waltham Forest and Redbridge has allocated 100 homes between them; Triathlon homes has allocation rights for 150 homes and the GLA has allocation rights for 70 homes with the view to allowing people to move within London.

A target has been set to ensure that 50 per cent of residents are in employment:

> This is an aspirational target and is higher than on our other developments where around 29–30 per cent are in employment. We are going to employ an employment support officer who will work to see if they need sign-posting into a training scheme; undertake a skills' audit, and generally support people through the employment process. So it's all around what we can do to achieve that target, rather than saying, "you're not in work, you can't have one."

Triathlon has identified four equal priorities for its 152 properties, along with scope for manoeuvre if demand is higher in one area than another. One priority is the military and ex-military personnel. This group of applicants are not required to have a local connection. Triathlon does not anticipate having any significant numbers of ex-service personnel with disabilities or high support needs as the MOD (Ministry of Defence) already have developed links with specialist providers for people in this category. Triathlon have attended promotional events with the MOD and demand is growing for the housing because of its transport connections and access to the Olympic Park. The other priority groups are those with decant status, hidden homeless (living with another household) and over-occupiers who will be giving up a bedroom.

The Mayor of Newham had previously reported that he wanted to ensure that priority went to military personnel and those in work and in September 2012 Newham revised its allocation policy to ensure that first priority went to military personnel or those who had previously been in the military, followed by those in employment with a maximum earning of £60k (Press Release, London Borough of Newham Armed Services and People in Employment to be Prioritised for Social Housing, 28 September 2012). Whilst Newham has given priority to the military, it is thought that reality very few properties will be allocated via this route as very few people from the military have a local connection with Newham. The focus on work is in line with Newham's policy of wanting to reward those in work. According to one councillor:

> We did a survey of residents living at Windsor Park (large housing estate funded by the London Docklands Development Corporation). We found the council who made nominations cleared their homeless families list by pouring them all onto the one place and 87 per cent were economically inactive. That really can't

happen with the Olympics Village and that's what our housing nominations process ensures.

For residents being decanted from the Carpenters Estate East Village has offered the possibility of remaining in the area. There are conflicting views as to whether there will be a significant demand to move to East Village. The Carpenters residents have attended promotional events run by Triathlon and Carpenters leaseholders are being advised on options to buy at East Village. One problem is that many residents on the Carpenters Estate are eligible for one bedroom properties and most of Newham's properties are larger and it may be that there can be some re-allocation between the different boroughs with regard to properties. The London Borough of Newham's approach to decanting is to encourage residents to apply through choice lettings as compared to offering first refusal which is a policy used by other housing agencies.

The Greater London Authority also has nomination rights to 68 properties. The allocation of 61 of the 68 units is through a pan London mobility scheme enabling residents to move from one part of the capital to another. The remaining seven properties have been allocated to former rough sleepers (GLA 2012). The remaining boroughs have allocated their properties through their formally agreed lettings policies and residents were able to bid for these properties through choice based lettings and details of opportunities to move to East Village have been widely promoted through the choice based letting system.[6]

The allocations process is complex in terms of scale, criteria and range of agencies involved. The employment targets and potential for a proportion of these properties to be utilised by people with disabilities has meant that a significant lead in period was needed to enable occupational therapists to identify people with disabilities who might move to the housing and undertake adaptations and therefore the allocation process commenced eight months prior to the tenant moving in. Interestingly the target of 50 per cent residents in work has been exceeded with 57 per cent in work largely explained as a result of Newham's amended housing policy.

Establishing a Mixed Community

East Village serves as an interesting case study for 'mixed communities as it is almost evenly balanced between market and affordable housing; includes family housing in both housing types and its design is intended to promote accessibility for people with disabilities (including wheelchair housing) and includes a magnet school aimed to be attractive to people from different socio-economic groups.

---

6   Choice based lettings provides details of available Local Authority or Registered Social Landlord owned properties that they can bid for properties which are allocated to those with the highest score on waiting lists.

At first sight then an exemplary model of inclusion and design. However it also reveals the underlying tensions of this approach. The affordable housing includes 50 per cent housing for social rent and another 50 per cent aimed at better off sections of those in housing need. Moreover, as we have seen whilst the public sector have effectively underwritten the Village, there has been a high degree of social engineering reflecting a sea change in attitudes away from prioritising those in greatest need to those who 'deserve it' and in the process effectively winds back housing policy fifty years. Newham's reform of its allocation policy will mean that the population of residents in housing need at the park are different from those in housing need more generally in the borough. Notwithstanding this it is important to recognise that a substantial number of new affordable homes will be available in a well designed scheme in an increasingly desirable part of London and if successful could act as a demonstration project for other parts of the Park and the UK more generally.

East Village – Concluding Thoughts

The level of thought and planning that has been invested in ensuring the success of East Village is impressive. The design, the public realm; the wider community offer and the social mix all make this an exemplar project. Whilst we can trace this housing to the initial Stratford City Scheme it is unlikely that the quality of this scheme would have been as high without the eyes of the world watching. On the other hand it is hard to imagine that with so much resource invested in it that it should be anything other than successful.

Stratford City

The athletes' village or East Village was part of the Stratford City Development that was granted outline planning permission in February 2005 and was also used as further justification for London being selected as host city. Ironically, a chicken and egg situation has arisen with regard to the construction of East Village and the Westfield Shopping Centre which were both part of this earlier Stratford City Planning application, but subsequently identified as a legacy benefit of London 2012. The Stratford City Planning application included a mix of retail, residential and business uses.

The application was submitted in 2004 by Stanhope (developer) and London and Continental Railways (landowner). Stratford City Developments was established which comprised a consortium of Stanhope; Westfield and Aldersgate. Westfield then bought Stanhope's share and became the majority shareholder. In 2009 London and Continental Railways went bankrupt with debts exceeding £5 billion and the government took it over for a nominal fee and therefore LCR became a government-owned company.

The Stratford City scheme initially included plans for 4,850 homes and included 30 per cent affordable housing increasing to 35 per cent if financial viability could be proved. The rationale for this relatively low proportion of affordable housing (significantly below levels indicated in the London Plan) was agreed partly because Stratford had a large proportion of residents living in social housing and they wanted to create a more 'balanced' community. The London Borough of Newham has been keen to ensure that the site is balanced both in terms of mix of properties and ownership to avoid concentrations of social housing in specific locations in what they have described as social housing ghettoes.[7]

The housing plans for the area are included in a Site Wide Housing Strategy that has been modified a number of times and was a conditional requirement of the original outline planning application. The Site Wide Housing Strategy was first produced in 2007 and by this time had increased to 5,453 and again in 2009 to 5,769 units. The Site Wide Strategy was updated in 2013 and total number of units planned increased to 6,500 including 1,987 (291 per cent) affordable units and 4,515 (71 per cent) market units. The affordable units comprise 950 intermediate units (up from 682 in 2009) and 923 Social rented units (down from 1,104 units in 2009). This lower level of social rented housing is offset in part through the funding of offsite affordable rented housing. The balance of affordable housing in the revised plan is now split evenly between intermediate and social rented housing (50:50) deviating from the original planning consent that stipulated a balance of 60:40 Social Rented to Intermediate Housing. The housing built at the Athletes Village comprises 2,818 of the total units planned and makes a significant contributiom to meeting the affordable housing requirements comprising 1,379 of the 1,987 affordable housing units planned. (London Legacy Corporation 2013a).

The recession and a failure for house prices to rise in this area has led to delays on other parts of the scheme. In 2011 an application was granted to allow an additional ten years (up from 2017 to 2027) to submit reserved matters agreed as part of this scheme with development to be commenced by 2030 rationalised by both the economic situation and the Olympics.

Stratford City's Seven Zones

For the purposes of planning, Stratford City comprises seven zones that set out the direction for development in that area. Zone 1 includes the Stratford Retail Centre and other leisure uses. Initially it was anticipated that 500 mainly one- and two-bedroom properties would be built as shop-top housing and therefore there were no plans for any social rented housing in Zone 1 due to claims about unsuitability. However, as the scheme developed distinctive residential areas emerged with the capacity to build up to 1,224 units located on Cherry Park (a 1.8 hectare site) and Angel Lane

---

7   See for example ODA Applications Consultation LBN Consultation response Plot N08, Stratford City Development ODA/90213 Remoda.

(a 0.7 hectare site). The planning consent for the Zone now comprises 35 per cent affordable housing including 47 per cent social rent, 53 per cent intermediate. It is anticipated that this Zone will comprise mainly one- and two-bedroom apartments (85 per cent) and a small number of three-bedroom units (15 per cent) (London Borough of Newham 2011a).

In March 2013 planning consent was granted for a 759-bedroom student hostel up to 14 storeys in height at Angel Lane, originally identified for residential housing. Newham rejected the proposal as they argue it will contribute to population churn and will use land that could be used to meet the needs of local residents in housing need and also questioned demand for this type of housing. In response to concerns about loss of residential floor space, the S106 agreement makes a stipulation that development cannot commence until residential land equivalent to that scheduled for use at Angel Lane is identified elsewhere (London Legacy Development Corporation 2013). This accommodation is in addition to planning permission granted elsewhere in Zone 1 for 900 units of Student accommodation (London Borough of Newham 2012).

Zone 2 is adjacent to Zone 1 and the intention is to develop a new 'financial quarter/commercial district'. It is anticipated that the development will create 15,000 jobs and a relatively small residential district. The zone was used for temporary purposes during the Olympic Games and handed back to London Continental Railways in the first quarter of 2013. Construction is scheduled to start in 2013 with the first completions by 2014. Current plans for Zone Two include the construction of a number of tall buildings up to thirty floors in height comprising 332 residential units. It is proposed that the scheme will include 20 intermediate units on site and a payment for off site affordable rented units elsewhere rationalised by its unsuitability for affordable/social housing (London Legacy Development Corporation 2013a).

Zone 3 includes Stratford International Station and the DLR station along with planned residential, hotel and office uses. This zone initially included 334 units of market housing and no affordable housing. Plans for the zone include tall, expensive buildings and these were deemed unsuitable for housing for social rent, in 2011 the amount of residential floor space was increased and a proportion of intermediate housing was included.

Planning Permission has been granted for a 42 storey tower in Zone 3. However, the particular plot that it is being built on has been removed from the Stratford City Planning Consent and treated as an independent planning application. The scheme comprises a hotel up until the 6th floor, a restaurant on the 7th floor and 248 apartments on the 8th to 42nd floors. The residential part of the scheme has been developed by the Manhattan Loft company and is due for completion in 2015 with units currently being sold off plan. The scheme comprises no on-site affordable housing and this was justified because of its lack of suitability for social housing due to the use of a single entrance, high-rise design, potential high service charges and limited space for family housing. A viability assessment indicated that the developer could finance 6–7 intermediate units on-site or 23 units off-site through a £1 million financial contribution. It was agreed that, given the likely time lag between reaching financial agreement and the scheme being built, a review mechanism be incorporated up to the value of 35 per cent affordable housing linked to the profitability of the scheme (up to the value of £8,700,000), though given the downward trend of contributions elsewhere and the ongoing recession it is hard to imagine that the scheme will deliver a reasonable financial contribution towards affordable housing (Greater London Authority 2010).

East Village is located in Zones 4 and 5. Zone 4 was initially scheduled to include 1,107 units. However, this increased to 1328 following the construction of the athletes' village and therefore residential land was redistributed from Zone 5 to Zone 4. Zone 4 is complete and comprises 1,328 residential units and a polyclinic. Zone 5 was initially scheduled to include 2,574 properties. Currently 1,491 units have been built. There is scope for more development here and six plots of land within Zone 5 are now owned by QDD. These plots were initially to have been developed for the athletes' village before it was cut. As we have noted above Stratford Village Property Holdings 2 Limited (trading company of Olympic Development Authority) submitted a planning application that included no affordable housing, rationalised by the high levels of affordable housing elsewhere:

> Whilst the application is presented as a stand-alone scheme, the applicant relates the affordable housing requirement to the committed provision within the Stratford City development as a whole. As such, no affordable housing is proposed on Plot NO8, ostensibly to dilute the concentration of affordable housing across Stratford City and contribute to the creation of a more mixed and balanced community that takes account of the already high proportion of social housing. (Greater London Authority 2011, para. 66, p. 6)

The GLA rejected this as a rationale and argued that the rejection of affordable housing had to be on the basis of economic constraint rather than social mix. The application was withdrawn in June 2012, however, it illustrates the tensions and contradictions between plan and outcome. Another argument that has been made on a subsequent planning application with regard to lower levels of affordable housing relates to the need for government to limit expenditure in this area given the extent of commitments arising from hosting the Games (Greater London Authority 2011).

At face value plans and policy documents for this area appear to guarantee substantial proportions of affordable housing. However, there are ways in which these commitments can be undermined and therefore policy should not be understood on the basis of reading plans, but as an outcome of complex negotiations between planners, developers and governing agencies.

Stratford City is an interesting case study with regard to exploring the relationship between states and markets. The initial application was for the private sector led redevelopment of a substantial part of Stratford. The private sector has delivered the shopping centre and has clearly benefitted from the substantial investment accruing from London hosting the Olympic and Paralympic Games. Redevelopment land has been bought by Government and private sector contractors have won contracts to build these schemes. Planning obligations for Stratford City were extensive and included 30 per cent affordable housing, a new school and health facilities and again it was anticipated that these obligations would be met by the private sector. However, when the government took over the contract from Lend Lease to develop the village many of these obligations became the responsibility of the ODA and not the private sector. Therefore, the Government has captured the risk and the private sector has selected the more profitable parts of the schemes.

The provision of 49 per cent affordable housing at East Village was facilitated by the public rather than private sector and a result of market failure rather than design. The housing itself clearly relates to the previous Stratford City project and arguments that this has been expedited through legacy are questionable and have been used to justify less affordable housing elsewhere in Stratford City. The justification for lower levels of affordable housing range from existing high levels of public expenditure in this area, high levels of social housing in the area, lack of viability, unsuitability of design and increasingly now as a result of fiscal austerity and a combination of lack of grants and new funding models to facilitate affordable housing. Either way there is a considerable risk to those original objectives of ensuring that the regeneration would be for the benefit of all who lived there. In the meantime developers are continuing to progress a range a schemes that are clearly at odds with these initial ambitions. In addition to plans for housing at Stratford City and on the Park, another substantial scheme, Chobham Farm is progressing at Stratford.

Chobham Farm

An outline planning application was approved in September 2013 for the development of Chobham Farm, an area adjacent to East Village and the Olympic Park though not within the Stratford City project. The scheme is divided into five zones and it is anticipated that it will be developed over a twenty year period. The developers of the scheme include East Thames Homes and London and Continental Railways. An outline planning has been approved for development of the five zones and includes planning permission of up to 1,046 units and 8,061 square metres of floor space across these zones. It is intended that the scheme comprises mainly low density family housing with 42 per cent of the units including three or four bedrooms. The Outline planning consent includes a minimum of 15 per cent affordable housing across the scheme comprising a mix of Affordable Rent (58 per cent) and Shared Ownership (42 per cent). This level of affordable housing is the minimum level that can be provided based on an assumption that no grant is available. However, there is a clause committing the developer to secure grant funding and a viability review mechanism to increase the level of affordable housing if sales values are higher up to a maximum of 35 per cent.

A full planning application has been submitted and planning permission granted for Zone 1 of the Chobham Manor scheme. This zone is located close to East Village and the Chobham Academy and development is expected to commence in 2014. This zone includes 173 residential units located in six blocks varying in height from three to ten storeys and 37 (22 per cent) affordable housing comprising a mix of Affordable Rent (20 units: 54 per cent) and Shared Ownership (17 units: 46 per cent). The affordable housing is to be funded through grant aid (London Legacy Development Corporation 2013b). This is then another example of another development that is likely to make a relatively negligible impact on the urgent need for genuinely affordable housing in the area.

References

Baroness Ford (2010). BBC News *Living on the Olympics Park will Dream Become Reality* – Thinkpiece, 5 December 2010 <http://www.bbc.co.uk/news/uk-11842550> (Accessed 3 September 2012).
Bernstock, P. (2008). *Making Neighbourhoods Work: Lessons from Thames Gateway* (London: Shelter).
Branson, A. (2012). The elusive finishing line, in *Planning*, 27 July.
Centre for Economic and Social Inclusion (2011). *Making Work Pay in London under Universal Credit* (London: Centre for Economic and Social Inclusion).
Coe, S. (2007). It's ludicrous to claim the Olympics will lead to evictions and Poverty, *Guardian* 15 June.
Farquhar, G. (2012). Village tests its readiness ahead of the Games, BBC Sports News Correspondent 30 June 2012 <http://www.bbc.co.uk/news/uk-18658814 London 2012: Athletes'> (Accessed 5 November).
Greater London Authority (2004). *Lower Lea Valley Plan* (London: Greater London Authority).
Greater London Authority (2004a). *An Inspiring Legacy: A Great Future after a Great Games* (London: Greater London Authority).
Greater London Authority. (2004b). *The London Plan: Spatial Development Strategy for Greater London* (London: Greater London Authority).
Greater London Authority (2006). *Draft Lower Lea Valley Opportunity Framework* (London: Greater London Authority).
Greater London Authority/London Development Agency (2007). *Lower Lea Valley Opportunity Area Planning Framework* (London: Greater London Authority).
Greater London Authority (2008). *Five Legacy Commitments* (London: GLA).
Greater London Authority (2010). Plot N24, Zone 3, Stratford City.
Greater London Authority (2011). Plot N06, Zone 5, Stratford City, Planning Application No 10 90560 OUMODA, 12 January 2011, Planning Report PDU 2578a/02, 22 December.

Greater London Authority (2012a). Housing Supplementary Planning Guidance: November 2012: London Plan 2011 Implementation Framework.

Greater London Authority (2012). DD853 Promotion and letting of the 68 Social Rented properties in East Village (London: Greater London Authority).

Hall, P. (2012). *How We Did It? Designing Olympic Homes.*

Hawkes, P. (2009). Athletes village gets 324 million Contingency Funding in Construction News, 13 May <http://www.cnplus.co.uk/alex-hawkes/1730.contributor> (Accessed May 2012).

House of Commons Media, Culture and Sports Committee (2007). London 2012 Olympic Games and Paralympic Games: Funding and Legacy: Second Report of Session 2006–7, Volume 1, 17 January 2007 (London: HMSO).

House of Commons Media, Culture and Sports Committee. (2010). Olympic Games and Paralympic Games Legacy, 3 March 2010.

Johnson, D. (2012). London assembly Member Press Release – Mayor failing on only two solutions to housing bill, 22 October 2012 <http://www.london.gov.uk/media/press_releases_assembly_member/news-darren-johnson-am-mayor-failing-only-two-solutions-housing-benefit-bill>.

London Candidate File (2004). *Theme 1 Concept and Legacy*, Volume 1, London Candidate File.

London Borough of Newham (2003). P03/0607 *Stratford City Planning Application*, Development Control Committee Papers, February.

London Borough of Newham (2011). *Zone 1 Stratford City Developments, Zone 1 Stratford Rail Lands*, 10/90061/OUTODA March 2011, Development Control Committee Papers, March.

London Borough of Newham (2012). *Application number 12/01957/ Angel Lane Zone 1*, Strategic Development Control Committee Papers, 30 November.

London Legacy Development Corporation (2012). *East Village Community Development Trust Legal Structure*, 12/00143/106, 3 September 2012.

London Legacy Development Corporation (2012a). 12/90458/FUMODA, Zone 1 (first detailed phase) land bounded by Leyton Road and Henrietta Street and including Wheelers Public House, 27 September 2012.

London Legacy Development Corporation (2013). Land at Angel Lane Bridge, Stratford Application (12/0021/Fum), 25 February.

London Legacy Development Corporation (2013b). Chobham Farm 12/00146/Ful) Public Item 5, Planning Decisions Committee, 23.7.2013).

Moore, R. (2012). Olympic Village Review, *Observer* Sunday 8 January 2012.

Newham Recorder (2013). Scramble for Social homes in East Village, *Newham Recorder*, 16 February.

Olympic Development Authority (2009). Final Agreements confirmed for Athletes village affordable housing, 22 June (London: ODA), <http://www.firstbase.com/downloads/2009/june2009/22june09.html> (Accessed 4 November 2012).

Olympic Development Directorate (2011). ODD31 Disposal of Lane at Sugar House Lane.

Olympic Park Legacy Company (2011). Legacy Communities Scheme, (London: OPLC).

Olympic Park Legacy Company (2012). *Legacy Communities Scheme: Regulation 22: Response and Additional Information Submission; Addendum, Housing and Social Infrastructure Statement* (London: Olympic Park Legacy Company).

Smith Institute (2012). *New Urban Living for London – The Making of East Village* (London: Smith Institute).

What house (2013). High Demand for Shared Ownership Properties at East Village, 18 March. <http://www.whathouse.co.uk/news/High-demand-for-shared-ownership-homes-at-East-Village-947> (Accessed 19 March).

Wellcome Trust (2011). Statement on the Olympic Park Press Release, 4 August (London: Wellcome Trust).

Chapter 6

Accelerated Regeneration – A Case Study of Stratford High Street

Planning gain has been a key mechanism for providing affordable housing in recent years. When London won the bid to host the Olympic and Paralympic Games in 2005 it was anticipated that this would trigger a process of accelerated regeneration that would trickle down and improve the lives of deprived communities living in the area. This chapter focuses on a case study of Stratford High Street which runs parallel to the Olympic Park. It provides an evaluation of each housing scheme of 50 or more properties built or planned since 2000 and the planning gain agreements associated with them. The chapter identifies a trend away from the 'mixed communities agenda', a decline in the value of planning gain, a substantial decrease in levels of affordable housing provided on site and a shift towards more off site affordable housing. More generally it highlights the significant weaknesses of current mechanisms for extracting and distributing 'public gain' from regeneration projects.

Much attention has been given to the scale of public investment required to host the Olympic and Paralympic Games in East London. The price tag of £9.3 billion is a considerable sum. The cost side of the equation is more amenable to precise evaluation than is the benefit. Estimating the latter is complex and capable of different interpretations arising from the difficulties in defining beneficiaries, discerning appropriate methodologies for capturing value-added and distinguishing Olympic-related developments from those that would have taken place anyway.

This chapter examines the process of urban revalorisation arising from the hosting of mega events and uses evidence from developments on the borders of the Olympic Park to draw attention to the inadequacy of existing legislative and policy frameworks in capturing value for community gain. This inadequacy arises for several reasons, including the scale of the regeneration project initiated by 'London 2012' (incorporating its 'overlap' with the London Thames Gateway project), the weaknesses inherent in the Section 106 arrangements designed to capture 'community gain' and the diversity of interests, public and private, that policy makers seek to reconcile and a more general failure to develop a satisfactory mechanism for defining relationships between the market and the state. The chapter is divided into three sections: The first examines the re-valorisation and value-added arising from London 2012 and places value capture in its current policy context. Second, the case study of Stratford High Street, bordering the Olympic Park, is discussed in relation to 'community gain' and, finally, the chapter draws some broader conclusions concerning London 2012 and its capacity to catalyse a pattern of social transformation that reduces social deprivation in East London.

London 2012: Revalorisation and Value Capture

The successful bid submitted to the IOC in 2005 to host the 2012 Games provided the opportunity for significant public investment to take place in East London. The bid organisers and stakeholders hoped that the private sector would share the burden not just via event sponsorship but also through the commitment of private capital in infrastructure development and facilities construction. This did not materialise.[1] The costs and the risks associated with East London's development fell to public investment and extensive policy commitments were required to legitimate the costs of the renewal of a significant part of East London. The impressive remediation of wasteland, the creation of the vast Olympic Park and the continued commitment to improving transport infrastructure was undertaken by public investment organised via quasi-government agencies, some created specifically for the purpose.

Revalorisation involves the replacement of the old (in the Olympic Park case, largely but not exclusively industrial wasteland) by a new urban infrastructure with the latter stimulating over time a rise in land and property values and creating the potential for a new round of economic competitiveness for the city. In the case of London, since the credit crunch and subsequent flat-lining of the economy, the process of urban revalorisation has relied significantly upon a combination of state investment (especially via the Games) and international investment (mainly in the city centre, involving iconic locations), attracted from growth regions in the world (China, the middle-east and other regions) and often taking the form of investment by Sovereign Wealth Funds.[2]

---

1   In March 2008, the House of Commons Committee of Public Accounts recorded in June 2005, the Department received further advice from Partnerships UK that there was little prospect of securing significant private sector funding to deliver the Olympic Park due to the tight timetable and a lack of clearly identifiable revenue streams. At the time of our hearing there were still no detailed legacy plans. In the March 2007 budget, the Department reduced the estimated private sector funding to £165 million, which comprised contributions to the media and broadcast facilities and to utilities on the Olympic Park'. See 'the budget for the 2012 Olympic and Paralympic Games', http://www.publications.parliament.uk/pa/cm200708/cmselect/cmpubacc/85/85.pdf, accessed 2 February 2012. In relation to the Olympic Village, LendLease, an international enterprise specializing in property and infrastructure development, was identified in 2008 as a partner with the public sector in creating the village. Lendlease pulled out, in 2009, in part because of the worsening economic conditions arising from the aftermath of the credit crunch. Arguably, this episode revealed the difficulty in securing private sector partners to share the costs of infrastructure development and the inherent instability in relying upon the partnerships with the private sector to fund major projects.

2   Fortune RE Group reported in March 2011 that 'Asian investors are the dominant force driving demand and should this year overtake the Middle East as the largest buying group. Jones Lang LaSalle said there was more than £52bn of equity seeking acquisitions, with 80pc focused on central London, China's influence on the London market, which

As a result of public intervention at the lower point in the cycle of depreciation, the state has managed the costs of transforming the Olympic Park area (broadly the Lower Lea Valley) from its final stages of capital depreciation through to the creation of the necessary conditions for subsequent private sector development. The hosting of the Olympic and Paralympic Games has provided a unique opportunity to bring together an unusually large area of land, especially for a city such as London, and establish the required planning powers to remove the old and lay the foundations for the new on a significant scale (Smith 2010, pp. 81–3). Urban transitions from old to new, we are reminded by Graham and Marvin (2001, pp. 176–7), are a complicated affair. In the case of 'London 2012', the Olympic Park's proximity to Canary Wharf and the transport infrastructure improvements to facilitate linkage between the Park and the city's financial centres, suggest that the former is an important component in expanding the spatial dimension of the latter's marketability. Equally, the proximity of the Olympic Press and Broadcast Centres to a cluster of high tech companies in the Shoreditch (Silicon Roundabout) area provides potential for a new commercial network to emerge. It seems that the accumulation of value added is part planned and in part an iterative affair. Before discussing the London 2012 case in terms of the capture and allocation of value, it is perhaps useful to commence with some broader observations on value creation and distribution arising from urban regeneration projects in the UK and, specifically, in London.

Urban regeneration projects since the 1980s have mainly been directed at addressing inner-city decay arising from de-industrialisation, the decline being marked by high concentrations of social deprivation in specific urban areas. Public investment, especially in transport, and physical infrastructure, has contributed to a rapid growth in the price of land especially where that land has been approved for housing construction. This trend has been particularly evident in the south and east of England, including London. The recent history of urban development/ regeneration in London has tilted toward the construction of high density, non-family accommodation; house prices have risen significantly and the combination of escalating land and house prices have reinforced their role in determining access to the most desirable and 'improving' neighbourhoods in the city.

In the wider national economy, at their peak in 2007, the market valuation of land, housing, utilities and other real estate assets made up 87 per cent of all UK tangible assets, massively outstripping those of productive industries, by 2010 this situation had not changed. In brief, the (scarcity) 'value' of housing and land reflected the operations of a highly unbalanced national economy and, at the micro

---

remains the biggest in the world, is poised to grow. The country's sovereign wealth fund made its first UK property investment in 2009 by backing the refinancing of Canary Wharf owner Songbird Estates. Investors are being attracted to central London properties by their trophy status, the standing of the UK as a global financial centre, a lack of supply of new properties, and the long lease lengths that UK rents offer'. See: http://www.fortuneregroup.com/2011/03/london-property-market-to-get-52bn-asian-investment/.

level, especially in London, regeneration projects reflected these imbalances, tending to fuel 'gentrification' rather than improving the living conditions of socially deprived communities.[3] Public investment in regeneration failed, at least in part, from the inadequacy of the measures designed to ensure that the benefits arising from this investment flowed on a sufficient scale to meet the needs of socially deprived communities rather than developers and landowners. The Barker Review of Housing Supply recognised this problem in 2004. She recommended the introduction of a planning gain supplement as a modification to the existing system of S106 agreements. Its aim to:

> capture a portion of the uplift in value accruing to land during the development process to fund enhanced investment in social housing, housing-related infrastructure, and to provide incentives for local authorities to deliver housing growth. (Barker: para. E45, p. 16)

Duncan Bowie's (2010) study of London's planning and house building during the period of Ken Livingstone's tenure as Mayor, provides detailed insights into the problems identified in the Barker Review. Despite the framework provided by the London Plan, the declared policies on social provision made by the Mayor and local authorities and the interventions made by the Housing Corporation, Bowie's analysis of 40 development schemes referred to the Mayor of London between July 2006 and June 2007, led him to conclude that community gain (largely triggered by Section 106 agreements) or public sector benefit was, at best, extremely limited:

> Ironically the main contribution of Ken Livingstone as Mayor to steering the market has been to encourage high-density and often high rise schemes, often in breach of his own published planning policy. Not only has planning policy as set out in the London Plan had limited impact on steering the market but also planning practice has had relatively limited success in managing the market in terms of achieving the best public sector benefit, the Mayor's planning practice has actually given greater support to the market to go in what in the short term was the most profitable direction. (Bowie 2010, pp. 193–5)

However, whilst acknowledging the limitations of planning gain in a period of relative boom Since 2007, the severe weakening of the city's economy arising from the credit crunch and the recessionary conditions that have followed, has created macro-economic conditions that have made the task of enhancing public benefit from major developments even more challenging. Therefore, the background

---

3 See Imrie, R.L. Lees and M. Raco (2009) *Regenerating London*. In their introduction to chapters providing case studies of regeneration projects in London, the authors argue 'it is important to recognise that since the early 1980s regeneration projects have not only failed to address such inequalities but has also played a significant role in creating and reproducing them' (2009: 9).

against which 'London 2012' is seeking to achieve significant public sector and local community benefit from Olympic-related investment is, it seems, unfavorable.

Value Capture and Olympic Development

Value capture, is also called 'betterment' capture. Public policy may deploy a variety of ways to capture betterment through taxation, regulation or by the introduction of frameworks for negotiation between public authorities and private developers.[4] By investing in infrastructure (transport, environmental improvement, and social amenities) the public purse improves an area from which developers subsequently benefit. This benefit does not derive from the new development that takes place but secures *unearned benefits* for the developer arising from the initial public investment in infrastructure. In public policy contexts the *unearned benefits*, or betterment, arising from public investment (e.g. land remediation, transport improvements) may be distinguished from other types of *development contribution* such as the provision of social housing or the contribution that may be placed on a developer as a direct result of the development itself, often called in the literature, *the impact fee*.

In the context of 'London 2012' the distinctions between unearned benefits and those derived from development contributions (such as social housing) and new development impacts have not been adequately recognised. Negotiations taking place between public authorities and developers have mainly focused upon the *development contribution*. As a result, developers have tended to secure agreements that are tilted decisively in their favour. While the public sector has borne the risks and costs inherent in a major project such as the Olympic development (involving compulsory land purchase, extensive land remediation and infrastructure development) the private sector has only entered into the revalorisation cycle at the point at which their interests are likely to prevail over what might be called the public good. The inadequacies of the current planning and legislative frameworks are exemplified in the following study of an area on the borders of the Olympic Park – Stratford High Street.

Stratford High Street

Stratford is changing at a rapid pace, accelerated by the construction of the Olympic Park and Stratford City. The High Street is characterised by the emergence of tall

---

4 There is a significant literature on value capture from the USA and more recently from Australasia; the value added by infrastructure improvements from transit systems to the proximity to sports stadiums have been studied. See for example: Smith A. and T. Gihring 'Financing Transit Systems Through Value Capture': An Annotated Bibliography" *American Journal of Economics and Sociology*, Volume 65, Issue 3, July 2006, p. 751.

towers whose construction is tending, in early 2013, to displace a varied but often run-down mixture of low rise buildings that have served as factories, workshops, offices, small retail outlets and cafes.

This section explores planning applications and S106 agreements completed or planned projects along Stratford High Street – including Burford Wharf, Stratford Icona and the Ikea/Landprop development that are located just off the High Street. We use two key measures that are central to negotiations around 'planning gain' – a financial contribution – which is captured on earlier developments as part of the S106 agreement and on recent developments through the application of a Community Infrastructure Levy aimed at mitigating the impact of the development and the proportion of the scheme that is designated as 'affordable housing' and or a contribution to 'affordable housing'.

Analysis of these schemes provide an insight into the regeneration that is taking place in this area and how this relates to the wider social goals arising from East London being host to the 2012 Olympic and Paralympic Games and, in the process, highlights limitations to the current approach to capturing value/community gain. We begin by reviewing the wider policy context and the agencies that have framed the approach of planning authorities to these applications.

Stratford High Street stretches from Bow Church to the Old Stratford Shopping Centre and covers an area of less than five kilometres. A number of agencies have been involved in making planning decisions about this area, as we have discussed in Chapter 4. The London Thames Gateway Development Corporation (LTGDC)[5] had planning powers between 2005 and 2012 for much of Stratford High Street. The London Legacy Development Corporation has since taken over these powers, whilst in 2011 development control for some parts of Newham including some schemes on the High Street were handed back to the borough.

The LTGDC's approach to planning gain has differed from the London Borough of Newham who have until recently applied a *heads of terms* approach to this issue, identifying the need to mitigate the impact of development across a wide number of areas. LTGDC on the other hand has applied a Planning Obligations Community Benefit Strategy (POCBS) linked to a cost per unit. This approach was first introduced in March 2008, and revised in July 2010 following an assessment of implementation and in response to the changed wider economic climate. The main amendment to the policy was to introduce a discounted POCBS. The LTGDC had been advised that in

---

5   As a result of the Localism Bill, the LTGDC will be transferring its assets and staff to the Mayoral Development Corporation and the GLA in the course of 2012. As it explains 'After the successful stewardship of planning and development activity in east London since 2005 which has secured over £6 billion of private sector investment along with planning consents with the potential to deliver over 18,000 homes and 15,000 jobs, LTGDC will transfer all its development assets and staff to the MDC and the GLA in April 2012 and will transfer its planning responsibilities for the Lower Lea Valley to the new Mayoral Development Corporation and the relevant local authorities in October 2012.' http://ltgdc.org.uk/ltgdc-news/ltgdc-asset-transfer-set-to-boost-mayor-of-london-regeneration-coffers-2/.

order to ensure new developments minimise impact, a standard charge per dwelling of £22,400 in the Lower Lea Valley should be applied. However, LTGDC argued that such a charge was unviable in the post-credit crunch context and instead adopted a discounted standard charge of £10,000 per unit, with the intention of reviewing the revised figure twice yearly for each major development.[6] The application of the standard unit cost was designed to avoid disincentivising the construction of larger schemes. It also introduced a deferred standard charge on schemes of 100 units or more, with the intention of enabling a renegotiation over contributions on schemes that have either been delayed or not progressed.

The LTGDC established two management groups, one for the Lower Lea Valley and one for London Riverside, with responsibility for determining expenditure and a landowner liaison group aimed at involving them in expenditure decisions, however, more generally it is acknowledged by LTDGC that the community gain monies will 'make a relatively small contribution to the overall infrastructure needs of the Thames Gateway' (LTGDC 2010a, p. 5). The approach of the LGTDC was to pool funds from specific infrastructure projects and this was relatively controversial as it meant that resources attracted in one area could be used in another LTGDC development location; such pooling could be interpreted more as a planning tax than a mechanism for mitigating the direct impact of developments.

The second main agency engaged in the planning process is the London Borough of Newham. Its Unitary Development Plan has guided policy since 2001 and has recently been updated. The plan had a specific vision for Stratford that involved rebalancing the housing mix as it was perceived that there was an over-supply of social housing. Planners, when considering new schemes were required to propose lower proportions of affordable housing and lower proportions of socially rented housing than was the requirement for Newham as a whole and below that set out in the Greater London Plan 2004. This was the approach that underpinned the Stratford City development and a number of the schemes discussed below. Newham revised its approach to planning with the adoption of its core strategy in January 2012. This strategy no longer stressed the need to rebalance the mix of housing as there had been considerable progress in this regard since 2001. However it did confirm the significance of Stratford as a key source of housing for Newham estimating that nearly 50 per cent of all new housing built in the borough between 2011 and 2027 will be in the 'Stratford and West Ham' district. The strategy also sets out its desire to ensure that each development secures between 35–50 per cent affordable housing, whilst acknowledging that current policy constraints are likely to lead to lower levels of affordable housing provision. In line with the GLA there is a policy intention of ensuring a 60:40 social rented – intermediate housing split, though again there is scope for negotiation. The Strategy sets out a clear commitment to secure more family housing with a target of at least 39 per cent family homes in recognition of

---

6   See LTGDC Planning Committee Report, 10 September 2010 at: http://ltgdc.org.uk/ltgdc/wp-content/uploads/2011/05/ITEM-4-Planning-Obligations-CIL-Update-Report.-09-09-10.pdf

the significant need in this area. The strategy confirmed that in assessing planning applications the intention would be to secure quality mixed and balanced communities. Other criteria applied included: scheme viability, the availability of subsidy, existing mix of housing in the area, individual conditions of the site and the availability of required infrastructure and community facilities for residents. Therefore there is considerable potential for negotiation between the borough and developers. A third important public agency impacting on the planning process is the Greater London Authority (GLA). Its policy is set out in the London Plan and this is discussed in detail in Chapter 4.

In summary, three key agencies have been engaged in guiding public policy on new developments along Stratford High Street between 2000 and 2012 – the LTGDC, the GLA and the London Borough of Newham. In October 2012 powers from the LTGDC and ODA transferred to the London Legacy Development Corporation with the aim of streamlining activities and creating a single point of contact for developments on the Park and surrounding areas.

These agencies have clearly faced significant challenges arising from a combination of the accelerated 'transformation' initiated by Olympic development occurring alongside the potentially decelerating effects of economic recession. Planning frameworks and housing targets have been reviewed and revised at city-wide and local levels, with important implications for the capacity of public agencies to achieve the scale of community gain required to significantly improve the living conditions of local people, especially those residing within socially disadvantaged communities.

The revisions to the frameworks for capturing community gain introduced by the Mayor, the LTGDC and Newham Local Authority in the wake of the credit crunch and subsequent economic recession suggests that the 'burden' placed upon developers to provide public benefit as a component of their construction projects has been diluted by the decisions of public agencies to, for example, discount 'standard charges', remove the 50 per cent affordable housing target and interpret more flexibly 'affordable housing' policies.

A more detailed, 'micro' insight into the balance struck between community benefit and private sector interests may be revealed through an examination of planning gain agreements on fifteen schemes developed or planned since 2000 either on or just off Stratford High Street (Burford Wharf and Stratford Icona, Warton Road). A further four schemes were submitted during this period, however, no S106 agreement has been signed and therefore, they have been excluded from our analysis.

New Housing and the London 2012 Effect

Between 2000 and 2012 some 2321 units have been constructed or are near completion along Stratford High Street and a further 2126 planned. Of these 24 per cent (1076) were categorised as affordable (See Appendix 1: Table 6.1). A number of regeneration projects have been significant in confirming the emergence of Stratford as an International hub.[7] Table 6.1 shows that housing activity increased considerably after 2005. Research undertaken on S106 agreements across Thames Gateway between 2000 and 2005 indicated that there was considerable interest in building new homes in this area prior to London winning the bid, though many of the applications were speculative (Bernstock 2006). Here it is suggested that London 2012 provided the confidence for developers to progress such schemes. The dominant architectural features are high density, tower constructions, with relatively few family size housing units, although more recent schemes have tended to include more family housing and less affordable housing. There have been concerns raised about the piecemeal/ad hoc nature of these schemes that have emerged along Stratford High Street.[8] Most significantly, the more recent major developments demonstrate a trend towards off site affordable housing or very low on site levels of affordable housing and significantly reduced financial contributions to 'community gain'.

Three Phases in Approaches to Affordable Housing on Stratford High Street

The analysis below divides the developments into three time phases that may assist in discerning the impact of both the Olympic Games and the recession prompted by the financial crisis (2007–2008). Period One is 2000–2005 prior to London winning the bid. Period Two (2005–2008) is when Stratford is confirmed as the Host location for the Olympic Park and the Third Period (2009–12) coincides with the impacts of economic recession and the emergence of particular problems affecting housing development and provision.

Affordable Housing: Period One 2000–2005

Table 6.1 indicates that three schemes were developed in this period. The first scheme demonstrates a minimal approach to capturing value through planning gain. The latter two schemes attempted to lever more value. The Registered Social Landlord delivered a greater proportion of affordable housing and a greater proportion of housing for social rent compared to the two private developers. In this period, a total of 484 properties were built. Of these, 21 per cent were designated affordable. However, very few were for social rent with a ratio of 75:25 intermediate housing to social rent. In this period there is a growing interest in development in the area. Planning gain from these schemes did not embrace the 50 per cent affordable housing; 60:40 social rent advocated in the London Plan. The London Borough of Newham was keen to rebalance the population of Stratford at

---

7 For example, Eurostar, Stratford City and London 2012.

8 See English Heritage's response to Planning application 09/07146 – 206-214 High Street Stratford.

this time due to a perceived over supply of social rented housing as compared to owner occupation.

Affordable Housing: Period Two 2005–2008

Table 6.1 reveals some interesting trends with regard to the provision and type of housing developed between 2005 and 2008. Most noticeable is the considerable rise in interest in developing projects. There were seven schemes of 50 or more properties completed or planned during this period. Three of these were led by developers in the private sector and four by Registered Social Landlords, though one of these was in partnership with a private developer. There were 1837 properties planned or completed with an additional 65 extra care units. A significant proportion of Affordable housing was included in these developments (38 per cent) and levels of affordable housing were similar both for private and RSL developed projects. The ratio of intermediate housing to social rented housing was 48:52. A small proportion of housing was built off site (15 units). One scheme developed during this period (Lett Road) initially included on site affordable housing i.e. ten shared ownership units. However, following a negotiation with the developer a contribution of £360,000 was made instead though it is hard to understand how this sum translates to subsidy for ten units.

Telford Homes developed two schemes and both included high proportions of affordable housing and at similar levels to those developed by Registered Social Landlords during this period. These schemes are illustrative of a number of housing schemes delivered in that period through public/private partnerships. They were underpinned by a commitment to 'mixed communities', financed through public subsidy and from a developers' perspective offered a degree of security about sales as the proportion of housing designated as affordable was funded via a Housing Association Grant. They also highlight a key tension in the use of limited public resources – despite the huge need for social rented housing the largest proportion of affordable housing was designated as 'intermediate housing'. These findings reinforce conclusions recently drawn by (Crook and Monk 2011). They reviewed national trends and identified an increase in the proportion of affordable housing required on schemes; a tendency to provide a greater proportion of shared ownership housing as compared to social rent and a reliance on government subsidies in order to deliver affordable housing to help realise the 'mixed communities' agenda.

The recession has taken its toll on two schemes in particular: 150 High Street Stratford, an ambitious project developed by Genesis, that ran out of cash half way through construction. They are privately renting the part of the scheme initially designated for owner-occupation. They were able to attract additional government funding by modifying the scheme to include 65 extra care units. Across the road at 160–188 High Street the credit crunch is also evident. Another block initially designated for owner occupation has been privately rented. The developers,

McFeely, have gone into receivership and private renters in the Stratford Athena block were decanted by receivers in May 2012.

Affordable Housing: Period Three 2009–2012

We can see from Table 6.1 some marked discontinuities between periods two and three. The table includes five schemes planned for Stratford High Street, a further scheme was submitted but it has been excluded from this analysis as it did not proceed to an S106 agreement. The schemes include a total of 2126 units. At the time of writing two of these schemes Unex Tower and Capital Towers are being marketed off plan with completion anticipated for 2015. The Capital Towers scheme was recently at the centre of a controversy when it emerged that it had been marketed overseas and using 'no social housing' as part of its marketing strategy (BBC News 2013). Progress is also being made on the Ikea/Landprop development. There are a number of marked differences between the schemes approved in this period. For example they mark a clear departure from the 'mixed communities' agenda, all five schemes are being developed by private developers with no involvement of RSL's. Three schemes do not include any on site social rented housing despite the huge need for it, the fourth a very low level of housing on site affordable housing for social/affordable rent i.e. between 4 and 5.5 per cent dependent on grant aid and 6 per cent on-site intermediate housing. There is also a trend to provide either no 'affordable housing' or off-site 'affordable housing' and the fifth includes a relatively high proportion of affordable housing in comparison to other schemes at 17 per cent on site affordable housing designated as 'affordable rent' whih can be charged at up to 80 per cent of market rent. This scheme has not commenced and may well be renegotiated in the context of agreements reached on other schemes. On two of the schemes developers have agreed to provide a financial contribution of £90,000 per unit for off-site affordable housing and on the third scheme a contribution towards affordable housing will be dependent on the profitability of the scheme.

Two of these schemes Broadway Chambers and Station House/Unex Tower were initially submitted in 2007 and then resubmitted with revised S106 agreements modified to reflect a very changed environment in comparison with earlier periods. Overage agreements are included linked to the profitability of these schemes. These schemes highlight some key tensions concerning the Olympic legacy. Stratford has benefitted from substantial infrastructure investment but with cuts to housing grants, the private sector is increasingly unwilling or unable to make any significant contribution to affordable housing development. Developers have successfully contested planning decisions, weakening the power of planning authorities to shape outcomes and these authorities, in a bid to attract development, are increasingly modifying their own rules. In the long term the development of sustainable mixed communities and a long term reduction in deprivation will not be achieved through such schemes. Crook and Monk (2011) have suggested that planning gain acts as a device for creating a form of inclusionary housing and whilst this was applicable to the period 2005–2008, there has subsequently been a substantial break from this approach. Far from building housing aimed at addressing deprivation and disadvantage it is likely that we will see more private housing aimed at the better off whilst the housing needs of those on lower income groups in the Legacy boroughs and London generally will be overlooked along with an abandonment of the 'mixed communities' agenda so central to the objectives espoused by successive governments in the form of legacy promises and policies, with the poor effectively removed by design.

Other Dimensions of Planning Gain 2000–2012

Table 6.2 explores other dimensions of planning gain linked to planning consent on these schemes. There are some interesting trends here reflecting in part the wider policy climate and the changing nature of planning gain. For example, during the period 2000–2005, significantly lower levels of planning gain were required and a less systematic approach applied. However, contributions increased significantly during the period 2005–2008 when a more systematic approach was taken and developers were making significant contributions as part of planning gain agreements to mitigate the impact of developments. From 2009 onwards, there has been a significant reduction in the level of planning gain applied – negotiations have led to a downward trend in contributions, significantly below levels deemed necessary in order to mitigate the impact of such developments. There also appears to be a considerable degree of bargaining evident in arriving at an actual sum reflecting less an analysis of the actual cost of mitigation but more a negotiation linked to the profitability of the schemes. We can see that payments have been made but not uniformly and in some instances it is likely that actual sums committed will not actually be paid.

Planning Gain 2000–2005

In the period 2000–2005, we can see that there was a very limited range of contributions required at 32–66 High Street and 72 High Street, Stratford. Moreover, the payment of £50,000 towards education specified in the S106 agreement at 72 High Street, Stratford was never made. A more comprehensive list of payments was required at Burford Wharf and in the main these appear to have been paid. There was some discrepancy between actual payments and expenditure. The sum required of all three schemes with regard to education contribution was broadly similar despite the variation in actual numbers of properties. We can also see that a range of sums specified in S106 agreements are not monetary i.e. they may relate to footpaths linked to the actual development and may be offset against a financial sum. The London Borough of Newham undertook an audit of expenditure of S106 monies and identified a time lag between monies being received and spent resulting in significant surpluses that were not utilised and this was evident here (London Borough of Newham 2011).

Planning Gain 2005–2008

Moving on to the period 2005–2008, we can see that significant sums were now being included as part of planning gain agreements with varying approaches to planning gain operated by LBN, who have applied a heads of terms approach identifying specific areas for mitigation, and the LTGDC who applied a levy linked to the number of units. We can see also that actual sums paid were considerably lower than that set out in agreements, with scope given in negotiations to offset the actual cost.

We also need to read with caution the substantial sums specified in agreements and what is then offset and defined as a non monetary contribution. This is evident on a number of these schemes. For example, a sum of £678,000 specified in the S106 agreement at 14–26 High Street, Stratford was offset by £380,000 with a final cash sum of £293,000 paid. Similarly, at 150 High Street, Stratford an indicative sum of £6,550,000 was specified in the S106 agreement with £4,584,213 offset, resulting in an actual payment of £1,712,866. This contribution has been paid and monies used to improve the Canning Town Roundabout (more than two miles from the actual site). The S106 agreement was negotiated twice following modification of the scheme and the inclusion of an additional 48 properties. Initially London Borough of Newham stipulated £675,000 in total of planning obligations, and a proportion that could be offset. The developer paid £245,000 to Newham in 2007 and part of this was used to improve the local school. The second part of the agreement linked to the expansion of the scheme applied a flat fee of £10,000 per unit which meant that an additional £480,000 was required, as of December 2012 £127,000 had been paid.

Across this period then considerable sums have been negotiated under the terms of various S106 agreements. There is clearly a gap though between the sums specified and those actually paid. The introduction of the Community Infrastructure Levy does appear to have enabled a more consistent approach to planning gain; collection of monies and expenditure. However, the recession has generated another complication with regard to the payment of monies and this is evident in the period 2009–2012 discussed below.

Planning Gain 2009–2012

There are currently five S106 agreements signed for this period. A review of these agreements demonstrates a significant departure from previous practice with what might be described as a 'race to the bottom' taking place in terms of planning gain. It is helpful to consider each agreement. Station House (Unex Tower) was originally presented in 2010 with a discounted standard charge per dwelling of £5,000. However, the scheme was revised in 2011 with a reduction in the total number of units and the discounted standard charge was reduced to £3,500 linked to scheme viability. We can see that the S106 agreement for Broadway Chambers has also been agreed at £3,000 per unit justified by scheme viability. This scheme includes an overage agreement linked to increased payments related to profitability. The scheme at 2–12 High Street (Capital Towers), Stratford has recently been signed by the ODA (the Developer) and LBN (who have a service level agreement to act as planning authority for this scheme). The agreement adopts a heads of terms approach totalling £923,000 with considerable scope for offsets to be applied. The scheme at Sugar House Lane provides an indicative sum of £8,543 per unit, and again significant scope for offsetting and therefore actual benefits are limited. The sum agreed at 68–70 High Street Stratford includes an indicative sum of 7.5k per unit.

The propensity then to capture value through developments has now been severely curtailed and new solutions are clearly sought if development is to make a contribution to reducing deprivation.

Conclusion

According to an image generated by 'Invest Thames Gateway' in 2009, Stratford High Street is set to become East London's new 'Manhattan Boulevard':

> Funding from the London Thames Gateway Development Corporation, with delivery by Newham Council, aims to breathe fresh life into the High Street, which is directly south of the Olympic Park, forms part of the Olympic Road Network and will be a major route to the Games.
>
> A new CGI of the future High Street, plots the new high rise developments which have been granted planning approval standing within a new boulevard along the 1 mile stretch. (http://www.investthamesgateway.com/thames-gateway-news/news_details.php?id=72)

The significant development in public infrastructure and the close proximity to the Olympic Park has facilitated the creation of a new residential area. It would seem that Stratford High Street richly illustrates the capacity of the private sector to secure the locational advantage (Stratford is recognised by the Local Authority as the most 'connected' part of the borough) afforded by public investment whilst, particularly in the context of the wider economic austerity, reach agreements with public agencies that commit them to the most modest contributions to 'community gain'.

Stratford High Street is but one development taking place within East London; several more are in the pipeline. It may be that the High Street constitutes a special case, a busy location and a transport hub, making it less family and 'affordable home' friendly. Such a view, however, cannot be assumed given that these trends are evident both elsewhere on the Park and across the country. It is possible that the emerging 'Boulevard' will be but one of several 'enclaves', sitting at the edge of the Olympic Park and benefitting from its proximity, largely housing new rather than existing communities in the borough and, through its uninspiring architecture, presenting all the outward features of the 'non-place'.

The urban development associated with the Olympic Park, the extensive public investment in transport infrastructure and the remediation of land previously declining in value has been impressively completed in the period of seven years. The large scale of the development has also highlighted the inadequacies of those mechanisms designed to capture public benefit or community gain. The case study of Stratford High Street illustrates changing priorities toward the provision of social and affordable housing and the concentration of value capture on development contribution and modest impact fees rather than reflecting the unearned benefits derived from the initial and significant public investment directly and indirectly associated with hosting the 2012 Olympic Games.[9]

Set in this context, the balance of private and public gain derived from the renewal of an area on the border of the Olympic Park has tilted decisively in favour of the former. Indeed, developers it seems have tended, in several cases, to accept the case for community gain (especially in relation to the provision of social housing) only as a means to access additional public funds for their specific developments. Equally, local authorities, such as Newham, are faced with the difficult task of securing specific public benefits from negotiations with each developer and ensuring that these modest 'gains' or fragments of infrastructure contribute to the achievement of wider area plans – rather like putting together a huge jigsaw puzzle when developers hold several missing pieces and are reluctant to give them to you.

Whether Stratford High Street will set the trend for future developments within the area remains to be seen; the underlying trends in economic and social policy suggest that it may well and more recent schemes at both Stratford City and plans for the park confirm rather than challenge these assumptions. The current government's cap on housing and welfare benefits, the continued rise in private sector rents and the on-going reluctance of banks and financial institutions to provide mortgages makes London, and increasingly parts of what was affordable East London, difficult places for relatively deprived communities to live. Such problems may be addressed if the mechanisms designed to capture value are radically revised and 'affordable', social housing provision considerably increased (along with the expansion of good quality private sector rented provision) in East London and other parts of the city. For value capture mechanisms to work, and reflect a better balance between private and public interest, scheme viability has to be assessed over the long term with the unearned benefits accruing to private enterprise reflected in the latter's contribution to urban development.

---

9   The 'capture' of the scale of public investment should also include that provided by the LTGDC in the area and the contribution of public investment for developments that obtained the minimum standard of social housing provision to attract public funds.

Such requirements fly in the face of the recent history of major projects associated with urban regeneration in the UK, and especially London, in which the private sector has sustained what might be characterised as a largely parasitic rather than productive relationship with the public sector. For the latter, the status accorded to 'public' provision, particularly social housing must be restored and re-conceptualised as an essential dimension of good city-building if the housing shortage in London is to be effectively addressed over the next decade so that the majority of people gain access to high quality, affordable homes with security of tenure. Such provision cannot be delivered, in the form it is presently organised, as the residual product of 'side-deals' between developers and public agencies. Such a re-conceptualisation should commence with an acknowledgement that successive rounds of city-wide and local government commitments to affordable housing targets have largely been honoured in their breach; in short planning policies have been riddled with inconsistencies and contradictions as a result of which low income families have become increasingly unable to gain access to, and move up, the 'affordability chain'. If London is to maintain its character as a city that is regarded as *home* by the relatively poor as well as the rich, new approaches to the creation, capture and distribution of value are urgently needed.

References

Barker, K. (2005). *Housing Policy: An Overview* (London: Crown).
BBC News (2013). Outrage over Capital Towers no Social Housing Advert, 19 September <http://www.bbc.co.uk/news/uk-england-london-24166974> (Accessed 20 September 2013).
Bernstock, P. (2006). Affordable housing in Thames Gateway: A study of S106 agreements. Commissioned by Davis Arnold Cooper.
Bowie, D. (2010). *Politics, Planning and Homes in a World City* (London: Routledge).
Crook, T. and Monk, S. (2011). Planning Gains, Providing Homes, *Housing Studies*, 26(7–8): 997–1018, October–November 2011.
Graham, S. and Marvin, S. (2001). *Splintering Urbanism* (London: Routledge).
GLA (2004). *London Plan* (London: GLA).
GLA (2009). The London Plan, Spatial Development Strategy for Greater London, Consultation, Draft Replacement Plan (London: GLA).
GLA (2012). Community Infrastructure Levy – Charging Schedule – Mayor London agreed Feb. 2012 takes effect April 2012 (London: GLA).
GLA (2009). *Strategic Housing Report* <www.london.gov.uk/mayor/publications/2009/docs/strategic-housing-report.pdf>.
Haurant, S. 'The Barker Review Key Points', *Guardian* 17 March 2004 <http://www.guardian.co.uk/money/2004/mar/17/business.housing>.
Imrie, R., Lees, L. and Raco, M. (2009). *Regenerating London: Governance, Sustainability and Community in a Global City* (London: Routledge).

Kavetsos, G. (2012). The impact of the London Olympics announcement on property prices, *Urban Studies*, 49(7), pp. 1453–70.

London Borough of Newham (2011). Strategic Development Committee, *Planning Obligations Report* (London: LBN).

London Borough of Newham (2012). Newham 2027 – Planning Newham, Core Strategy – adopted January 2012, (London: LBN).

London Thames Gateway Development Corporation (2010a). *Revised Planning Obligations Strategy*, July 2010.

London Thames Gateway Development Corporation (2010b). LTGDC Planning Committee Report <http://ltgdc.org.uk/ltgdc/wp-content/uploads/2011/05/ITEM-4-Planning-Obligations-CIL-Update-Report.-09-09-10.pdf> (Accessed 10 September 2010).

London Thames Gateway Development Corporation (2010c). Application Number 09/01746/LTGDC/LBNM 206-214 High Street Stratford.

London Thames Gateway Development Corporation (2011). Planning committee minutes, July 2011 <http://ltgdc.org.uk/ltgdc/wp-content/uploads/2011/07/2011-07-14-Planning-Committee-Minutes.pdf>.

Smith, N. (2010). A Short History of Gentrification, in *The Gentrification Debates*, edited by J. Brown-Saracino (London: Routledge), pp. 31–6.

Whitehead, C. (2007). Planning Policies and Affordable Housing: England as a Successful Case Study?, *Housing Studies*, 22(1): 25–44, January 2007.

Appendix A

Table 6.1 Housing schemes completed or planned along Stratford High Street – numbers and proportions of affordable housing 2000–2012

Housing completion timeline	Scheme	Number of units	% and no of affordable housing units	% and no of affordable housing units – intermediate	% and no of affordable housing units – social rent
Housing completed prior to London being confirmed as host city (July 2005)	32–66 High Street Stratford. Permission 1999. S106 signed 2000. Developer: Barratts. Planning authority: LBN.	193	0.5% (12) affordable	100% (12) shared-ownership	0
	Burford Wharf. Permission and S106 2004. Developer: Acton Housing Association. Planning authority; LBN.	161	35% (56) affordable	67% (38)	33% (18)
	72 High Street. Permission and S106 2004. Developer: Bellway. Planning authority: LBN.	130	25% (32) affordable	78% (25)	22% (7)
Period one: total 2000–2005		484	21% (100)	75% (75) 15% of total	25 (25%) 6% of total
Housing planned between July 2005 and 2008	Stratford Icona, Warton Road. Application submitted 2004. S106 signed August 2005. Developer: Telford. Planning authority LBN.	249	35% (87 units) 49.8% SO/IR: 50.2% social rent. 35.4% shared ownership = 31 units. 14.3% Intermediate Rent = 12 units.	35.4% (31) shared ownership. 14.3% (12) intermediate rent.	50.2% (44)

14–26 High Street Stratford. Planning permission 2006. S106 signed March 2006. Developer: Telford. Planning authority: LBN.	301	42% (133) On site funded via HAG.	69% (84)	31% (34) (5 off site)
160–188 High Street Stratford. Planning consent October 2007. S106 signed March 2009. Completed. Developer: McFeely Group and L and Q. Planning authority: LBN and LTGDC.	298	43% (127)	62% (79)	38% (48)
150 High Street. Planning permission granted 2007. Scheme modified 2010. Completed. Developer: Genesis Housing Group. Planning authority: LTGDC.	639 and 65 extra care units	33% (229)	40% (191)	Social rent 60% (138)
236–252 High Street. Scheme submitted 2007. S106 signed March 2010. Completed. Developer: One Housing Group (initially Community Housing Association). Planning authority: LTGDC.	113	50% (57)	25% (28)	50% (28)

Table 6.1 continued

	1a Lett Road. Planning permission granted May 2007. S106 signed November 2007. Deed of variation May 2010. Developer: Thornsett Developments. Planning authority: LTGDC.	64	Initial agreement. 36% 10 on site intermediate. Deed of variation resulted in no on site affordable housing.	0	13 off site social rent 1,290,000. Deed of variation added 360k towards 10 off site units. 532k had been paid as of April 2012 and a further 1,118k is due in instalments from 2012–2013.
	223–231 High Street. Outline planning permission 2004. Planning permission granted 2008. S106 signed December 2008. Developer: One Housing Group. Planning authority: LBN and then LTGDC	173	36% (62) Ratio of shared ownership: social rent 40: 60 40% (25) intermediate	40% (25)	60% (37)
Total Housing on Schemes submitted 2005–2008		1837 plus 65 extra care units	38% (695) 342 shared ownership. 19.5% (354) 12 intermediate. Ratio of social rented: intermediate 48:52	19.5% (342) shared ownership and 12 intermediate units.	18% (329) on site. 15 off site social rented units and 360k to refurbish 10 units*. Total social rent including offsite (19%).
Schemes submitted after 2009	Station House, Unex Tower. Planning permission granted December 2008. S106 signed May 2010. Scheme resubmitted with reduction in properties. This was approved in 2011 subject to signing new S106 agreement.	260 homes cut to 220	Initially 36 (14%) on site intermediate homes. Now cut to 22 (10%) on site. 26% (58) affordable units including on and off site.	Initially 14% (36) shared ownership. Reduced to 10% (22).	Off site housing for social rent. Initially 21% (55) @ 90k per unit. Now 16% (36) @t 90k per unit. (16%) = 26%.

Broadway Chambers (MCRP no 1 LLP). Two applications were submitted the latter with lower levels of community gain in 2009. Fraught negotiation resulting in developer appealing to Secretary of State. Planning permission granted 23rd November 2009. S106 signed Feb. 2010.	342	18% (61) (34) 10% on site intermediate units.	(34) 10% on site affordable housing and 100% of all on site affordable housing.	0 on site affordable housing. 27 units at 90k per unit. (8%) = off site.
2–12 High Street. Planning permission granted May 2011. S106 Signed March 2012 between ODA and Developer with Newham council beneficiaries of agreement. Developer: Stratford High Street Limited. ODA is planning authority, however, they have a service level agreement with Newham.	191	0 on site affordable housing. Contribution to off site affordable housing specified.	First affordable housing contribution 200k (prior to commencement of development) plus 3k to employ an independent valuation consultant to undertake valuation with 50% of sum payable on sale of the 95th unit. Monies to be used for off site affordable housing tenure type not.	Second contribution linked to profitability of scheme up to a maximum of 6,685,00 and 70% of the profit once the development has reached the break even figure of 63,400,000.
Sugar House Lane. Planning permission granted September 2012. S105 signed between Developer and London Thames Gateway Corporation September 2012. Developer: Landprop Holdings.	1200	Varying options dependent on grant aid. If no grant aid is available 8% (96) units affordable housing. If grant aid available 11% (132 units).	4% (48) discounted market. Sale if no grant is available. 5.5% (66) if grant is available.	4% (48) affordable rent if no grant is available. 5.5% (66) if grant is available.

Table 6.1 continued

68–70 Stratford High Street Planning permission and S106 signed March 2012 Planning Authority: ODA Service agreement with LBN. Developer: Lancaster PLC.	173	17% (30) 22% on habitable room basis as AH includes some larger units.	0	All Affordable rent.
Total planned 2009–2012	2126	13% (281) including off site affordable housing. 7% (152) on site.	6% (122) on site intermediate.	96 (4.5%) on site. 63 (3%) off site. Total 7.5%. Ratio of intermediate: social rent 49:51. Excludes affordable rent.
Total all three periods	4447 plus 65 extra care units	.24% (1076) Includes on and off site housing 22% (988) on site only	12% (551)	10% (450) on site. 2% (88) off site* Total: 12% (538). Plus 65 extra care units = 603 Ratio of intermediate: social rent 45:55 Excludes affordable rent Ratio of intermediate to social rent if extra care units excluded 52:48

*Excludes affordable housing at 2–12 High Street Stratford given uncertainties about delivery and assumes grant aid is available at Sugar House Lane and therefore includes higher figure.

Table 6.2 Other dimensions of community gain on schemes along Stratford High Street

Housing Completion Timeline	Scheme	Number of Units	Other dimension of Planning gain	Financial value of Planning gain
Housing completed prior to London being confirmed as host city (July 2005).	32–66 High Street Stratford. Permission 1999. S106 signed 2000.	193	Clause in lease to ensure affordable housing remained affordable.	£70k Highway, £48k Education, £20k Improving footpath. Total = £138k Paid
	Burford Wharf permission and S106 2004. Acton Housing Association Developer.	161	Sets out nominations for both sub regionally via the East London Allocation system. Includes definition of affordability and specifies target rents.	£42,500 controlled parking zone, £50k DLR, £50k education to be used for grant payment to train people in the locality, £50k environmental improvements, £200k highways = 392,500 Monies were paid and spent as follows: £6,600 spent on environmental improvements 2007/8, £50k to support town centre management activities 2006/7, £45k to support Town Centre management activities 2007/8, £87,601 spent on improvements to Channelsea road and path (2008/9), £37,106 parking (2008/9), £29,501 laying out Cam Road. Training budget: £10k training for electrical safety 2007/8, £40k on training at workplace council's job brokerage and recruitment service.

Table 6.2 continued

	72 High Street. S106 2004.	130	Local labour agreement. One affordable commercial unit nominated by council. Sets out Income levels for intermediate housing and targets affordable intermediate housing at key workers using OPDM (2004) definition.	£150k riverside walkway, £50k education = 200k. The education contribution was not paid by the developer.

2000–2005		484		
Housing planned between July 2005 and October 2007	Stratford Icona, Warton Road. S106 signed August 2005.	249	Local Labour clause. Specified purchase price of affordable housing at 9,250,000. Specified target rent as 70% of market rent.	£175,000 affordable workspace payment to be used to subsidise leaseholders of the affordable work space, £145k Education payment, £150k Open space payment, £72k primary care payment = £542k. £156k paid to Newham 20.10.2005.
	14–26 High Street Stratford. Planning permission 2006. S106 signed March 2006. Telford. Completed.	301	Specified price of purchase of homes to be acquired by RSL at an agreed cost of 5,424,450 for the building lease including 32 car parking spaces, all affordable housing reached by lift wheelchair standard, all lifetime homes, affordable service charges, car club, local goods and services clause	Agreement specified: £2k bus infrastructure – paid, £20k controlled parking zone extension – £10k paid, £10k cycling improvements paid, £202k education, £380k open space, £20k CPZ extension, £10k cycling and pedestrian improvements paid, £12k feasibility study for carbon emission reduction – paid, £20k waterspace strategy – paid. Total = £678k. Total monies paid was: £293k. Highway improvements and public realm valued at £380k were non monetary obligations and were complied with.

160–188 High Street Stratford. October 2007 planning consent. S106 signed March 2009. Completed. McFeely Group and L and Q.	298	Wheelchair adaptable housing, lifetime homes, energy strategy.	Initial agreement negotiated by Newham under heads of terms: £250k education including £150k for phase two of Carpenters Estate, £70k open Space, £50k health, £90k environmental public realm, £50k transport information boards, £40k local labour in construction, £35k cycle pedestrian infrastructure, £40k CCTV Signage, £40k CPZ expansion = £245k paid to Newham 15/03/2007, £27,734 spent on modernisation to Carpenters School (2007/8) and then £67k on modernisation work 2008/9. Scheme was modified with additional 48 properties resulting in additional payment of £480k modified with LTGDC with £10k per unit charge applied. Estimated as of April 2012 £127k had been paid and the developer had gone into receivership raising questions about any additional payments. Expenditure of money determined by Lower Lea Valley Management Fund.

Table 6.2 continued

150 High Street. Planning permission granted 2007. Scheme modified 2010. Completed. Developer: Genesis Housing Group.	639 and 65 extra care units	Green travel plan, car club, local goods and services commitment, affordable business space.	£6,550,00 based on £10k per unit £4,584,213 offset against River Wall and improvements to public facilities including landscaping and associated works: **£1,535,000.** Greenway pedestrian link: **£145,000.** Pocket Park (including walkway alongside): **£445,000.** Children's play area: **£141,550.** Public Square: **£195,000.** Contingencies (in respect of the above items): **£123,578.** Capitalised contribution to repair, maintenance, management and insurance: **£1,989,085.** **TOTAL: £4,584,213 (offset)** Paid – £1,712,866 has been paid and used for Canning Town Roundabout improvement works – Level of offset will be linked to actual sales. Monies used for improvements to Canning Town Roundabout.
236–252 High Street. Submitted 2007. S106 signed March 2010. Completed.	113	Commitment to local goods and services, 10% renewable energy, Very good standard regarding eco-homes, Monitor and mitigate effects on TV reception in the area, Commitment to reduced car development £2k admin, commitment to a car club.	£10k per unit contribution estimated at *1,2650.* Actual amount in agreement £560k. £560k has been paid and allocated to Carpenters Road improvement works.

	1a Lett Road. S106 Signed November 2007. Deed of variation May 2010.	Lifetime homes, 10% wheelchair adaptable, local commitment scheme – setting out details and mechanisms for securing use of local labour, contractors and goods and services both during construction and occupation of the development to be approved by the Local Planning Authority.	£100k towards environmental improvements, education, traffic order amendments and skills training. This money has been paid and has been used for: environmental improvements, skills training, bulk to Carpenters School.
	223–231 High Street. Outline planning permission 2004. Planning permission granted 2008. S106 signed December 2008. Deed of Variation signed 2009. Completed. Developer: One Housing Group.	173 Travel plan, local goods and services.	First S106 specified: £100k education, £50K transport, £135k home zone, £51,500 environmental improvements, £150k health care, Deed of variation specified: £490k total infrastructure cost, £490k has been received, £100k education, £185k transport improvements, £351.5k environmental improvements, £3150k healthcare provision, £2.4k environmental health.
Schemes submitted after 2009	206–214 High Street. Submitted 2009. Planning permission granted Feb. 2010 subject to S106. This has not been signed. Developer: Newling UK Ltd.	147	No S106 signed.

Table 6.2 continued

Station House, Unex Tower. Planning permission granted December 2008. S106 signed May 2010. Scheme resubmitted with reduction in properties. This was approved in 2011 subject to signing new S106 agreement.	220	Local labour agreement, local goods and services agreement, on site car club, Section 278 related to footpaths, amendment, controlled parking zone.	May 2010 first S106 signed specifying a contribution of £7.5k per unit. Scheme resubmitted in December 2011 with a revised contribution of £5k per unit based on financial viability and this was approved subject to deed of variation for S106. Total infrastructure cost = £1,000,000.
Broadway Chambers (MCRP no 1 LLP). Two applications were submitted, the latter with lower levels of community gain in 2009. Fraught negotiation resulting in developer appealing to Secretary of State. Planning permission granted 23 November 2009, S106 signed Feb. 2010.	342	Local labour, contractor, goods and services, and young people clause, parking traffic management, TV reception mitigation.	LLV pooled fund of £3k per unit = £1,026,000. Overage agreement.

2–12 High Street. Planning permission granted May 2011. S106 signed t May 2011.	191	Employment and training, submission of and adherence to a Local Labour Commitment Scheme – 25% of construction staff to be Newham Residents; of this 10% apprentices. Leasing Units to ACME (management company for artist studios) for three years at no cost (value 209,5250).	£90k waterways, £19k health, £120k highways, 187k education, £60k for future CPZ and provision of pedestrian/ cycle crossing facility under the A12, £60,000 to Transport for London to provide improvements to buses and real time information boards within the development, £175k public realm, £3k to pay for tendering of independent Viability Assessment, consultant to provide detail of the second affordable housing contribution up to £20k £95,500 towards skills and training, £90,000 towards improvement of the waterway environment to be undertaken by British Waterways, £19,000 towards health, £2,000 towards reduced car parking. Total = £923k.
Sugar House Lane. S106 signed September 2012.		Aspirational target of 25% jobs for local people and where possible (workplace) advised of jobs and quarterly monitoring. 4000 square metres of community floorspace rented at no more than 7.50 per square foot, 7.00 per square metres.	£8,543 per unit includes actual payments and capacity to offset work in kind against this figure to the value of around £6.5million (work in kind relates to bridges and junctions; park area; water bus and community floor space £70k bus infrastructure payment for Crossrail, £2,390k education contribution, Energy Study to meet carbon dioxide reduction targets, River Lea Tidal Mill Trust £150k, £150k training contribution, £1.2 million TFL contribution, £3,642,640 CIL Mayoral Contribution to Crossrail.

Not yet commenced	68–70 Stratford High Street Permission and S106 signed March 2012	173 units	25% local labour target for construction including 10% apprentices • Ensure loacl businesses benefit directly from commercial opportunities in mixed use development • 731 square metres of commercial space to be let as affordable work space.	• Education contribution 324k • Health 183,611 • 50k public realm • 20k TFL contribution • Waterways contribution • Total 616,311 quates to 7.5k per unit
Planned 2009–2012		900		

Chapter 7
New Migrants to Stratford City

In this final chapter we explore who is moving to Stratford and why they are choosing this area. This is based on primary research undertaken in Stratford with estate agents, developers and people who are either purchasing or renting properties in the new developments along Stratford High Street. The intention was to understand more about the characteristics of people choosing to live in Stratford and their reasons for moving to the area. Initially we had hoped to interview people who had purchased housing in Stratford High Street, however, it very quickly became clear that most people living in the new developments had bought properties with a view to letting them as opposed to living in them. Nevertheless we were able to identify a small numbers of purchasers who had bought properties to live in either for outright sale or shared-ownership and we also included some residents who had chosen to rent in Stratford High Street. Therefore our sample includes both buyers and renters. Whilst this was a small-scale study it was possible to draw some very clear conclusions about the characteristics of people moving into these new development; why they had chosen Stratford and how this fits with wider debates about 'gentrification' and social class change in East London.

The terms 'gentrification' and 'polarisation' are increasingly being applied to East London and Stratford more generally (Brownill 1990; Hamnett 2009; Watt 2013). Ruth Glass pioneered the concept of 'gentrification' in the 1960s in her analysis of neighbourhood change in areas such as Islington and Notting Hill. Here she observed a transformation of what were working-class neighbourhoods into middle-class neighbourhoods and the subsequent displacement of working-class and unskilled groups and in 1973 predicted that 'gentrification' posed a significant risk for the future of working-class communities in Inner London. For Glass 'gentrification' was characterised by physical improvement of the stock, the transfer from private renting to owner-occupation and social class change. This early 'gentrification' was facilitated by the availability of mortgage finance; a growing group of professional workers seeking to live in inner city areas, and the availability of a suitable stock of nineteenth and early-twentieth century houses that could be renovated and improved, with owner occupation a more attractive proposition for landowners as rent control had limited profitability (Glass 1964; Glass 1973). There is also a substantial literature that has debated whether the term 'replacement' is more helpful than 'displacement' for understanding the changing class structure of these neighbourhoods, in other words were working class communities pushed out of these neighbourhoods or where they simply replaced over time. Clearly both are true, with many working class residents opting to leave London to move to the suburbs and new towns.

Simultaneously there were also a number of high profile campaigns around Kings Cross, Docklands, Coin Street and more recently Clays Lane Housing Cooperative and the Carpenters Estate that demonstrate quite clearly resistance to displacement and the desire of many 'working class' families to remain in inner London and as Watt (2013) suggests we should not mistake the changing appearance of class structure with the disappearance of class antagonism. Moreover, whilst only a small number may have been directly displaced through eviction and decanting a process of indirect displacement occurred whereby working class residents were simply priced out of those areas, through a mix of rising house prices and the declining availability of public housing. Moreover, in response to 'gentrification', Housing Associations such as The Notting Hill Housing Trust played an active role in purchasing properties in areas such as Notting Hill and converting them into low-cost, high-quality housing in response to the poor housing conditions and as a way of ensuring that working-class residents had a future in these areas.

There is not time to explore in detail the literature on 'gentrification', however, there are a number of key themes that have shaped the approach adopted in this research. One theme that runs through the literature focuses on 'gentrification' from a consumption perspective exploring the cultural practices and drivers of the 'gentrifiers' themselves. Initial assumptions were that 'gentrification' would have a positive impact on what were perceived as disadvantaged areas. However, there is an increasing recognition that there is considerable diversity amongst the 'gentrifiers' themselves and that the process itself is dynamic and has changed over time. For example, Lees and Butler (2006) distinguish between the more progressive values of early gentrifiers who sent their children to local schools, integrated into the local community and rejected traditional suburban values of domesticity with the growth of 'super gentrifiers' who are more wealthy, more likely to socialise with people like themselves, opt for private education and hold 'suburban' as compared to 'urban values' on attitudes related to gender and work, with many of the mothers giving up work to stay at home (Lees, Butler 2006). They argue that the 'early gentrifiers' who moved into areas such as Notting Hill and Islington have been replaced by 'super gentrifiers', who are distinct from 'early gentrifiers' in terms of wealth and attitude to neighbourhood. Moreover, Butler and Robson (2008) have suggested that far from integrating with local communities, 'gentrifiers' tend to live separate lives, using the metaphor of 'tectonic plates' to describe ways in which they are spatially adjacent and socially separate (Butler, Robson 2008).

Most relevant to Stratford High Street is Butler's work on incomers in Docklands, as there is some evidence that Stratford High Street is soaking up an overspill of demand from the Docklands. He argues that Docklands has been identified as a classic case of 'gentrification'. However, he observed clear distinctions between the docklands 'gentrifiers' and those in other areas with the Docklands 'gentrifiers' having more in common with those who had previously opted for suburban living. He argued that they were not interested in the provision of services or social interaction with their neighbours; their housing served as an urban dormitory located close enough to work to avoid being late and return to sleep; and they sought a type of security and safeness normally associated with suburban living and concluded that these aspirations echo that of the classic 'suburbaniser' (Butler 2006).

There is now a substantial international literature on 'gentrification' where it is argued that it is a feature of a number of major/world cities that have undergone a process of industrial restructuring reflected in a shift from manufacturing to financial and business services, a significant growth in the number of professional workers and a decline in traditional working-class employment. Nevertheless the decline in traditional working-class employment has been replaced in part by other forms of low-skill employment (Hamnett 2003). There has also been a substantial shift in the nature of what constitutes 'gentrified' housing. The supply of period houses for family occupation was limited and by the 1980s had shifted to the conversion of period houses into flats followed by warehouse and factory conversions, along with the wider transformation of places such as London Docklands. Boddy and Lambert have suggested that applying the term 'gentrification' to all of these forms of development is effectively stretching the term beyond any usefulness and it is more helpful to use the concept 'residentialisation' where space is converted for housing purposes. Hamnett has also suggested that 're-urbanisation' may be more applicable where development takes place on derelict land or former Brownfield sites (Boddy and Lambert 2002; Hamnett 2003). Nevertheless, its usefulness or value is in helping us to understand the replacement/displacement of lower income groups from a range of areas and their replacement with higher income groups as part of a process of social class change and the reordering of cities.

Hamnett argues that one of the most marked changes in London is for 'gentrification' to have changed the social geography of London. In the 1960s much of London was dominated by the working-class and over time a process of middle-class colonisation has occurred, spilling out into more and more areas including parts of Haringey, Hackney, Docklands and parts of the East End closest to the city. He argues that whilst the East End remained predominantly working-class the trend towards 'gentrification' is also evident as a process of 'spatially displaced demand' reflecting the lack of affordability in some areas that has pushed purchasers further afield. He concluded that whilst areas in East London such as Waltham Forest and Newham continue to be relatively cheap, they have experienced the greatest percentage increases since 1995 and he suggests that this does not relate to specific factors within East London but is a result of London's position as the centre of financial capital in Europe which in turn has created a crisis in affordability that has trickled out across the whole of London and created sub markets reflecting 'income constrained' 'gentrification' (Hamnett 2009). We can see than that over time 'gentrification' has spread across inner London and has made it more problematic for low paid and indeed middle income workers wishing to live in inner London or indeed its surrounding areas. The London labour force continues to comprise a substantial proportion of low skill, service sector type jobs with an estimated 16 per cent of London's population earning below the London Living Wage coupled with substantial numbers who are unemployed or economically inactive, and whilst rising house prices have impacted on all groups it is the ability of these groups to continue to live in London that is now in question (Hamnett 2003; New Policy Institute 2012).

There has also been a debate within the 'gentrification' literature about drivers of 'gentrification'. Initial explanations tended to point to the changed preferences of middle-class, professional university graduates who had rejected suburbia and traditional gender roles; whilst others have focussed on the role of capital. For example Smith argues that the process of 'gentrification' was triggered by capital in response to a 'rent-gap' thesis in terms of profitability which was addressed by converting homes from private rental to owner occupation and Watt has applied the 'rent-gap' thesis to public housing in London where public/subsidised housing is located on high value land such as is the case at the Carpenters Estate (Watt 2013). Others have explored the role more generally of 'capital' in promoting a form of property led regeneration aimed at the middle classes in areas such as Docklands. More recently the focus has shifted to the role of the state in promoting socially mixed neighbourhoods or revitalisation/urban renaissance of cities linked to property led regeneration with an implicitly 'gentrifying' agenda (Smith 1987; Slater 2006).

The regeneration of Stratford High Street has not involved any direct displacement and is characteristic of what we might describe 're-urbanisation' or 'residentialisation' as housing has been developed in the main on former industrial sites. As we have also seen in the previous chapter the wider policy context has shaped the mix of schemes with a clear shift away from on site affordable housing on more recently approved schemes. The schemes vary in quality, scale and proportions of market and social rented housing. Up until 2002 the High Street was a classic case of disinvestment with lots of disused premises and a sense of decline, overtime it has been transformed into an emerging high density residential district:

> Before 2005 there wasn't too much on the high street ... warehouses, industrial and quite a few derelict buildings ... but since we won the bid it's totally transformed with new high rise blocks, hotels and cafes. (Estate Agent)

> They have spent a lot of money now. In years gone by when we have been working here local residents were up in arms about the state of Stratford ... Then as time went by we saw the area was being cleaned up. For example, there was a small piece of graffiti we were trying to get rid of for years. Two days before the Olympic bid was decided they came in and said we will clean that up for you. We have had vast improvements to the walkways and roads, public art and then there is all the regeneration stuff going on at the Olympic Park. (Estate Agent)

Moving to Stratford High Street

As we have seen in the previous chapter, Stratford has a differentiated tenure system offering housing for social rent, shared ownership, intermediate rent and outright sale. The move for social renters and purchasers to Stratford High Street was often at the end of a considerable wait, for example:

> I lived for ten years at a number of different places in temporary accommodation, Plaistow, East Ham, Canning Town. My last housing was bed and breakfast where I lived for three months. I was making bidding every week, bidding, bidding (through choice based lettings) the occupational therapist and the physiotherapist they told me to bid for this property. (Social Renter)

> I lived with my parents for ten years while I was saving a deposit. I was looking for a property for about eighteen months ... I looked at so many properties over a period of years, I looked at around ten properties in one day. (Owner Occupier)

Why Were People Choosing Stratford

There were four main reasons why people were choosing Stratford High Street. A key driver for purchasers was the sense that Stratford would be the next place to experience a sufficient uplift in value and potential capital gains that might accrue. Affordability was also significant both for private renters and purchasers in terms of value for money and access, with Stratford effectively operating as a more affordable overspill from Bow and Canary Wharf, outstanding connectivity in terms of transport links and the wider benefits of living in an area undergoing substantial regeneration and new facilities such as Westfield and the Olympic Park and most residents cited all of these as significant in choosing to move to the area. London 2012 and the associated infrastructure investments provided confidence in the area and the anticipated long term benefits were also a factor.

The potential capital gains of a regenerated Stratford were a strong driver and as we have already observed much of this demand has translated into a buy-to-let rather than buy-to-live market, however, those choosing to buy were clearly anticipating significant capital gains:

> We wanted to go for an area that had the biggest chance to improve over the next few years, as a good investment. We made a decision really quickly. Stratford was the best place we thought. (Owner Occupier)

> I bought my flat to live in, but in the long term I think it is a good investment. (Owner Occupier)

> It is kind of like Islington in the process ... its moving towards that and Islington is a lovely area and everybody would love to live there ... I did a lot of research. (Owner Occupier)

The potential capital gains had also been attracting a large number of buy to let investors:

> Around 50 per cent of our inquiries are for buy to let investors, some from overseas and they are mainly looking for new build. (Estate Agent)

However, there was also sense that perhaps there had been over provision of housing for sale and that the anticipated capital gains were not materialising:

> Lots of developers had to sell it at a knock down price, they were originally going to sell it for extortionate prices, but there are not enough buyers out there. In terms of valuation it is slightly lower than they thought it would be.

> I think a lot of people thought that the prices would drastically increase and a lot of the people decided to buy in Stratford for a good investment. I think it's those people that tend now to sell as we approach the Olympics and they think it's coming to the end of their investment series where they can maybe cash in and get a little bit more than they originally paid for these properties. (Estate agent, Stratford)

The substantial amount of new housing for sale linked both to the Olympic Park and in places such as Stratford High Street have as we have seen in previous chapters created concern about over supply and its impact on the value of housing. This perceived oversupply was evident in the decision of one RSL to privately rent a block of flats scheduled for market sale and another block of new apartments along Stratford High Street remains empty with only security guards in residence, possibly with the intention of selling them when the market improves.

Transport connectivity was a key dimension in London winning the bid and has improved dramatically since that time. Transport has made Stratford an attractive location and this has clearly been strengthened by the wider improvements to the area. Estate Agents and Interviewees universally expressed the benefits of transport as a key selling point both for renters and purchasers:

> Most want to be near transport links. They say I want to be as close to the station as possible. Property that comes available rents out within two weeks. Transport connections are more important than the Olympics in acting as a draw to the area. (Estate Agent)

> We have noticed a lot of young people moving in and finding that Stratford is not as far east as they think. It is just three stops from Liverpool Street on the Central

> Line and has great transport links. We have a lot of people who are working in the centre and thought I can move a few stops east and save quite a bit of money. (Estate Agent)

> We were looking for anywhere on the Central Line. I liked Stratford because of the DLR which takes me directly to Canary Wharf. (Private Renter)

For three of the sample the location was suitable as it not only enabled access to work but the inter-city services made it easy to visit family:

> The location is ideal, I work in Liverpool Street, and my parents live in Suffolk, so it is easy to jump on the train and visit them or get into work. (Owner Occupier)

There was also evidence of what Hamnett refers to as 'spatially displaced demand' with Stratford perceived as more affordable and offering better value for money both for owner occupiers and private renters:

> The area is attracting residents that may previously have gone to Canary Wharf, it is cheaper and transport links are the best. People pay much less for larger properties. (Estate Agent)

> I have a lot of people coming from Bow ... it's cheaper, they don't want to live in Stratford but they move here because it is on the Central Line. (Estate Agent)

> I spent months visiting places in Bow but they were all really expensive. I fell in love with one but the car parking space alone was £30k ... I had looked at five properties in Bow and I was driving back up to Ilford. As I was driving along I thought Blimey there are a lot of improvements here ... I started looking and I thought it has potential and you get much more for your money.

> East London was cheaper, I would have liked to live in South London but there wasn't much going in shared ownership ... It was a good area close to the station it was all up and coming ... It had a lot of newly developed flats we are hoping the area is going to go up. (Owner Occupier)

> We originally moved to Limehouse ... The rent was about £1350 pcm and that became just too much for the space. So, that's why we moved to Stratford. We got a much nicer apartment for less money. (Private Renter)

Clearly Stratford has undergone significant transformation with the opening of Westfield; improved transport links and the construction of the Olympic Park and the sense that this was an area that would be significantly improved was clearly a pull factor for those buying in the area with a sense of optimism about how the area might change:

> One of the key factors for choosing Stratford was the urban regeneration strategies, once the Olympic Park is up and running property prices will go through the roof I remember Stratford when it was not a very nice place to live, but there are lots of improvements here now ... I go for fantastic walks on the canal or do my shopping at Westfield, there are new restaurants opening up on the high street. (Owner Occupier)

> I knew it wasn't awful I didn't think it was the best area either, I thought it was a bit dull to be honest, I thought it will probably get more interesting. I am also interested in watching the regeneration. (Owner Occupier)

> We had the transport links. Now we have the shopping and social facilities and this has made the area grow in popularity. It is so popular it is just so busy. (Estate Agent)

> We have lots of corporates picking Stratford because it is much more than just a residential area, it has Westfield, Restaurants etc. There is more life here. (Estate Agent)

Who is Moving to Stratford

We were interested to explore the characteristics of those moving to Stratford in comparison with the existing population of Stratford. Prior to the construction of the new housing developments along Stratford High Street, the area comprised a mix of industrial and residential uses. The residential housing was in the main social housing constructed by the London Borough of Newham and included the Carpenters Estate to the North of Stratford High Street and two towers and low rise flats to the south of the High Street.

Whilst a proportion of the new units along Stratford High Street have been allocated for social rent, we would suggest that those people moving to Stratford High Street as either owner occupiers; private renters or buying through shared ownership are distinctive from those already living there.

Estate agents and those selling units directly on Stratford High Street were keen to stress the diverse nature of people looking for housing either in Stratford or specifically on the High Street, evenly balanced between those wishing to purchase as investors and those wishing to purchase or rent to live in:

> You have all different types of people, buy to let landlords, Chinese investors, we get every creed and colour coming into the office. (Estate Agent)

On further analysis it was clear that the profile of residents interested in living in the area tended to be young professionals from a range of ethnic groups, who were in the main childless. The 'new migrants' we interviewed were all graduates and some had post graduate qualifications. They worked in a range of jobs such as social media; finance, law; urban planning and healthcare and were from a range of ethnic groups:

> The majority are professionals some working in the city and others in a range of professions. (Estate Agent)

> It depends what time of year ... We have professionals and then we get a lot of students from Queen Mary and UEL in September. (Estate Agent)

Estate Agents confirmed that very few residents moving into Stratford High Street were on housing benefit as the housing benefit restrictions meant that they would need to pay a substantial top up. There was also a complete absence of what we might describe as the White working class, with this group leaving Stratford over time:

> A lot of the Eastenders had already gone. They have been moving out for the last twenty years, there are very few of them left to be honest with you. We have offices in Essex, we work with them to find somewhere out there in places like Rainham, Dagenham, Braintree, and Chelmsford.

> I think that we have seen white, working-class moving further away and commute into London now for work.

The other group that was in the main missing from those moving to the area were families with children, explained in terms of a lack of good schools:

> We get some families but as they go to secondary school they tend to leave the area ... They want to move to places like Redbridge where they have better prospects. (Estate Agent)

> When I was in Hackney you used to get people asking for a catchment for a particular school. You don't get that here. (Estate Agent)

In the main there was a consensus that it was relatively rare for families to come to Stratford.

As we have described in the previous chapter 'affordable housing' included a mix of social rent, shared ownership and intermediate rent and sale products. For those on low incomes there are significant barriers to accessing 'affordable housing' through shared ownership and intermediate rent options and therefore, residents moving into this type of housing were often young professional workers taking their first steps onto the housing ladder. One sales representative described the target market and screening process for an Intermediate market rental unit illustrating the increasing barriers to affordable housing for those on low incomes and a trend to subsidise workers on higher incomes:

> If you are living with family and friends you get higher priority over someone who is private renting, if you are a teacher or nurse you get higher priority, if you are Ministry of Defence or on a council waiting list that really ups your chances. We assess their bank account for the last three months, their loans and bits and pieces they might have. We will speak with their employer and assess their last three months bank statements. For a two bed you have to be earning around £39k and not in excess of £62k. These units have a massive uptake we have no problem shifting our intermediate rent units ... we have provided housing for retail workers and chefs at Westfield. (Registered Social Landlord Sales Agent)

We were interested in finding out whether residents living in Stratford High Street felt that they were similar to people living in their blocks and similar to people living in Stratford more generally. There was a general consensus that whilst there were some social renters in the blocks, residents in the block were more like them in terms of being young professional workers and less like people living in Stratford. For example:

> The people living in the block are more like me, but we are very different from the people already living in Stratford.

Staying in Stratford

We were interested in exploring how long residents moving to Stratford High Street planned to stay and it was clear that for the majority it was a stepping stone and a foot on the housing ladder with most planning to move on quite quickly. Some expressed concern about bringing up a family in Stratford:

> I don't imagine that the people buying here are going to stay here for very long, they are young professionals who see this as a stepping stone. (Estate Agent)

> We are hoping to be here a couple of years and then move out of London, if we start a family ... At the moment we definitely wouldn't consider bringing up a child in Stratford or even in London ... we would prefer to go outside of London. (Owner Occupier)

> I would like a garden and a bigger property, I don't think we could afford that here so we would move further out. I don't think I would want to have kids here. People from work that have kids say that some of the London councils because they have more issues to deal with and they have a lot less money for education and child care that kind of thing. Whereas, if you go further out, there's a lot more money available in the council. (Private Renter)

> We are thinking of moving out of London. I would like to be able to afford a big house at least five bedrooms, a big garden ... we might move to Sittingbourne for that. It is not very cheap to get that in London. We might rent the flat out we will see how it goes. (Owner Occupier)

> My impression is that is great for singles if you have a job in the city, but if you were thinking about kids and settling down you would want to move out of Stratford. (Private Renter)

One interviewee felt that they would wait and see how the area changed and another was willing to consider more family friendly parts of Stratford:

> This is a stepping stone for me. I would think about staying in Stratford but maybe not on a main road if I had a family I would have to find out more about local schools. (Owner Occupier)

Overall then despite the policy aim of reducing population churn through the construction of market housing as a way of making Stratford a more attractive place to live there was a sense that these new migrants would in the main have all moved on within five years possibly adding to the supply of private rental property. Therefore it is likely that the High Street will be a relatively transient place, ironically those who have longstanding connections to the area in places such as Carpenters Estate and a desire to stay in Stratford may be being moved on.

'Space', 'Place' and 'Neighbourhood'

We were interested in exploring connections with space, place and neighbourhood. Stratford is increasingly a place of two halves. A new Stratford with parkland, Westfield shopping centre and lots of new apartments and an old Stratford characterised by the old shopping Centre; disinvested Local Authority run housing and deprivation.

What became very clear was that residents in the main tended to locate themselves spatially in a new Stratford distinctive from the old Stratford, visiting places such as Westfield to shop and spend leisure time or simply connecting to more desirable parts by boarding a train. A small minority indicated that they may sometimes visit the old centre to access bargains but that in the main they used Westfield:

> I try to stay in the new part of Stratford for example when I am walking to the station I walk next to Olympic Park, I very rarely go to the old parts, sometimes I go to the old parts for value, I mainly go to Westfield to go out shopping. (Owner Occupier)

> When I think of myself in Stratford I just think about me in my flat and Westfield. Those are the only two things that I really use in Stratford. If I fancy going for a walk, it wouldn't be a walk around Stratford. (Owner Occupier)

> We tend to shop in Westfield but walk through the old Stratford Centre to get there. (Owner Occupier)

One interviewee explained that whilst they do make use of Westfield for shopping they felt it was too crowded for socialising and would prefer to socialise outside of Stratford:

> Today, I went to the old Stratford Centre, but I mainly use Westfield. The good thing is there are a lot of people I know moving here. But there aren't any places for you to kind of go drinking, or do social things. Once you get to Westfield, it's absolutely packed ... I tend to go out drinking where I work in Liverpool Street. (Private Renter)

> The people that are coming to look round they are not looking to socialise in Stratford. They will commute ... We have all the shops they need but if they want to go out they will head in the centre of London. I get a sense they wouldn't socialise or go to bars in the older part of Town. (Estate Agent)

A small minority were using other parts of Stratford associated with regeneration:

> I like the Greenway, I like the travel route north and south. There is a new Moroccan/ Lebanese place open on the high Street, I go there with friends. I go to Westfield in my personal time.

> When my friends come over we go out for fantastic walks along the canal. When I lived in Essex we just used to stay at home when people visited but now there is so much to do.

Use of Local Services

In the main those interviewed were young professionals and they tended not to make use of local health services and in the main had not registered with a local GP. In two instances this was explained in terms of concerns about quality:

> I have to confess I kept my GP with my parent, this might be an erroneous prejudice but I think they would be less stretched than here, the second reason is that I have been with that practice for years and I didn't want to leave. (Owner Occupier)

> We didn't sign up for the doctor here because the hours were awful. Whereas our old doctor had pretty good hours and Saturday appointments, stuff like that. So, we just haven't told them. It's just easier not changing over. (Private Renter)

Interaction with Neighbours

We were interested to understand more about relationships with neighbours. Residents tended to report minimal but positive contact with neighbours in their block and more than one indicated under occupancy of the block:

> I've been here three months, I haven't got to know my neighbours. I have seen people in the corridor a couple of times ... you tend to come home and shut the door to the world and not have much interaction. (Owner Occupier)

> I see people getting in and out of the lift. People are polite. Everyone seems to work long hours. The block seems half empty. (Private Renter)

> We send cards at Christmas and my neighbour has my key, but we don't go round and have cups of tea. (Owner Occupier)

> The people in this building are perfectly friendly. It's definitely not an unfriendly area. But there is an aura of professional disinterest. It is an element of city life, people just ignore each other's existence. (Private Renter)

> I have to say I was disappointed to find that I was one of only a few people that had bought a home to live in, I would like to set up some kind of residents' association but people don't seem interested. (Owner Occupier)

The buildings all included shared gardens as a way of offsetting high density buildings. However, the use of these areas seemed to vary from building to building. One of the blocks had invested in a strategy to promote the use of the communal garden including child free times.

> I have made a lot of friends here with older ladies, We go and sit in the communal gardens ... The garden is very safe because it is upstairs and I am not scared my daughter is going to go anywhere. (Social Renter)

Whereas in another recently completed block we observed an outdoor communal area that clearly met planning requirements but did nothing to ensure the area was utilised. There was no seating and some plants fading after only six months of occupation:

> I think I've only been out there once and I didn't meet any one. I've never seen anybody out there. That's the shared area. I imagine, if it was all grass and maybe had a barbecue pit and stuff people would use it. The one thing that I thought of that could really change that is roof tops. In New York, which you would imagine would be quite unfriendly and similar, it's not, because there's shared areas. (Private Renter)

The schemes in which we undertook interviews would all be categorised as 'mixed communities' schemes as they comprised a mix of affordable and market housing. However, there was often segregation between those purchasing market housing; those social renting and those purchasing shared ownership with some arguing for a need to separate such group and others recognising that sound management is the key to successfully integrated 'mixed communities':

> Throughout our schemes it is a running issue that people aren't as tidy in the social rent and from our point of view it is much easier to have corridors and lobbies separate. There can be vandalism and noise pollution we find that someone who buys a property with their own money tends to respect it. Sounds harsh. That is the way it is. People do have worries about social renters and we make residents aware that there will be social renters. (Sales Agent, Registered Social Landlord)

On the other hand:

> We try to do everything tenure blind to be honest, but we tend to cluster six or eight units together. There was a time when people were concerned about the impact on sales. I think so long as the units are well managed. I think house purchasers are accepting it in a way they wouldn't have ten years ago. (Private Developer)

> A few weeks ago I visited an estate in West London. We went in there and I had never been there before. Half of the estate was pristine-clean, with tables and chairs on the balcony, the other half had pushchairs and stuff like that. I said to my colleague look 'social housing' bit there and he said no, They are the buy to lets, that is our block there (Points to pristine part) it's well managed. (Manager, Registered Social Landlord)

One shared ownership purchaser expressed concern at the way in which residents in social rent were presented as a problem:

> The only think I don't like about this block is that it feels like a bit of an apartheid, because we have a separate entrance and a separate lift and the social renters have a different door. There was some remark about how that was designed so we almost wouldn't have to see them, I found that slightly odd, I would rather

be integrated, it felt like we were looking down on them. I didn't like that but I didn't design it.

Overall then whilst these schemes reflect a commitment to 'mixed neighbourhoods' beneath the surface they reveal the ways in which social divisions are reinforced rather than offset in the design of new developments, moreover, whilst social renters dominated the old Stratford they are effectively marginalised in the new Stratford.

The Carpenters Estate – Perspectives of 'New Migrants'

Towards the end of our research it was confirmed that residents would be decanted from the Carpenters Estate. We were interested to explore the views of new migrants to this as it provided an insight into their knowledge of the area and engagement with existing residents and local issues. However, not all interviewees were asked their views on this as some of the interviews took place prior to this decision being made. There was a mixed response ranging from not knowing anything about it through to indifference and a sense that perhaps it was fair as they lived in social housing and did not pay any rent.

> I didn't know about that. Do they pay rent? It seems unfair that they have to move when the area is starting to improve, but then again if they are in social housing. (Private Renter)

> I've seen signs about that. I don't have a particular problem with stuff being knocked down. But if they're knocking things down, and those people don't have anywhere to live within effectively like a five-minute walk where they're living now, so they have to change their whole lives, that's different ... There are two different questions to me. One is relocating people. Then again, it's a council estate does that mean that it's all people who are not necessarily paying for it. (Private Renter)

> Well I think the UCL campus is a great idea for the area and let's face it they won't be homeless. (Owner Occupier)

One new migrant was supportive.

> I don't know that much about it, what I hear I don't like, I walked around the Carpenters Estate and I really liked it, it reminds me of where I come from in Essex. It has that post war design that I really rate and I don't understand why there is so much talk about how it is a failed estate, I am not really happy about it.

Clearly then there were mixed views with an assumption that perhaps it was acceptable as those moving may be on benefits and lived in social housing and this highlights the resurgence of notions of the 'undeserving poor'.

Housing Conditions

Stratford High Street comprises a number of tower blocks owned by a mix of Registered Social Landlords and Private Developers. They were all relatively new properties and all of the 'new migrants' interviewed were the first occupants of their apartments. There was a consensus that the move to Stratford High Street had led to an improvement in housing conditions:

> It's easy for me I have a lift inside so I don't have to carry my daughter up the stairs. In temporary accommodation I was carrying her upstairs and downstairs. It is really nice. My family are much happier. (Social Renter)

> It has a nice feel it feels a really comfortable place without issues, such as drainage, or being old, dirty or grimy it feels new and nice. (Owner Occupier)

> It feels like it is done to quite a high standard, it has good views, it is a good place to entertain. I have a balcony, it feels fresh and new. (Owner Occupier)

However, whilst satisfied with their new housing there were concerns about housing management and it was clear that the approaches to housing management varied greatly in these schemes ranging from exemplary to poor. Each scheme had its own approach to housing management: two schemes developed relatively early on by a Private developer included on site concierge and maintenance of these blocks appeared to be of a high standard. The largest scheme on the High Street had invested heavily in housing management and maintenance:

> We have an awful lot of glass which needs cleaning. We could have asked the residents to clean that but in practice we have some very short residents and people in wheelchairs, so we thought right we will do the window cleaning for a reasonable cost and put it in the service charge ... We put blinds in every single property to make it tenure blind and it looks much better than having all different types of things up at the window. We have a 24 hour concierge and an on-site maintenance person so that jobs can normally get done the same day ... We have our own cleaner that we pay the London Living Wage so nothing is sub contracted and we have control and can ensure residents aren't passed from one person to another if they have a concern. We can do this because it is a large scheme and we have economies of scale. (Manager, Registered Social Landlord)

However, along the road from here it was clear that maintenance has not been taken as seriously, with a limited management presence and a significant number of individual buy to let investors:

> The owners are basically partial douche bags, they haven't been that responsive to the community. The building is numbers on a spread sheet to make money there is no investment. They have put bike sheds in and they are great but they have not got any long term care strategy of any kind. They haven't invested a huge amount of money in the peripherals. That door over there fell off because of the wind. All of our windows the latches have come loose they have not put a huge amount of money into the finish. The service level is not good. Luckily I don't pay the service charge but I imagine it is worked into my rent. As far as getting things done it is pretty appalling. (Private Renter)

We observed a handwritten notice on the notice board from one of the residents giving an update on the problems that had been widely reported to us about the Combined Heating and Power system. However, what was noticeable in its absence was any formal response from the Registered Social Landlord that owned the building. Over the road at another block we encountered a similar issue, this time in a block built by a private developer:

> I fought my arse off basically just about getting them to not charge us for it. So, we don't get charged it at all because I said it's ridiculous (referring to heating system). There is no kind of power in this building. Our letting agency passes everything off to the developers, then we speak to them they say it is not us, it's not our fault.
>
> I think that's one of the biggest obstacles to developing a professional private rented market is individual buy to let landlords. Because if they are going into a block, and they are buying up, one-two-three-four units, whatever it is, immediately you've broken up that block and therefore you can't provide a uniform service. More and more people are having to go into the private sector or choosing to rent. And what we want to do is we want to actually distinguish ourselves from others in the market place. So we are developing a letting service. We will offer people a five year lease, which would normally happen in the private sector. It's a 24-hour service. There's a named property manager. It's an ethical landlord. That's how we want to distinguish ourselves. (Manager, Registered Social Landlord)

It will be important to address the ongoing maintenance issues to avoid parts of the High Street becoming quite run down in a relatively short period of time. More generally there is a feeling that Stratford High Street has evolved in an unplanned fragmented way and that there was a need for greater attention to be played to place making. This is evident in the range of vacant premises that sit beneath many of these buildings along Stratford High Street, included as a way of getting planning permission and then left vacant as there is little incentive to lease them:

> Stratford High Street is littered with flats in front of shops. And there are two problems with that. One is that if housing developers and RSLs have no interest in what happens on the ground floor, in any commercial activity, all they are interested in is housing numbers and margins. They put boards up and walk away and leave shops empty for years. They don't care if there are voids on the ground floors. What we want now is for schemes that put the lights on the ground floor before anything else happens. You can't let anything until you've occupied the ground floor. If that means letting it to somebody for free, then that's what you do. Having activity on the ground floor is crucial, commercial activity sheds light on the street. I think affordable workspaces are almost as important as affordable housing. (Local Councillor)

There is increasing activity on the high street and new residents were clearly encouraged by the opening up of a new restaurant and hoped for more activity. However, as one estate agent warned:

> I am excited to see what happens on the ground floor of all of those developments. At the moment there is not a lot happening. There are lots of empty units, and I think they hold the key, if you had coffee shops/restaurants, it could be not quite Manhattan but it depends on the retailers. If you have cash and carry and betting shops that could ruin the high street. The quality and type of thing that goes in holds the key. (Estate Agent)

Ironically both of these uses now have a presence on Stratford High Street and it felt that this strange relationship between market and state with regard to planning needs to be more effectively aligned to ensure successful place making.

Will Stratford Become Gentrified?

Finally then there is the question of how this area might develop – will Stratford develop in two halves, the old Stratford marked out by its disadvantage and a new Stratford home to a growing group of middle class professionals who have bought into a particular version of Stratford? Will the 'gentrification' evident in Bow trickle down to Stratford? There was clearly a sense that the area would change with an increase in the number of professional workers:

> One of the slight oddities of Newham I suppose, as opposed to Islington or Hackney, is that deprivation tends to be evenly spread across the borough where in Islington or Hackney you have lots of posh bits and lots of not so posh bits ...

> Within Newham, I expect some areas will be richer than others. There will be different economic patterns across the borough. The docklands parts of Newham were previously the poorest now they have some people earning in excess of 100k per year. I think that's probably a good thing and it doesn't worry me. In Stratford, a block of flats is being built by a designer which will be remarkable and they will be very expensive and that's fine! I don't mind. I mean they are bringing their buying power to the area, etc, and they are changing how the area is perceived and making it more economically viable for other businesses to come. I don't mind at all. (Local Councillor)

There was also a sense that it would be important to attract more middle-class workers whilst not pushing out the poor:

> I think people from different classes have a right to live anywhere. However, what you want as a property owner is a concern that your property prices increase so you want people who are going to care about the area. People in social housing don't care as much for their property. It is not politically correct thing to say but if there are more middle class people in Newham that is not a bad thing. I want more middle class people to live here but I want a mix it would not be fair if the poor people were pushed out as the area improved. There should be people on social housing living here as well, to push them out would be a real mistake. (Owner Occupier)

> I think it might become gentrified I don't think it is automatic in the way people suggest you can only have so much gentrification. I appreciate places like Bethnal Green and Stoke Newington have become gentrified and there may be parts of the developments around the Olympic park that might be gentrified. However, there is a hell of lot of poverty in London and that is not about to be addressed and people have to live somewhere. (Owner Occupier)

> I know that part of the original plan was that there would be affordable housing, so there will be a mix but I do think it will become more comparable with places like Docklands. (Estate Agent)

One respondent suggested that Stratford lacked the necessary intrinsic qualities for successful 'gentrification':

> It won't become cool. At best it will become young professional. It will be like your Jersey City in New York. It won't be the cool, hipster place to be because it's too far out and it's going to be too new and modern. But I think it will definitely attract lots of young professionals. (Private Renter)

Conclusion

This study demonstrated that Stratford is now attracting a growing number of professional workers, with much of this a reflection of what Hamnett might refer to as 'spatially displaced demand'. There is clearly evidence of a process of social class change in the area. As we can see planning policy has had a protective effect in that it has ensured a presence of social renters in many of these new developments. However, the changed policy climate means that overtime this presence will diminish and another area that has typically housed working class residents will become the reserve of the better off. As this is a re-urbanised area there is no evidence of direct displacement though this is likely to be indirect through the price mechanism and supported through a changed housing benefit system. The new migrants tended to interact very little with their neighbours or neighbourhood and associated themselves with the new rather than old Stratford. There was little sense that their presence made a contribution to the area and for most it was just a brief stepping stone. More generally there had been a lack of place making and whilst there was a sense in which this area would be gentrified the possibility that parts of the high street might constitute the slum housing of the future was also a potential risk and limit to 'gentrification'. Stratford is clearly changing and there is a sense that low income groups are moving from being the 'dominant' group to being the tolerated group.

The real question is that given this part of Stratford was unoccupied and given that this new housing is clearly meeting a housing need does it matter? It is suggested that it does matter because both housing and land are in short supply in London and this is an area that has traditionally housed lower income groups and has the potential to continue to do so. However, every time a new development is built with limited potential to house low income groups it results in a redistribution of scarce land and in the process threatens the existence of such groups in the area, moreover, there is a domino effect with activity in one scheme shaping what happens on the next. Slater has argued gentrification is embedded in a process of class struggle, however, what is noticeably absent in Stratford (notwithstanding the Carpenters Residents) is a voice/movement that is arguing against this process of area change, as Slater has argued the language has shifted from 'gentrification' to regeneration, renaissance, revitalisation and in the process has obscured the underlying class conflict at its heart.

References

Boddy, M. and Lambert, N. (2007). *International Journal of Urban and Regional Research*, 31(4): 759–81, December.

Butler, T. and Lees, L. (2006). Super-'gentrification' in Barnsbury, London: globalisation and gentrifying elites at the neighbourhood level. *Transactions of the Institute of British Geographers* NS31: 467–87.

Butler, T. (2007). Re-urbanizing London Docklands: 'gentrification', Suburbanization or New Urbanism? *International Journal of Urban and Regional Research*, 31(4): 759–81.

Butler, T. and Robson, G. (2008). Social Capital, Gentrification and Neighbourhood Change in London: A Comparison of Three South London Neighbourhoods, *International Journal of Social Research Methodology* 11(2): 141–9.

Glass, R. (1964). *Introduction to London: Aspects of Change*. Centre for Urban Studies, London. Reprinted in Glass, R. (1989) *Cliches of Urban Doom* (Oxford: Blackwell), pp. 132–58.

Glass, R. (1973). The mood of London, in *London: Urban Patterns, Problems and Policies,* edited by Donnison, D and Eversley, D. (London: Heinemann). Reprinted in Glass, R. (1989) *Cliches of Urban Doom* (Oxford: Blackwell), pp. 159–83.

Hamnett, C. (2003). 'Gentrification' and the Middle-class Remaking of Inner London, 1961–2001, *Urban Studies*, 40, (12): 2401–26.

Hammett, C. (2009). Spatially displaced demand and the changing geography of house prices in London 1995–2006, *Housing Studies*, 24(3): 301–20.

Ley, D. (1996). *The New Middle Class and the Remaking of the Central City*. (Oxford: Oxford University Press).

Marcuse, P. (1985). 'Gentrification', abandonment and displacement: connections, causes and policy responses in New York City. *Journal of Urban and Contemporary Law* 28: 195–240.

National Policy Institute. (2011). *Low Pay over time* <http://www.londonspovertyprofile.org.uk/indicators/topics/low-pay/low-pay-over-time/>.

Raco, M. and Imrie, R. (2003). *Urban Renaissance? New Labour, Community and Urban Policy* (Policy Press: Bristol).

Slater, T. (2006). The eviction of critical perspectives from gentrification research, *International Journal of Urban and Regional Research*, 30: 737–57.

Smith, N. (1987). Gentrification' and the rent-gap, *Annals of the Association of American Geographers,* 77(3): 462–5.

Tonkiss, F. (2005). *Space, the City and Social Theory* (Cambridge: Polity Press).

Watt, P. (2013). It's not for us: Regeneration, the 2012 Olympics and the Gentrification of East London, *City*, 17(1):99–118.

Conclusion
Imagining the Housing Futures of London 2012

In July 2012 as we watched the Olympic ceremony unfold on our television screens I was, like many others, captivated by the opening ceremony that portrayed a sense of Britishness that had at its heart inclusion and social justice; that celebrated multiculturalism and working class history and highlighted the success rather than failure of a key British institution, (the NHS) that symbolises the concept of social citizenship and equality. The opening ceremony managed to balance the future with the past looking forward as well as back and its attention to detail and technical brilliance demonstrated the possibility simultaneously of innovation, excellence and inclusion. The ceremony reflected and embraced those initial commitments to legacy central to London winning the Games. Moreover, it generated an Olympic and Paralympic fever, with sell-out venues for both the Olympic and Paralympic Games which again demonstrated widespread support for the type of inclusion that had made our bid compelling when presented in Singapore. The closing ceremony of the Olympic Games was, on the other hand, a more lacklustre albeit technologically competent event built on a notion of a past Britain and reinforcing hierarchy through its reliance on celebrity, and noteworthy for its lack of images that promoted inclusion and multiculturalism. These two ceremonies serve as a useful metaphor for the former reflecting those initial housing legacy intentions and the latter embracing the now more likely outcomes.

As was stated in the introduction this project set out to interrogate housing legacy by asking a number of questions:

1. What were the housing legacies of other host cities? How does the experience of London compare?
2. What were the experiences of travellers and residents at Clays Lane decanted from the park? How much housing was lost? Were other residents displaced as indirect effect of London hosting the games?
3. Would London 2012 result in accelerated regeneration of East London and what would be the nature of that accelerated regeneration?
4. How would the athletes' village be financed, developed and converted into housing after the games? Who would have access to this housing?
5. Would the area attract a more professional population and would this displace existing populations?

6. What kinds of plans and policy instruments would be developed to realise the housing 'legacy'? Would they be adequate? How would they change over time?
7. How and in what ways would the massive investment in this area translate into benefits for deprived communities living in East London?
8. What would be the relationship between state and market in terms of delivering London 2012 and its intended legacy?
9. How would this part of London change over the coming decades?

In Chapter 1 we provided an overview of housing legacies in other host cities. It is clear that much of what we associate as being specific to London's legacy such as the conversion of the athletes' village into housing after the Games was not unique to London but was a feature of other host cities. In Barcelona (Barcelona included affordable housing elsewhere), Beijing and Sydney their respective athletes' villages were developed by the private sector and converted into housing for sale after the games. Athens, Vancouver and London on the other hand included affordable housing. However, each of these cities was faced with significant problems with regard to delivery. In the case of London and Vancouver it was anticipated that their respective villages would be developed by the private sector. However, both required significant additional financial investment by the taxpayer than was originally anticipated. In the case of Athens, the village was developed by the 'third sector' due to lack of alternatives and was unique in providing 100 per cent affordable housing. However, here the village has been plagued by financial problems and poor planning. These case studies highlight the limitations of mega events in ensuring more equitable housing outcomes. As we have seen in the case of Beijing, Barcelona and Sydney less inclusive approaches are more affordable (to the taxpayer) and more inclusive approaches come at a significant cost and raise questions about whether this is the best use of resources and most appropriate vehicle for securing transformative change for low income communities.

Displacement was a feature of mega events in Barcelona, Atlanta, Beijing, Athens and London and as we have seen in the case of London the level of displacement linked to hosting London 2012. Displacement has tended to affect the most disadvantaged populations with Roma and Traveller groups disproportionately affected in a number of host cities and as we have seen the treatment of the displaced has varied from breaching legal conventions through to satisfactory. Displacement has occurred both for reasons directly related to specific regeneration sites; more general beautification of areas and in the case of Atlanta as an opportunity to use the games to demolish much of its public housing.

The victimisation of the homeless (in particular rough sleepers) was another feature that occurred to varying extents in host cities. There was evidence of victimisation of rough sleepers in Atlanta, Athens and Beijing. Sydney, Vancouver and London sought to distance themselves from these kinds of activities with Sydney introducing a homelessness protocol, Vancouver an inclusivity statement and a commitment in the bid to end homelessness and London it's 'no second night out' strategy and a range of strategies to manage a potential increase in homelessness. Despite these commitments, homelessness statistics indicated an actual rise in the number of families classified as homelessness in Vancouver and London, and in both Sydney and London there was evidence of landlords evicting tenants in order to rent their properties out at substantially inflated prices, which in the case of London was entirely legal. Ironically, as London hosted the games and implemented strategies for rough sleeping it coincided with an exodus of residents on housing benefit from inner London to outer London and beyond.

An increase in the value of properties in host cities has been evident to varying degrees across each host city. However, whilst the Olympics and Paralympics may have contributed to this increase it is not the key explanatory factor. Barcelona is the outlier in this regard with substantial house prices linked to the transformation of the city arising from hosting the games. In other cities such as Sydney and Athens price increases were more marked on schemes some distance from Olympic venues. Similarly, in Vancouver the huge increase in population has increased demand for properties. Therefore, any assumption that such events translate into increased property prices should be viewed with caution. On the other hand evidence from Barcelona, Beijing and Sydney suggests that housing at the athletes' village itself may benefit from above average increases in property prices, though this has not been the case so far in Vancouver. Similarly, it appears that whilst London has experienced a mini housing boom in the period lead up to the games, this boom has little to do with London hosting the games and is associated with other factors with negligible increase in property prices in the areas closest to Olympic venues, such as Stratford, which may limit the amount of private sector interest in schemes on the Park. Rental values have increased at a much higher rate in areas such as Stratford making this an attractive proposition for buy to let investors as this does little to resolve the issue of population churn identified as a key problem for this part of East London. This also means that following the introduction of the affordable rent model this will translate directly into higher rents and make it difficult for those on lower incomes to live in the area. One dimension of inclusion that cuts across the housing legacies of host cities that transformed the athletes' village into housing after the Games was the socially inclusive design with regard to disability which has meant that those who were able to afford it in the case of Barcelona, Sydney and Beijing were able to access this well-designed housing. Similarly, in London the village has been designed with a strong focus on ensuring equal access for people with disabilities and this is clearly a substantial benefit for building lifetime neighbourhoods and an exemplar for other regeneration schemes.

We also explored in detail London Docklands arguing that there is considerable overlap between the approach adopted at Stratford and London Docklands, alongwith some distinctive differences. In both cases there has been a tendency to present the areas as urban wastelands in need of wholesale transformation, understating existing land uses, such as local industry and longstanding communities. Whilst it was argued that London Docklands should be developed in the 'national' interest because of its strategic significance and proximity to the City, Stratford on the other hand was presented as national project with a strong focus on local need. However, as we have seen there has been a dilution of these earlier commitments; a promotion of mainly market housing and increasing costs of intermediate housing options that mean that there is a similar risk that Stratford will be characterised by the same divisions of wealth and poverty evident on the Isle of Dogs and reflected in a 'new' and 'old' Stratford.

There was a substantial decanting programme undertaken in preparation for hosting the Olympic and Paralympic games. This meant that 425 individual tenancies were lost and 327 additional social housing units used to rehouse them equating to 752 social housing units used to facilitate the construction of the Park. As has already been noted there is still the possibility that the whole of the Carpenters Estate may be decanted. Moreover the social housing lost was much more genuinely affordable than additional affordable housing at the Park and at a time when the government is anticipating a cut in welfare payments this can mean even further hardship for residents or an increase in the housing benefit bill.

For those decanted there were mixed experiences. Clearly for those residents on the housing waiting list who planned to move out of the Clays Lane Housing Cooperative the decision to decant the estate would have enabled them to access self-contained accommodation and have a considerable degree of choice over destination. Nevertheless the process of establishing relevant systems even for this group was slow and therefore residents experienced a considerable degree of anxiety about their futures particularly given the pressure to leave the estate by July 2007 and this pressure cannot be underestimated. There was a more serious failure to realise the preferences of a significant proportion of residents who wished to move as a group/collective who had to settle for individualised housing options resulting in the fracturing of a strong community that offered social support and perceived as the necessary price to pay for the longer term legacy benefits that would accrue. The need to more effectively consider and integrate systems of emotional support into decant systems was a clear finding, with this important dimension overlooked until relatively late on in the process.

There was clearly a significant financial impact for most residents and whilst an enhanced financial compensation package was reached this would not have covered the additional costs over a significant period and therefore we can assume for many financial hardship was a key problem following the move. Moreover, evidence given at the inquiry into the Compulsory Purchase Order by the LDA underestimated the additional financial costs to residents. More generally what was lost was a relatively unique form of affordable housing available for single people living in East London at a time when there is serious shortage of such housing. The LDA had a job that had to be done – residents had to be evicted from the site by July 2007 and systems were put in place to ensure this happened with compensation withheld for any residents that had not moved. From the perspective of the LDA it was a success in part because there were no forced evictions. However, the fact that a public inquiry was initiated into the processes of relocation and that the inspector acknowledged a range of problems is evidence that the re-housing process was problematic. Essentially the LDA had to square the circle between ensuring the project was delivered on time and meeting the needs of residents and compromises were made in favour of the former. For those with relatively straightforward needs i.e. individualised housing options in the local area it was relatively easy to meet those needs. Whereas for those seeking something more complex i.e. a group move this was more problematic. Nevertheless residents interviewed as part of this study were generally happy with their new housing.

The two groups of Travellers shared some common experiences such as considerable anxiety about finding suitable sites, uncertainty and delays in moving. The LDA had commissioned research to identify the preferences of Travellers, however, these preferences were ultimately disregarded and two groups of Travellers were forced to move to sites unacceptable to them and where there were serious concerns about hostility in the immediate neighbourhood. The Hackney Travellers separated into smaller groups and this again caused considerable anxiety.

Both groups of Travellers had input into the design of sites and specific units, however, Travellers in Hackney appeared to be more satisfied with their new housing. The presence of an additional source of support in Hackney was important in securing more satisfactory outcomes with Travellers talking positively about a range of agencies supporting them ranging from Hackney Homes through to the Hackney Learning Trust and the London Gypsy and Travellers Unit. Travellers in Newham on the other hand felt unsupported by their Local Authority and indeed their relationship appeared to be conflictual rather than supportive. The perceived or alleged legacy benefits to the whole area acted as a trump card enabling policy makers to move Travellers off of the site before new permanent sites were ready irrespective of their rights.

What is clear is that residents living at the Clays Lane Housing Cooperative and residents living on Traveller sites found themselves in the way of a prestigious national project. Anxiety about the need to complete the project on time meant that there was a relatively short time period between London winning the Games and the final decant (two years). The need to expedite the project meant that both sets of residents had to respond to a very tight and highly pressurised timetable which created added pressure and led to less desirable outcomes.

Ironically whilst the trump card of long term benefits was crucial in London winning the bid and clearing the area, actual commitments and specific details about housing legacy were vague (beyond the Athletes' Village) and linked both explicitly to housing on the park and then as part of the accelerated regeneration of the Lower Lea Valley, therefore, whilst Sebastian Coe suggested that 30,000–40,000 homes would be built many of which would be affordable' this was simply based on the potential housing capacity of the Lower Lea Valley rather than any specific housing plans or schemes in place to deliver this housing. The concept of housing legacy operates essentially at three levels, at one level then there is the anticipated accelerated regeneration of the Lower Lea Valley and we can see that there is clearly some evidence of this acceleration in terms of housing production and this is discussed below. Secondly there is the legacy housing at the athletes' village and thirdly there are housing plans for the park.

Let us consider then the legacy housing at the athletes' village or what is now known as East Village there has been considerable slippage here between original plans and outcomes. In 2004 the GLA indicated that up to 4,600 homes would be converted into housing following the Games. In 2007 plans for the athletes' village and Stratford City (which had been approved prior to London winning the bid and already included nearly 5,000 homes) were merged into one scheme leading to concerns about the net gain in additional housing and double counting with the ODA arguing that it was legacy housing as it had been accelerated by the scheme. The final number of units was cut first to 3,300 and then 2,800 units and therefore the actual legacy linked to the athletes' village was substantially reduced. The scheme was initially to have been developed by a private developer and included 30 per cent affordable housing as per the Stratford City Planning consent. However, as we saw the government was forced to step in and bail out the scheme transferring the risk from private to public sector whilst the same private developer profited from the contract to build the Village. Moreover, as the ODA acted as developer it inherited the substantial planning obligations that would have been the responsibility of the private developer increasing the cost to the public sector.

The ODA underwent a process of competitive tender for the 51 per cent market housing at the athletes' village and there was considerable interest in this. The Wellcome Trust bid offered the potential for fundamental transformation of this part of East London and for London more generally with its plans to create a potential Silicon Valley. However, this was not ultimately pursued and QDD were awarded the contract. A major attraction of the QDD bid were its plans to rent rather than simply sell off the housing which means they have an interest in ensuring the long term success of the scheme and they have established the first Private Management Investment Fund developed since the deregulation of the private residential sector in 1988 which was positively received given the dominance of individual buy to let investors.

The design of the village is an area of potential division, with those who either love or loathe it. A considerable amount of attention to detail has been invested in the scheme with high density living offset by outstanding high quality public realm with a view to liveability. There are some unique features of this project in that most projects are built in stages and this scheme is unprecedented in the release of 2,800 homes in a short period of time creating both logistical and financial challenges in terms of oversupply. East Village will be relatively unique in that, as a 'mixed community', it is almost evenly split between market and affordable housing and includes a significant proportion of family and wheelchair housing. Residents living in market and affordable housing will share courtyards avoiding some of the social separation evident elsewhere. Significant infrastructure has been put in place as a result of extensive planning which means that the Village benefits from outstanding transport links and a new school and health facilities. There is an impressive attention to detail with regard to housing management and maintenance systems and community development and infrastructure. However, the high density living and shared communal gardens necessitate a much more active management policy.

The scheme includes four types of affordable housing. The largest proportion of affordable housing is available for social/target rent and this means that it is more genuinely affordable than had it been funded under the 'affordable rent' model. The scheme whilst described by some as the last bastion of housing has more in common with early council housing schemes in places such as Becontree that were targeted at the 'respectable working classes'. Indeed concern about who would live at the Village has generated such concern that housing allocation policies were rewritten in Newham to ensure that the scheme favoured those in work and initial targets of 50 per cent of residents in work or training have been exceeded. This prioritisation of those in work has taken place against a backdrop of increasing unemployment which may appear punitive for the badly housed who are not in work.

Notwithstanding this the availability of a substantial supply of social rented housing is clearly welcome and whilst it does not compensate numerically for the housing lost it does provide self contained accommodation as compared to shared accommodation and includes much needed family and wheelchair housing.

Other dimensions of the affordable housing offer at the East Village are substantially more expensive and are likely to be available only to those on much higher incomes. Overall then we can see that there is a relatively extensive affordable housing offer and it may be that this becomes the Jewel in the Crown of an otherwise disappointing housing legacy.

Another key dimension of housing legacy is associated with plans for the park. The benefits of a single-minded agency focussing on legacy was evident in 2010 when an ambitious Masterplan for the park was produced by the newly-established Olympic Park Legacy Company setting out a clear direction for the subsequent legacy. This plan placed considerable emphasis on high quality neighbourhoods; family housing and at this point an indicative 35–40 per cent affordable housing. In 2012 the OPLC produced a revised Masterplan (Legacy Communities Scheme) setting out the potential to create five new neighbourhoods and up to 6,870 homes. The 2012 plan indicated that more ambitious affordable housing targets had been reviewed reflecting the fast changing policy context of austerity and housing finance reform and the need to capitalise on the sale of lands to pay back debts and included for the first time a minimum level of affordable housing across the park of 20 per cent. This raises a very real question as to whether 20 per cent affordable housing would have provided such a compelling legacy argument, and raises serious questions about how this will help to alleviate the huge levels of housing deprivation in the 'Legacy' boroughs.

We have seen that one way of implementing legacy plans has been through the design of successive plans and policy documents ranging from the Lower Lea Valley Plan, the London Plan, the Stratford Metropolitan Master Plan and the Legacy Communities Scheme through to convergence frameworks. However, these plans lack substance. They are simply a way of imagining how land might be developed and as successive examples have shown throughout this book the recommendations and stipulations of the Plan are consistently deviated from.

There are a number of tensions with regard plans and implementation and one of the most important is that whilst legacy was a central part of London's bid, there was never any budget allocated for subsequent legacy. It is assumed that the remediation of land (a key part of legacy) will attract developers with affordable housing derived either through planning gain or delivered by Registered Social Landlords. However, as we have seen these policy instruments central to housing delivery in 2005 are less likely to deliver genuinely affordable housing in the current context. As we have seen planning gain is less able to lever contributions to affordable housing. The replacement of the Target/Social rent funding model with the so called 'Affordable Rent' model reinforces market principles and raises very significant issues about the possibilities of providing genuinely 'affordable' housing in more expensive areas and whom the potential beneficiaries of such might be. The Policy context then of 2005 was very different to that of 2013.

The policy context that underpinned the bid promoted the notion of social inclusion and social democratic principles with regards to space and place. The emphasis has now shifted to a more rampant market individualism with a sea change in attitude towards disadvantaged groups and housing for social rent more generally.

The other key issue has been the ever-changing array of agencies and individuals charged with legacy and their changing emphasis which in itself presents a challenge in following through those original goals. The establishment of the London Legacy Development Corporation does provide the potential for a much clearer focus on legacy. Their role both as landowner and planner this puts them in a strong position to shape what happens on the land and to ensure that it meets those original policy intentions and clearly it will be important to ensure they are held to account for those initial commitments. However, they will have to square the circle in a context of fiscal austerity of awarding planning consent to schemes that deviate substantially from the plan or having no development at all.

As we have seen then the housing legacy was to be realised through the development of housing at the athletes' village, the Park and the wider Lower Lea Valley Area through a process of accelerated regeneration.

There has clearly been a substantial amount of accelerated regeneration as a result of urban transformation facilitated by the decision to host the Olympic and Paralympic Games. UCL and Loughborough both plan to have campuses on the Park creating the potential for a knowledge economy to emerge on the Park, BT are leasing substantial space at I CITY (a new technology hub). Plans for Stratford City preceded the Park though it is clear that there has been considerable activity at

Stratford city both already developed and planned and we will never know if this would have happened anyway and there are debates as to whether the Olympics accelerated this project. It is also clear that the Olympic and Paralympic project has accelerated the regeneration of Stratford High Street with it increasingly becoming a desirable place to live. In Chapter 6 we examined planning gain agreements on new developments along Stratford High Street and highlighted a number of weaknesses within current planning frameworks to capture value and benefits for local communities and declining contributions over time. This highlights the peculiar relationship between state and market. The state has invested in extensive public investment in transport infrastructure and the remediation of land leading to increased land values impressively completed in a seven year period and creating the potential for a new residential area. Stratford High Street richly illustrates the capacity of the private sector to secure the locational advantage afforded by this public investment whilst, particularly in the context of the wider economic austerity, reach agreements with public agencies that commit them to the most modest contributions to planning gain that don't even cover the actual impact of those developments on the local area in terms of additional health and educational infrastructure resulting in the need for further public subsidy for these schemes.

The case study of Stratford High Street illustrates changing priorities toward the provision of social and affordable housing and the concentration of value capture on development contribution and modest impact fees rather than reflecting the unearned benefits derived from the initial and significant public investment directly and indirectly associated with hosting the 2012 Games. Set in this context, the balance of private and public gain derived from the renewal of an area on the border of the Olympic Park has tilted decisively in favour of the former. Indeed, developers it seems have tended, in several cases, to accept the case for planning gain (especially in relation to the provision of social housing) only as a means to access additional public funds for their specific developments. Equally, planning authorities such as Newham or the London Legacy Development Corporation are faced with the difficult task of securing specific public benefits from negotiations with each developer and ensuring that these modest 'gains' or fragments of infrastructure contribute to the achievement of wider area plans.

Whether Stratford High Street will set the trend for future developments within the area remains to be seen; the underlying trends in economic and social policy suggest that it may well and more recent schemes at both Stratford City and plans for the park confirm rather than challenge these assumptions. The current government's cap on housing and welfare benefits, the continued rise in private sector rents and the on-going reluctance of banks and financial institutions to provide mortgages makes London, and increasingly parts of what was affordable East London, difficult places for relatively deprived communities to live. Such problems may be addressed if the mechanisms designed to capture value are radically revised and 'affordable', social housing provision considerably increased. For value capture mechanisms to work, and reflect a better balance between private and public interest, scheme viability has to be assessed over the long term with the unearned benefits accruing to private enterprise reflected in the latter's contribution to urban development.

We also explored the concept of social class change and gentrification in Stratford High Street. The concept of 'spatially displaced demand' is helpful for understanding why these new migrants are choosing Stratford as a spill-over from places such as Bow and Docklands which adds further legitimacy to the notion that a process of 'gentrification' is under way. The planning gain agreements that underpinned much of the new housing reflected the 'mixed communities' agenda where planning policy was used to ensure a social mix through the inclusion of affordable housing with planning policy having a protective effect on the extent of gentrification. However, it is clear that even within these mixed communities evidence of social class change is apparent and this will be accentuated further in later developments that include negligible proportions of affordable housing and will ensure that another area that has typically housed working class residents will become the reserve of the better off.

As Stratford High Street is a re-urbanised area there is no evidence of direct displacement though this is likely to be indirect through the price mechanism and supported through a changed benefit system. The new migrants tended to interact very little with their neighbours or neighbourhood and associated themselves with a new rather than old Stratford. There was little sense that their presence made a contribution to the area and for most it was just a brief stepping stone. More generally there had been a lack of place making and whilst there was a sense in which this area would be gentrified the possibility that parts of the high street might constitute the slum housing of the future was also a potential risk and limit to 'gentrification' and suggested that the state had a role to play here in conjunction with private developers to ensure a place was more than the sum of individual schemes.

The real question is that given this part of Stratford was unoccupied and given that this new housing is clearly meeting a housing need does it matter? It is suggested that it matters because both housing and land are in short supply in London and this is an area that has traditionally housed lower income groups. Moreover, as we have seen elsewhere in this book there is an urgent need for new affordable housing and every time a new development is built with limited potential to house low income groups it results in a redistribution of scarce land that traditionally served lower income groups to higher income groups and in the process threatens their very future, it also has a ripple effect shaping what happens elsewhere. Slater has argued gentrification is embedded in a process of class struggle, however, what is noticeably absent in Stratford (notwithstanding the Carpenters Residents) is a voice/movement that is arguing against this process of area change, as Slater has argued the language has shifted from 'gentrification' to regeneration, renaissance, revitalisation and in the process has obscured the underlying class conflict at its heart.

As of September 2013 there is a sense that the housing legacy is taking shape both inside and outside of the Park with East Village becoming occupied, but what of the future? What will this part of East London look like in 10 and indeed 20 years time? There are clearly a number of possible scenarios for housing legacy. However, on current trends it is suggested that this part of East London will increasingly become an island of relative prosperity with little impact on deprived communities in East London. East Village may be the exception rather than the rule and used as justification for building less affordable housing elsewhere. The impact of Universal Credit may mean that much of the affordable family housing planned for the park will simply not be feasible and where affordable housing is provided it will increasingly be available only to the better-off. Private developers will progress schemes but will increasingly exclude affordable housing, justified by a mixture of financial viability and inappropriateness of design in these schemes. The Park may develop in an uneven way with interest in building on those sites closest to Stratford. Cuts to budgets may mean that the kind of place making activities crucial to making this area a success are not undertaken, resulting in a sterile environment, and an array of formulaic housing projects purchased either by overseas or buy-to-let investors and targeted at young professionals creating a transient place. Moreover there is a risk that other estates may be demolished to facilitate other projects elsewhere and justified because of a lack of the necessary resources needed for regeneration. Another possible scenario is that the increased supply of mainly market housing leads to market collapse resulting in a decline of the area and a lack of interest from the private developers in building new schemes of course the corollary of this is that RSL developers may be able to build affordable housing relatively cheaply which may result in more affordable housing.

On the other hand the success of East Village presents the possibility that mixed communities, appropriately managed, offer a solution that squares the circle between housing need and new housing provision and serves as a demonstration project elsewhere on the park and more widely.

Looking ahead it is suggested that there are three main goals for what needs to happen on the Park if more inclusive goals are to be achieved. The first is that it should become a desirable area to live with families and individuals from a range of socio-economic groups choosing to locate in Stratford for the long term addressing the issue of population churn. Secondly that genuinely affordable housing is provided on the park that meets the needs of existing residents living in deprived communities whether in or out of work. Finally that there is a focus on ensuring that there is a growth in employment opportunities and strategies to ensure that existing residents living in the legacy boroughs are able to take advantage of these opportunities.

What is also clear is that mechanisms for delivering affordable housing are in crisis and what is needed is a radical rethink of how we fund and deliver affordable housing whilst simultaneously reducing welfare dependency. One key dimension of the growing welfare bill has been the growth of housing benefit. The shift from subsidising bricks and mortar to housing benefit has resulted in a growth in welfare dependency as lack of supply has pushed up costs and the government has spent finite government resources on a growing housing benefit bill. The 'Affordable Rent' model will either exclude low income households from more expensive parts of London or force more people to claim benefits to meet the increasing costs of housing. Those in lower income groups are forced to suffer the housing consequences of years of neglect and are now increasingly blamed for their own misfortune and for those not in work their eligibility to decent housing is increasingly being brought into question

The land at the Park could be used to create a test bed for new models of housing finance that create truly affordable housing related to income rather than land values. This would reduce welfare dependency and in the long term the housing benefit bill. Instead of focusing energy on seeking to discriminate between the deserving and undeserving poor, the focus should be on breaking down barriers to work and ensuring that local residents access local employment and relevant training.

There has been a substantial amount of construction work and training in the area and there is the potential to encourage self build and more innovative construction and ownership methods. These approaches will ensure the long term future of low income residents in the area and will ensure a model of convergence based on transforming the opportunities of existing populations. It will also be important to ensure that no additional affordable housing is lost as a result of 'Legacy' related projects. This study has focussed on those ambitious policy goals related to housing Legacy. Initial plans were underpinned by social democratic notions of place and space and these are now being unsettled and reformulated to emphasise market based entitlements. The contradictions of a market based housing model are increasingly evident in London with stagnant wages, rising house prices and high levels of housing need. In London's bid application, it was claimed that the legacy would lead to: 'The regeneration of an entire community for the direct benefit of everyone who lives there'. The real risk is that the area will be regenerated but with very little benefit to those existing communities.

Index

affordable housing
  Barcelona 1992 7
  behavioural criteria for residents 106–7, 130
  Chobham Farm 135
  Chobham Manor 103
  dilution of in East Village 118
  downward shift in expectations 93–8
  East Wick 104
  economic climate, impact of 106
  extent of across the site 105–7
  finance for the athletes' village 115
  flexibility over levels of 107
  London Plan 96–8
  Lower Lea Valley regeneration 94–8
  Marshgate Wharf 104
  mixed communities agenda 100
  new, in the legacy boroughs *81*, 81–2
  planning gain 140
  Pudding Mill 105
  Stratford City 131
  Stratford High Street 147–52, *156–60*
  Stratford Metropolitan Masterplan 101
  Sugar House Lane 99–100
  Sweetwater 105
  types of at East Village 120–21
  Vancouver Winter Games 2010 17–19
affordable rent model 97
agencies overseeing legacy 83–7
Agenda 21 5
allocation of housing at East Village 127–9
Altmann, Andrew 127
Ambrose, B. 8, 9
Athens 2004, housing legacy 12–15
athletes' villages
  Athens 2004 12–15
  Atlanta 1996 7–10
  Barcelona 1992 6–7
  Bejing 2008 15–17
  Sydney 2000 10–12
  see also East Village
Atlanta 1996, housing legacy 7–10

Barata, D. 66, 69
Barcelona 1992, housing legacy 6–7
Barker Review of Housing Supply 2004 142
behavioural criteria for residents 106–7
Bejing 2008, housing legacy 15–17
Bernstock, P. 98, 122, 147
betterment capture 143
Boddy, M. 171
Bounds, M. 11
Bowie, D. 142
Butler, T. 170

Cabinet Office 87
Carpenters Estate 65–9, 129, 183–4
Centennial Place 9
Chobham Academy 123–4
Chobham Farm 135
Chobham Manor 103
Clays Lane Housing Cooperative
  collective move, failure of 35–8
  community, sense of 47–9
  costs of housing 46–7
  destinations following decant 42
  disabilities, number of residents with 34–5
  dissatisfaction with support during decant 39–42
  emotional support 42
  financial support 42–3
  management of 32
  practical support 42
  quality of replacement housing, issues with 35
  reaction to London winning the bid 38
  rejection of concerns from 32–3

routes into 38–9
satisfaction with housing 44–5
size and organization of 31–2
survey of residents views 33, 34
system and strategy for relocation 34–5
Clays Lane (Newham) Travellers
community, sense of 56–7
compensation fee 53
compulsory order inquiry 52–3
delays relating to move 55
identification of sites for relocation 51, 52–3, 53–5
issues with site relocated to 57
return to previous accommodation 57–8
satisfaction with accommodation 56
support and advice given 51–2
closing ceremony of the Olympic Games 191
communal areas
charges for 126–7
Stratford City 181–2
community, sense of
Clay Lane (Newham) Travellers 56–7
Clays Lane Housing Cooperative 47–9
development of at East Village 122–4
Hackney Travellers 62
Stratford High Street 153, *161–8*, 181–2
Community Development Trust at East Village 124
compensation packages
Carpenters Estate 67–8
Clay Lane and Irish Travellers 53
Clays Lane Housing Cooperative 42–3
convergence agenda 87–8
costs of housing for residents 46–7
counselling services 43–4

debts, pressure to repay 109
decanting. *see* Clays Lane Housing Cooperative; Clays Lane (Newham) Travellers; displacement; Hackney Travellers
decent homes standard 32n2
design of the athletes' village 118–19
displacement

Athens 2004 12–13
Atlanta 1996 8–9
Barcelona 1992 6
Carpenters Estate 65–9
impact of 30–31
as ongoing in East London 30
resistance to 170
see also Clays Lane Housing Cooperative; Clays Lane (Newham) Travellers; gentrification; Hackney Travellers
Docklands, London
gentrification of 170–71
regeneration of 20–23
Dwyer, W. 11

East Village
allocation of housing 127–9
behavioural criteria for residents 130
Carpenters Estate residents 129
charges for public realm and services 126–7
Chobham Academy 123–4
community development 122–4
Community Development Trust 124
conversion from athletes' village 119–20
design of 118–19
dilution of affordable housing 118
employment opportunities 123
financing the athletes' village 114–15
governance and management 124–6
infrastructure 121–2
military personnel as potential residents 128
as mixed community 129–30
private sector organisations 115–17
QDD Athletes Village UK Limited 117
rental prices 127
revisions to initial scheme 113–14
and Stratford City 130–34
Triathlon Homes 125–6
types of housing at 120–21
Wellcome Trust proposal 116–17
East Wick 103–4
emotional support 42, 43–4
employment opportunities at East Village 123

Equality and Diversity Forum 84
evictions, increases during lead up to Games 74

family housing, commitment to 98
finance for the athletes' village 114–15
financial support to residents 42–3, 53, 67–8

gentrification
   concern over 31
   consumption perspective 170
   Docklands 170–71
   drivers of 172
   early/super gentrifiers 170
   origin and definition of term 169–70
   resistance to 170
   and social geography of London 171
   and types of housing 171
   usefulness of term 171
Glass, Ruth 169
governance of legacy 83–7
   East Village 124–6
Grigsby, W. 8, 9

Hackney Travellers
   community, sense of 62
   compensation fee 53
   compulsory order inquiry 52–3
   design of new homes 60–61
   identification of sites for relocation 51, 52–3, 58–60
   option of return 59
   satisfaction with housing before and after move 61–2
   separation into different groups 58–9
   support and advice given 51–2
   support received 60
Hall, Peter 126
Hamnett, C. 171
homeless population
   Athens 2004 14
   Atlanta 1996 8–9
   Bejing 2008 16–17
   in the legacy boroughs 74–6, *76*
   Sydney 2000 12
   Vancouver Winter Games 2010 17–19

house prices
   Athens 2004 14
   Atlanta 1996 8–9
   Barcelona 1992 7
   Bejing 2008 16
   as legacy 71–3
   Sydney 2000 11

inclusivity in legacy bids 17
Irish Travellers. *see* Hackney Travellers

Keating, R. 8
Keogh, Laura 83

Lambert, N. 171
Landprop 99
Lees, L. 170
legacy
   Athens 2004 12–15
   Atlanta 1996 7–10
   Barcelona 1992 6–7
   Bejing 2008 15–17
   Chobham Manor 103
   convergence agenda 87–8
   debts, pressure to repay 109
   developers' concerns 108
   East Wick 103–4
   extent of affordable homes across the site 105–7
   family housing 107–8
   governance of 83–7
   homelessness 74–6, *76*
   house prices 71–3
   Legacy Communities Scheme 101–5
   Lower Lea Valley regeneration 94–8
   Marshgate Wharf 104
   new affordable homes *81,* 81–2
   overcrowding *79,* 79–80
   poverty 76–7
   Pudding Mill 105
   realising the plan 108–9
   satisfaction with neighbourhood 82
   Stratford Metropolitan Masterplan 101
   Sugar House Lane 99–100
   Supplementary Guidance 98
   Sweetwater 104–5
   Sydney 2000 10–12

tenure of housing 77–9, *78*
Vancouver Winter Games 2010 17–19
waiting lists *80,* 80–81
see also East Village
Legacy Communities Scheme 101–5
Lend Lease 114
Li, B. 15
Livingstone, Ken 93–4
London 2012 Equality and Diversity Forum 84
London Borough of Newham 145–6
London Development Agency 84–5
London Docklands
　gentrification of 170–71
　regeneration of 20–23
London Legacy Mayoral Development Corporation 86, 102, 144
London Organising Committee for the Olympic and Paralympic Games (LOCOG) 84
London Plan 96–8
London Thames Gateway Development Corporation 85, 99, 144–5
low income groups
　Athens 2004 14
　Atlanta 1996 8–9
Lower Lea Valley 94–8
Lupton, R. 100

Mallik, G. 11
management of East Village 124–6
Marshgate Wharf 104
Mayor of London 83–4
migration to Stratford City
　Carpenters Estate, views on 183–4
　characteristics of migrants 176–8
　communal areas 181–2
　duration of stay in 178–9
　gentrification 169–72
　gentrification of Stratford 186–7
　housing conditions 184–6
　local services, use of 180–81
　maintenance of housing 184–6
　management of housing 184–6
　mixed communities 182–3
　motivation for 173–6
　neighbour relations 181–2

　space, place and neighbourhood 179–80
　wait for accommodation 173
mixed communities 100, 182–3

Nation and Regions Group 84
Newham Travellers. *see* Clays Lane (Newham) Travellers
Newman, H.K. 9

Olympic Board 84
Olympic Development Authority (ODA) 84
Olympic Park Legacy Company 85–6, 99
Olympic Park Regeneration Steering Group 84
Olympics, opening/closing ceremonies 191
opening ceremony of the Olympic Games 191
overcrowding in the legacy boroughs *79,* 79–80
oversight of legacy 83–7
owner occupation in the legacy boroughs 77–9, *78*

planning gain
　and affordable housing 140
　London 2012 142
　Stratford High Street 150–52
poverty
　in the legacy boroughs 76–7
　and mixed communities agenda 100
Poynter, G. 3, 7
prices, house and rental
　Athens 2004 14
　Atlanta 1996 8–9
　Barcelona 1992 7
　Bejing 2008 16
　Clays Lane Housing Cooperative 46–7
　as legacy 71–3
　Sydney 2000 11
private sector
　funding by 140, 140n1
　involvement in East Village 115–17
public realm and services, charges for 126–7
Pudding Mill 105

QDD Athletes Village UK Limited 117, 124–6

Raco, M. 30
regeneration 140–43
rental prices
   Barcelona 1992 7
   Clays Lane Housing Cooperative 46–7
   East Village 127
   increases during lead up to Games 74
   as legacy 73
   social/affordable rent model 97
research
   methodology 29–30
   questions 1–2
revalorisation 140–43
Robson, G. 170
Roma families and Athens 2004 12–13
rough sleeping in the legacy boroughs 74–6, *76*

satisfaction with neighbourhood 82
Shin, H.B. 15
Smith, N. 172
social rent model 97
Stratford City
   downplayment of prior usage 31
   East Village 130–31
   gentrification of 186–7
   seven zones of 131–4
   see also migration to Stratford City
Stratford High Street
   affordable housing 147–52, *156–60*
   agencies involved with planning 144–6
   community gain on schemes 153, *161–8*
   housing schemes completed/planned *156–60*
   planning application and S106 agreements 144–6
   planning gain 150–52
   vacant premises 186
   and value capture 153–4
Stratford Metropolitan Masterplan 101
Sugar House Lane 99–100
Supplementary Guidance 98
Sweetwater 104–5
Sydney 2000, housing legacy 10–12

Techwood Homes 8
tenure of housing in the legacy boroughs *78*
Travellers, *see* Clays Lane (Newham) Travellers; Hackney Travellers
Triathlon Homes 115, 125–6
Tunney, E. 30
Tunstall, R. 100

value capture 143, 153–4
Vancouver Winter Games 2010 housing legacy 17–19

waiting lists in the legacy boroughs *80*, 80–81
Watt, P. 170
Wellcome Trust proposal 116–17